Get Rich Slow

Your Guide to Producing Income & Building Wealth with Rental Real Estate

millrock
PUBLISHING

Cover Design	Gary Bandfield
Interior Design	Design Type Service
Copy Editing	Carol Rose
Production Team Leader	Jason Hintze
Accuracy Checking	Elin Kappus
Marketing	Richard T. Hercher, Jr.

ISBN 978-0-615-55703-8

E-mail: *info@getrichslowwebber.com*
Website: *getrichslowwebber.com*

Cover photo by Posh Photography, courtesy of Daybreak Eastlake Village Condominium Owner's Association.

ACKNOWLEDGMENTS

This book reflects the efforts of many people. I extend my thanks to the entire Millrock team for putting their hearts and talents into the book. They have made this a top-quality product.

A big thank you to Mark Papanikolas, CPA, for valuable input on income tax laws, accounting-related issues, mortgage loan brokering, and other matters related to the overall book.

Thanks to experts in their field for technical assistance: Bruce J. Nelson, attorney-at-law, for valuable input on legal topics and landlord/tenant issues; Sage Sawyer, ARA National, for practical suggestions on what's happening in the apartment house/investment community; and Toni Nilson, Epic Property Management, for constructive ideas on property management topics.

A special thanks to reviewers for their valuable feedback: Phil Berry, Jr., Anne Greer, Mary Jo Lund, Angie Papanikolas, Christine Lynn, Christina Jones, Tom Pfaff, Richard W. Block, Burke Staker, Kyle Papanikolas, Chris Metos, A. O. Headman, Jr., and Chris Chatzis. This is a much better book because of their input.

Thanks to the staff at Hewlett Packard, and to the staff at Texas Instruments.

I am indebted to my many mentors in real estate development and investing, and to all of my investment partners along the way.

Thanks to the education staffs of the Utah Association of Realtors and its local boards, along with the Salt Lake Community College, for allowing me the chance to share my enthusiasm for investing. And thanks to my many students over the years, for their valuable feedback and suggestions.

A final thanks to my family and friends, who have been major cheerleaders—especially to my cute wife Debbie and my children Wendy, Robin, Toni, Tara, and Casey.

ABOUT THE AUTHOR

John is a successful real estate developer and investor. In addition to being a personal investor, John has represented hundreds of investors by finding investment properties that fit their needs.

John has been teaching real estate investment seminars to Realtors for many years and serves as an adjunct professor at Salt Lake Community College, teaching financial mathematics, personal finance, and accounting.

John has served on the board of directors for the Salt Lake Board of Realtors, as chairman of the Education Committee for the Utah Association of Realtors, as Regional Governor for the National Association of Independent Fee Appraisers, and as a partner in a tax-consulting business.

John is the author of a college textbook, *Math for Business and Life*, currently in its fifth edition.

A NOTE FROM JOHN

If you are looking for a book that will turn you into an instant millionaire, this book isn't for you! As the title to the book—*Get Rich Slow*—implies, I consider wealth-building through rental real estate to be a *slow* but *reliable* process. While some real estate investments do provide quick profits, be prepared to have patience when it comes to building wealth through real estate investments. And don't be surprised if there are periods when values even go down.

Some people don't like investing in stocks because of the risk. If they lose money they feel bad. If they make money they may feel no personal satisfaction—they just feel lucky. Some people don't like investing in bonds because bonds don't respond to inflation. Many people caught in this dilemma invest in real estate—good judgment is a big part of success, and real estate can be a hedge against inflation. One big advantage of investing in rental real estate is, after making a down payment and getting a mortgage loan for the difference, our tenants help us pay off the mortgage. And during the process we can raise rents when the market allows and hopefully watch the value go up.

This book is different from other real estate investment books: it gets into the nitty-gritty that other books ignore. We will project cash flows (reflecting income taxes) and calculate a rate of return (IRR) on the projected cash flows. We will even discuss how to select good tenants. You may be saying, Hey, some of this stuff sounds complicated, but as you will see, the process is pretty simple because of the way the concepts are introduced: slowly, thoroughly, and one step at a time:

Step 1	Weigh the Pros and Cons
Step 2	Get Your Ducks in a Row
Step 3	Eliminate the Duds
Step 4	Estimate Net Operating Income (NOI)
Step 5	Get to Know Your Hidden Partner—The Tax Man
Step 6	Crunch Numbers Like a Pro
Step 7	Figure the Bottom Line: Cash Flows & Rate of Return
Step 8	Buy It or Walk Away: Decision Time
Step 9	Help the Money Tree Thrive: Effective Landlording

(cont. on next page)

By following the approach of the book and doing a careful analysis up front, we can avoid bad investments. A well-seasoned real estate developer once told me,

If a potential investment doesn't work out on paper,
it won't work out in real life.

I have tried to use that advice in my investment decisions and recommend the same to you. If you believe in the carpenter's advice, Measure Twice and Cut Once, this book is for you. Run the numbers carefully, and don't be afraid to walk away from potential investments that don't meet your criteria.

I hope the concepts of the book will be financially rewarding. I would love to hear from you about how the book helps you personally, or about any ideas or suggestions you may have.

John Webber
jwebber@getrichslowwebber.com

CONTENTS

Weigh the Pros and Cons

We'll Explore

- Investment Alternatives

- The 8 Investment Criteria

- Do I Really Want to Be a Landlord?

For most people, the greatest earning period is from age 35 to 55. During these years, people may have extra money; some spend it on fun stuff, while others invest part of it for the future. For the average person, earnings peak near age 50 and then decline until, at some point, earnings fall *below* the cost of living. Many of those who fail to invest for the future end up not having enough income when they retire to maintain their standard of living. That's when they approach their kids to see if there is room for them in their kids' basement! Those who do invest along the way can use money from their investments to maintain their standard of living.

For the money we invest, we have lots of choices. We will explore some of the choices and things to consider before selecting a specific investment. Then, we will consider some pros and cons of investing in rental real estate so you can figure out if becoming a landlord is for you.

Investment Alternatives

Investors can choose among a variety of investments. A few are shown below. If you are well-versed in investment alternatives, feel free to skip the next few pages.

Stock

When we invest in stock we become an owner of the corporation. As an owner, we are entitled to a share of the company's profits. Corporations often distribute part of the profits as dividends and keep part for future development and contingencies. Stock investors also hope for an increase in the value of the stock they own.

Bonds

Corporations, the U.S. government, and local governmental agencies often need large sums of money. They often raise the money by selling bonds to the public. When we invest in bonds we are lending money to the corporation or governmental agency.

Corporate bonds are often in denominations of $1,000, generally pay interest semiannually or annually, and pay the $1,000 maturity value on the maturity date (which could be anywhere from 6 months to 20 years from the date issued).

U.S. government bonds, called U.S. securities, have different names depending on the maturity date. *Treasury bills* (*T-bills*) mature in 1 year or less and pay no interest until maturity. *Treasury notes* mature between 2 and 10 years and pay interest semiannually. *Treasury bonds* mature in 30 years and pay interest semiannually. *Savings bonds* are purchased at half of the face value; interest is paid in one lump sum when the bond matures.

Municipal bonds are issued by states, counties, cities, and other municipal agencies. Many municipal bonds have at least a 20-year maturity and are often sold in denominations of $5,000.

As an example of how bonds work, suppose you buy a $5,000 municipal bond that pays 6% interest annually and has a 20-year maturity. You would receive an interest check at the end of each year for 19 years of $300 ($5,000 × 6%). At the end of Year 20, you would receive a check for $5,300 ($300 for Year 20 interest + $5,000 principal repayment, called maturity value). Some bonds, referred to as zero-coupon bonds, pay all of the interest when the bond matures. For example, you may purchase a $1,000 zero-coupon bond for $400 and collect the $1,000 maturity value when the bond matures in 15 years.

Mutual Funds

A mutual fund is a company that pools money from investors (shareholders) and invests in a variety of securities (stocks, bonds, etc.). Some mutual funds specialize in a particular type of investment. For example, one mutual fund may invest only in U.S. government bonds, another only in well-proven stocks, and another only in municipal bonds. One reason people invest in mutual funds is to spread their risk; when we invest in a mutual fund, we own a small portion of several different things, rather than a larger portion of one thing. Another reason people choose mutual funds is that they don't have to worry about specific investment decisions; the mutual fund company makes the decisions.

Money Deposits

Some people keep their money under a mattress or in a jar. By doing so, they fail to earn interest on their money. They would be better off depositing their money in any one of the accounts typically offered at their local bank. They could deposit their money in a *passbook savings account* and withdraw it any time. They could purchase a *certificate of deposit* (*CD*), which generally requires a minimum deposit, for a fixed period of time and earn a higher rate than passbook accounts. Or they could deposit the money in a *money market account*, which requires a minimum balance, offers limited check-writing privileges, and earns rates higher than passbook savings but lower than CDs.

Loans

We can loan money to others, charging interest and front-end fees for making the loan. If we make a secured loan and the borrower quits making payments we can take the collateral they have pledged (like a car or real estate), or have the collateral sold and use the sales proceeds to help pay off the loan. Instead of making a loan, we could buy the promissory note from the person who originally made the loan; we step into that person's shoes, collecting the remaining payments from the borrower. Depending on the note rate (the interest rate the borrower pays), we might have to buy the note at a *premium*, or we may be able to buy the note at a *discount*; we calculate the price to pay for a note in the Appendix.

Real Estate

Real estate is land and buildings that are attached to the land. Many people who invest in real estate do so by first investing in a home to live in. Then, they might buy a small residential rental property, such as a duplex or triplex. As time goes on, they invest in larger properties, such as apartment buildings or commercial properties (like office buildings or retail properties). People also invest in vacant land (such as a subdivided lot or a large parcel for future development).

Currency

We can invest in a foreign currency, hoping that the currency goes up in value, relative to our own currency. For example, let's assume that you buy Swiss francs at an exchange rate of 0.8664, which means that you can exchange 1 U.S. dollar for 0.8664 francs. If you invest $2,000 you will get 1,732.80 Swiss francs (2,000 × 0.8664 = 1,732.80). Then, suppose 2 years later the exchange rate has changed to 0.7120. You can sell your Swiss francs for $2,433.71 (1,732.80 Swiss francs ÷ 0.7120 = 2,433.71). You made $433.71.

Precious Metals

People invest in gold, silver, and other metals in hopes that they will increase in value.

Collectibles

People buy art, trading cards, stamps, coins, memorabilia, and other items in hopes that the demand (and, therefore, value) will go up.

The 8 Investment Criteria

When deciding on one investment over another, there are several factors to consider, including (1) management, (2) liquidity, (3) cash flow, (4) appreciation, (5) tax consequences, (6) risk, (7) leverage, and (8) rate of return.

Criteria 1. Management

Not all investments require the same degree of involvement. For example, owning stocks, bonds, and mutual funds requires very little involvement. Owning an apartment building requires substantial management (and a lot of aspirin!); even if the owner hires a property management company to oversee the property, the owner must select and oversee the property management company. Some investors do not mind a high degree of involvement; others want an investment requiring minimal management.

Criteria 2. Liquidity

In some cases, investors must sell (liquidate) an investment because of changes in investment goals, to take advantage of new investment opportunities, or because of a financial emergency. Some investments—such as stocks, bonds, and mutual funds—can be liquidated very quickly. Other investments, such as real estate, take considerable time to sell; that is one of the drawbacks of investing in real estate.

Criteria 3. Cash Flow

Investors want to receive more cash back from an investment than they put into it; otherwise they are losing money. Some investors need substantial cash flow during the investment period, while others don't care about cash flow *during* the investment as long as they get plenty of cash when the investment is *sold*. The need for cash flow during an investment narrows an investor's choices. For example, an investor who needs lots of cash flow during an investment would probably not want to invest in vacant land or zero-coupon bonds.

Criteria 4. Appreciation

Fixed-return investments, such as a savings account or CD, do not have the potential to appreciate; we know exactly what our return will be. Fixed-return investments do not increase in value; the investor is paid interest with no additional profit. Equity-type investments, such as stocks and real estate, have the *potential* to appreciate. Values can also decrease. For equity-type investments, an investor's return is uncertain.

Some investors prefer fixed returns because fixed returns take some of the uncertainty out of investing. But during periods of inflation, we can lose buying power with fixed-return investments. For example, if we invest in a 5-year CD paying 4% interest, and inflation is 6%, our investment is not keeping up with inflation. Equity-type investments, on the other hand, have historically increased in value as the price of goods has increased; using investment terminology, equity-type investments are a "hedge" against inflation.

Many young investors choose equity-type investments. But when they get older they say, It has taken 40 years to accumulate this money and I don't want to lose it! So they invest some, or all, of their portfolio in fixed-return investments.

Criteria 5. Tax Consequences

Not all investments have the same income tax consequences. Here are some income tax consequences (as of the writing of this book) for a few investments:

- For savings accounts or corporate bonds, interest is fully taxable.
- For U.S. savings bonds, the owner can make the election of reporting a pro-rated portion of interest annually or can report interest the year in which the

bond is redeemed. Under certain conditions, interest from U.S. savings bonds that is used to finance a college education is totally exempt from taxation.

- For loans we make, the interest portion of the payments we collect is taxable; the principal portion is not taxable.

- For qualified municipal bonds (some are not qualified), interest is exempt from federal income tax. Some states do tax the interest if the bonds were issued from certain states (those without a reciprocal agreement).

- For stocks, most dividends are taxable. This is a form of double taxation. Here's why. Corporations must pay federal and, in most states, state income tax on their profits. Whatever is left over can be distributed as dividends. Then, stockholders must pay income tax on the dividends they receive. Corporate dividends may, however, be taxed at lower rates than ordinary income; they are taxed at the same rates as capital gains (see Step 5 of the book).

- For the sale of stocks and real estate, gains may be taxed at lower rates (see Step 5 of the book).

- For rental property, we must report rents and we can deduct expenses of the property (like repairs, property taxes, utilities, insurance, interest, etc.). We can also deduct depreciation as an operating expense even though depreciation is not a cash expenditure; we discuss depreciation in detail in Step 5.

- For the home that we live in, we can deduct interest (generally limited to interest on mortgages of $1,000,000 or less) and property taxes as itemized deductions (Schedule A). Another tax benefit—a huge advantage—is the right to exempt the first $250,000 of gain when we sell the home, provided we have lived in the home for at least 2 of the last 5 years ($500,000 of gain if we are married filing jointly). Suppose, for example, that you and your spouse purchased your home 8 years ago for $300,000 and spent $100,000 on qualified improvements. Your total cost (called adjusted basis) is $400,000. Suppose you and your spouse have lived in the home all of that time, just sold the home for $980,000, and incurred selling expenses (real estate commissions, title insurance, etc.) of $50,000. Your gain is: $980,000 - $50,000 - $400,000 = $530,000. Since $500,000 is tax exempt, you must report only $30,000 of the gain.

- For an investment in vacant land, we can claim interest and property taxes as itemized deductions.

Criteria 6. Risk

Risk is perhaps the most important factor to consider when making an investment. Before investing ask, What can go wrong with this particular investment, and can I survive financially if that happens? The following situations could cause an investment to be a financial flop:

Stock

- The company you invest in has inefficient or dishonest management.

- The company gets sued. For example, you may invest in a nuclear power company just before a power plant explosion, in an oil company just before an oil spill, or in a pharmaceutical company just before a customer is poisoned from the company's product.

- A competitor invents a better product, making your company's product worthless.

- Often, many stock prices rise or fall together, depending on how investors feel about the overall economy and stock market. When investors are optimistic, stock prices rise; this is referred to as a bull market. When investors are pessimistic, stock prices fall; this is referred to as a bear market. If you bought your stock just before the start of a bear market, you could lose money.

- Just after you buy your stock, the company announces its quarterly profits. If the profits are less than anticipated, or the company had a loss, your stock price could go down.

- A change in interest rates can affect stock prices. An increase in interest rates is bad news for the stock market. Not only do corporations have higher interest costs on borrowed money, but higher rates discourage consumers from spending and/or borrowing to buy corporate products and services. Also, higher interest rates generally result in an increase in bond rates, which increases the demand for bonds, taking investors away from the stock market.

Bonds

- The company or municipality goes broke, leaving bondholders with bonds worth pennies on the dollar.

- Many beginning investors think that a $1,000 bond is always worth $1,000. While a $1,000 bond is worth $1,000 at maturity, the same bond may be worth more or less than $1,000 *prior* to maturity, depending on the prevailing rate for similar bonds. For example, if you own a bond paying 4% and new bonds are paying 6%, investors will buy the 6% bond instead of yours; to attract a buyer you will have to sell your bond for less than $1,000 (a *discount*) so that the buyer can earn 6%.

Mutual funds

- The mutual fund company may invest your money in things that decrease in value. For example, a mutual fund company that invests in stocks would likely have values drop during a bear market.

- The mutual fund company's management fees may be greater than profits from the fund.

Rental property

- Population in your area decreases, resulting in higher vacancy rates and lower rents. The main culprit for a population decrease in an area is a loss of jobs; when jobs go away, so do the people. Areas with one major employer are at higher risk than areas with a diversified employment market.

- Wages decrease or a recession occurs. When money is tight, tenants "double-up" with friends or move in with family, reducing the tenant population.

- Apartment construction booms, resulting in too many apartments in your area. The increased supply will result in higher vacancy rates and lower rents.

- You suffer a loss due to fire, flood, or earthquake. If you do not have adequate insurance, the results could be devastating.

- Unfavorable tax laws are enacted, reducing the demand for owning rental property. As a result, values drop.

- Landlord/tenant laws change in a way that is unfavorable to landlords.

- Mortgage rates drop dramatically. As a result, lots of tenants buy homes, which decreases the tenant population and, therefore, rents.

- Expenses of maintaining a rental property increase dramatically. Because investors are interested in the "bottom line," the property value will go down.

- The yield for alternative investments increases dramatically. When this happens, investors gravitate toward the alternative investment and away from real estate; less demand for real estate results in a drop in value.

These what-ifs are not intended to discourage investing; the purpose is to encourage prudent investing, making sure the risk is not more than we can handle. Historically, some investments have done well during periods of inflation; some have done well during a recession. Most investors place their money in a variety of investments to reduce overall risk. The following proverbs definitely apply to investing.

Don't bite off more than you can chew
&
Don't put all your eggs in one basket

Criteria 7. Leverage

You may remember from physics that leverage can be used to lift heavy objects. For example, a person might have trouble lifting a 100-pound rock. With leverage, the same 100-pound rock can be lifted easily. Leverage is similar in investing. Leverage is using borrowed money to control more investments than could otherwise be controlled. Leverage has a dramatic effect on cash flow.

Suppose you and your brother Reed each have $150,000 to invest. Reed uses his $150,000 as a down payment on a 54-unit apartment building. The property costs $3,000,000; Reed pays the seller $150,000 down and agrees to pay the seller the remaining $2,850,000 @ $23,000 per month ($276,000 a year). During the first year, Reed collects a total of $455,300 in rents and has expenses totaling $141,800. You use your $150,000 as a down payment on a 6-unit apartment building. The property costs $400,000; you pay the seller $150,000 down and agree to pay the seller the remaining $250,000 @ $2,000 a month ($24,000 a year). During the first year, you collect a total of $58,700 in rents and have expenses totaling $18,500. You each invested $150,000, but who comes out ahead in terms of cash flow? Here are the results:

Reed: $455,300 (rent) – $141,800 (expenses) – $276,000 (mortgage payments) = **$37,500**
You: $58,700 (rent) – $18,500 (expenses) – $24,000 (mortgage payments) = **$16,200**

Using leverage, Reed gets $21,300 more than you did. Now, suppose that at the end of the first year, a major employer moves to another state, causing an increase in vacancy rates and a decrease in rents. During Year 2, Reed is able to collect a total of $302,400; his expenses increase to $157,900. You collect a total of $39,000; your expenses are $20,600. Here are the cash flows for Year 2:

Reed: $302,400 (rent) – $157,900 (expenses) – $276,000 (mortgage payments) = – **$131,500**
You: $39,000 (rent) – $20,600 (expenses) – $24,000 (mortgage payments) = – **$5,600**

In the second year, Reed (who used leverage) must subsidize his investment a whopping $131,500! You need only $5,600. If Reed does not have $131,500 sitting around, he will be forced to sell other assets, borrow on other assets, or face the consequences of a foreclosure on his 54-unit apartment building.

As you can see, leverage works to the advantage of an investor when conditions are right, but leverage can lead to financial ruin under adverse conditions. Using our physics analogy, it is possible for the "lever" to break or the rock to slip. Be careful in selecting the right size rock (investment) and amount of leverage (loan) so that if something goes wrong, the rock will not crush you as it comes tumbling down.

Criteria 8. Rate of Return

Comparing rates of return is valuable in helping to decide between different investments. For example, if you can get an 8.06% rate of return on one bond and a 7.95% rate of return on a second bond, you may want to invest in the first bond (assuming all other factors are equal) because it provides a greater rate of return.

Comparing investments with the same income tax consequences (like corporate bonds to corporate bonds) is pretty straightforward. But what if the investments have different income tax consequences? Assume, for example, you are in a 28% tax bracket and are trying to decide whether to invest in a corporate bond providing a yield of 8.06% or a tax-exempt municipal bond providing a yield of 5.95%. For each dollar of interest from the corporate bond, you must pay 28 cents (28%) as federal income tax; you lose 28% of your earnings to the tax man. Your after-tax rate on the corporate bond is

Total rate	8.06
Portion to taxes: 8.06 × 28%	−2.26
Remainder (after-tax portion)	**5.80**

Your after-tax rate on the corporate bond is 5.80%. The municipal bond provides the greater after-tax rate (5.95%).

TIP   **don't rely exclusively on a rate of return**

While calculating a rate of return is an important investment tool, don't disregard the other investment criteria. On page 113, we will use the 8 Investment Criteria to compare an investment in rental real estate with another type of investment.

Do I Really Want to Be a Landlord?

I am a strong believer in building wealth through investing in real estate, particularly with rental real estate. I have seen lots of people from a variety of backgrounds build wealth by investing in rental real estate. They have done it slowly but surely, and in most cases the monthly cash flow from their real estate investments exceeds their wages and other income. Real estate has become their major source of income and retirement.

Not everyone is cut out to be a successful investor in rental property. Here are some questions you should ask yourself.

Do I Have the Time?

Researching, purchasing, and owning rental real estate takes time. You may feel like you are already stretched too thin with work and family. Chances are, however, you can probably find time for things you *really* want to do. If investing in real estate is one of those things, you can probably find the time.

Can I Handle the Stress?

The process of researching a property, negotiating a purchase, and working with tenants can add some stress to your life. Some people (myself included) get a bit stressed when going on vacation to a new destination. Once we get there and get settled, the stress is replaced by relaxation. That's what it can be like when venturing into rental real estate. The research and number-crunching can be exciting, hoping the numbers turn out nicely. Negotiating with the seller can be painless if we are respectful and honest with the seller; it doesn't have to be a confrontational relationship. And the stress of managing a property (ordering repairs, working with tenants, etc.) can be minimized if we remember to treat other people the way we would like to be treated. We can, if we want, hire a property manager to help with the day-to-day management.

Do I Need a Huge Amount of Money?

Some people think investing in rental real estate takes a large chunk of money to get started. That is not the case. I am *not* a fan of buying real estate with nothing (or very little) down. Highly leveraging a property dramatically increases an investor's risk. But that doesn't mean we need a fortune before starting to invest. We could, for instance, start out by buying a small property. And we could invest with some friends. For example, let's say you are thinking about buying a $180,000 duplex. If you put 20% down and borrow the remaining 80%, your down payment would be $36,000. If you buy the property with two friends, and each of you puts up one-third of the down payment, you would need only $12,000. As an added bonus of investing with others, you have less risk because you have other people to share in any unexpected decrease in cash flow.

I recommend that before beginning to invest in rental real estate, you pay off your credit card debt and have an emergency fund set aside. Most financial planners recommend an emergency fund that will cover up to 6 months of living expenses; the emergency fund should consist of liquid assets (money that you can get your hands on quickly). Having an emergency fund will provide a sense of financial well-being, and will also help with mortgage applications. If you have not yet paid off your credit cards and do not have an emergency fund, start now. Meantime, you can begin using Steps 2 through 7 of the book before ever making an offer on a property!

Do I Know Enough?

Most successful people, in any field, start out knowing very little about what they get into. This book provides a good foundation for investing in rental real estate. If you do your research, listen carefully to others, and use common sense, you will soon be able to distinguish a "good" deal from a "bad" deal. Before long, you may be the expert that others seek out.

Do I Have to Know How to Fix Things?

While it is nice to have a mechanical touch, most landlords don't. Most do what the rest of us do: call someone who knows how to fix things—a general handy-man (or handywoman) who knows how to fix a variety of things or a specialist for more difficult repair jobs. For larger properties, the owner may employ a repair person by paying a weekly or monthly salary.

Over time, most landlords learn how to fix some basic things without having to call a repair person; for example, a clogged sink or drain can often be fixed by you or your tenant using a plunger.

Will There Be Surprises?

Yes! You may get a call from a tenant in the middle of the night saying water is coming through the ceiling. Or market conditions may change, resulting in higher vacancy rates and lower rents. But remember, all investments have draw-backs. Owning rental property has its rewards. We can increase rents when the market allows, and hopefully the value of the property increases. After making a down payment and getting a mortgage loan for the remainder of the price, our tenants help us pay off the mortgage loan; after the loan is paid off, our cash flow increases dramatically! Owning rental property provides some nice tax advantages that other investments do not offer. And it is rewarding to be responsible for upgrading a property to provide a nice place for people to live.

 Moving forward. Hopefully, you've decided you would like to look further into rental real estate. On to Step 2!

Get Your Ducks in a Row

We'll Explore

- Assembling a Team of Experts
- Finding Properties
- Finding Money
- Partners & Forms of Ownership

Before investing in rental real estate, you should do some basic ground work, like finding experts to help make decisions, deciding which types of rental property to invest in, understanding market trends in the area, and finding a lender. Then you will be ready to "pounce" on a good deal when it becomes available.

Assembling a Team of Experts

When investing in rental real estate, (1) make sure that a property is worth buying *before* making the purchase, (2) maximize cash flow during the investment, (3) sell at the right time and for the right price, and (4) pay the least amount of income taxes along the way. That requires making *lots* of decisions. Investors who think that they can make all of the decisions without any help are at a big disadvantage. It's like trying to be a one-person football team, doomed from the opening kickoff. No matter how knowledgeable you become, you will not know as much as individual experts in their field. Even well-seasoned investors have a team of experts to help make decisions. Having help along the way may cost a bit more in the short term but will likely save lots of money in the long term. Neglecting to hire a property inspector before buying a property will save an inspection fee, but may cost a fortune later when the roof collapses! Here are a few general qualities to look for in team members:

- *They are good listeners.* They should understand our situation and what we are trying to achieve.

- *They care.* There are lots of people who don't have the ability to put themselves in other people's shoes. Many people look out only for themselves. It's important that the people we select put their hearts into working on our behalf.

- *They are interested in having a long-term relationship*, rather than being focused on making some quick money.

- *They are honest.* To illustrate, a good real estate agent will talk us out of a deal that doesn't make economic sense, even though the agent will lose a commission on the deal.

- *They specialize in rental real estate.* This is especially important when selecting a real estate agent and attorney.

- *They aren't afraid to share their opinions.* We don't want yes-men who will agree with everything we suggest. We don't have to agree with all of their advice, but we are paying them to give it, hopefully without being asked.

Get basic team members lined up right from the get-go: an attorney, income tax advisor, real estate agent, and property management company.

Attorney

Having an attorney for your real estate investments may seem like an unnecessary expense. But there are several things you may need advice on:

- How to own the properties: as an individual, a limited liability company (LLC), corporation, or some other business entity? A qualified attorney can advise us how to best protect our personal assets and provide maximum tax benefits.

- Help with landlord/tenant issues, including disputes with tenants.

- In some locations, buyers and sellers are required to have an attorney for any real estate transaction. In many locations, preprinted forms are used, but even in those cases some things will require the advice of an attorney.

Chances are, one attorney may not be an expert in all areas mentioned, so you may need a different attorney for each purpose. Remember, you want *expert* help in all areas.

Income Tax Advisor

Income tax laws constantly change so it is important to have the advice of someone who keeps current on tax rules. A good tax advisor can help minimize income taxes by suggesting how to treat income and expenses, and in structuring a purchase or sale. A good tax advisor can also complete the necessary forms at tax time each year.

Few tax advisors fully understand the tax laws that apply to rental real estate. When selecting a tax consultant, make sure the person is an expert on rental real estate tax laws.

Real Estate Agent

If you are not familiar with how real estate agents are paid, here are a few basics. Real estate agents are paid a commission, generally by the seller, due when a sale is completed. Commissions are negotiable, but are often about 5% to 7% of the sales price for homes and condos, about 4% to 6% for small investment properties, and about 1% to 3% for large investment properties.

Real estate agents are licensed by the state in which they do business. Each real estate office has a broker who is responsible for all of the agents in that office.

In many transactions, two agents are involved—one representing the seller and another representing the buyer. If, for example, a $24,000 commission were split equally between the two offices, the listing office (the one representing the seller) would get $12,000 and the selling office (the one representing the buyer) would get $12,000. Each office would then share its $12,000 with its agent, on an agreed-upon basis: agents often get about 50% to 90% of the total received by their office; the company keeps the remainder to cover overhead.

In some cases, the listing agent not only works with the seller but also shows the property to a buyer. This is called dual agency. When an agent acts as a dual agent, representing both the seller and the buyer, he or she must divulge this to the seller and buyer, since it is difficult to fairly represent both the seller and the buyer at the same time.

Some investors prefer to buy unlisted properties directly from a seller. Doing so allows them to negotiate directly with the seller and they figure that if a property is listed for sale through a real estate company, the price may be higher (to cover the real estate commission). Most investors, however, prefer to work with a top-notch real estate agent who specializes in investment property. Top-notch agents know the market. They understand what's happening with vacancy rates and rents. They understand which areas of town tenants are moving to. They also know what's happening to values. Top-notch agents can help buyers find properties they might not find on their own, can often help identify problems with properties, and can help with the negotiations, financing, inspections, and the closing. Finally, top-notch agents can help investors figure out when it's time to sell and can help find a buyer.

Property Management Company

Many owners of rental property do their own property management. Others hire a property management company to do the day-to-day management. For smaller properties, a property manager is generally paid a percent of rents collected (about 6% to 15% of rents, depending on the property). For larger properties, the owner may hire a property management staff, paying each member of the staff a salary.

A good property manager has relationships with repair people and vendors, and can get them to respond promptly. They know how to communicate fairly and effectively with tenants and others. Many property managers oversee several properties, allowing them to get better pricing from vendors and repair people. In some cases, a property manager can save an owner more than the owner pays in property management fees—by increasing rents when needed, by renting vacant units quickly, by selecting tenants who will pay their rent and take care of the property, and by getting repairs done efficiently and at competitive prices. And a good property manager relieves the owner of headaches along the way.

How to Find Key Team Members

You may be asking, How do I find these team members? Here are a few ideas. Ask other real estate investors who they use, and why. Go to larger properties that have management offices and inquire. Or call landlords or property managers who place "for rent" ads. Let them know that you want to become a landlord and would appreciate their help.

Once you find an expert in his or her field, chances are that person can suggest experts in other fields. A real estate agent who specializes in rental real estate will likely have suggestions for property managers, tax consultants, and attorneys who specialize in rental property.

Check with local organizations like the local Board of Realtors (for a real estate agent) or the state Bar Association (for an attorney).

Finding people on the Internet may not be the best way to find experts in their field. The people listed may be hungry for business because they are *not* experts in their field.

Once you get names, meet with the people and ask plenty of questions about their experience and views. Ask for permission to contact some of their clients; then call those clients to see how pleased they are. You may get lucky and find a great person on the first try; if not, keep looking.

Finding Other Team Members

In addition to having basic team members, you will need the help of others. You can find most of these people by getting recommendations from your real estate agent or property manager. Here are a few people you will likely need help from along the way:

- *Property inspector.* Before buying a property, hire a competent inspector to evaluate the condition of the buildings and their components. The inspector may recommend contacting specialists (like a roofing company to give a more detailed report on the roof).

- *Contractor/Remodeling specialist.* To maximize rents, you may want to upgrade the exterior and interior of the property, which will require a contractor or remodeling specialist.

- *Repair specialists.* Most landlords have a handyman who can do a variety of repairs, plus specialists (like plumbers and electricians) for jobs the handyman can't do.

- *Suppliers.* You will need sources to buy products like appliances, floor coverings, and light fixtures.

- *Insurance agent.* You will want an agent who can provide insurance coverage on your properties at reasonable prices.

- *Appraiser.* You may want to have a qualified appraiser tell you what a property is worth before you buy or sell it. If you are getting a loan on a property, the lender will get an appraisal; some buyers get their own appraisal anyway, because they would rather rely on the opinion of their appraiser than the one the lender hires.

- *Architect.* If you make substantial improvements to a property you may need to hire an architect.

- *Structural engineer.* If a building has a structural problem you will need a structural engineer to recommend a solution.

Finding Properties

Now let's consider the type of rental real estate to invest in, which geographical areas will work best, if the timing is right, and how to find specific properties.

Types of Rental Real Estate

Once you make the decision to invest in rental real estate and have put together a team of experts, you can start looking for properties to invest in. Ask yourself which types of rental real estate you feel most comfortable with. You could invest in something as simple as a single family home or residential condominium, and rent it out. You could invest in a residential duplex, triplex, fourplex, or larger complex. Or, you could invest in a commercial property, like a retail building, an office building, a neighborhood shopping center, a warehouse or manufacturing building, or a large shopping mall.

The common thread for all of these investments is that you would be the owner of the property and collect rent from your tenants. Each type of property has some pros and cons. Here are a few things to consider:

- Smaller properties require less cash and have smaller mortgage payments.

- As a general rule, the more affordable a property is, the more buyers line up to buy it. More demand means an elevated price. While this works against a buyer of a smaller property, it will work to that investor's benefit when he or she sells the property.

- As a general rule, larger properties have an economy of scale when it comes to expenses. For example, landscaping expense may not be much different on a large office building than it is on a lower-priced duplex.

- As a general rule, commercial tenants stay longer than residential tenants and there are less day-to-day headaches overseeing commercial tenants than there are overseeing residential tenants.

- It is generally easier to find residential tenants than commercial tenants. Finding a commercial tenant may require enlisting the services of a commercial lease specialist and paying a lease commission. And it might take considerable time to fill the vacancy.

- Single-tenant properties are easier to manage than multi-tenant properties, but the risk is greater because a vacancy in a single-tenant building results in a 100% vacancy rate.

Most people who invest in rental real estate start out with something simple, like a duplex, then gradually invest in larger properties. Some investors get into real estate development, finding vacant land and developing the land with new residential or commercial buildings; as you might imagine, developing a site involves lots of work, including getting a building permit, getting plans from an architect, arranging financing, getting a contractor, overseeing construction, and finding tenants.

Where to Invest

Once you have decided what types of rental real estate you feel comfortable investing in, you must decide which geographical area(s) to invest in. Most investors agree that it is safer to invest in an area they are familiar with. It is difficult enough trying to understand the dynamics of the rental market in an area you know; imagine trying to figure out the trends in an unfamiliar area. And consider travel time and the drawback of not being able to visit the property on a regular basis. If you are thinking of investing in an area you are not familiar with, get a team of experts to help understand the rental market in that area.

Most towns have some nice areas, and some that are not so nice. Prices of rental property are generally lower in the run-down areas than in the nicer areas. You may be able to buy a 12-unit apartment building in a distressed area of town for, say, 70% of what it would cost in a nicer part of town. That may make it enticing to buy a property in a distressed area, but here are a few things to consider. First, you can spend tons of money to upgrade a property but doing so will not change the neighborhood; you will be limited on how much you can increase rents because of the neighborhood. In addition, the property will not appeal to top-quality tenants because of the neighborhood; marginal tenants typically do not pay their rent as promptly, require more attention, and may not take care of the property as well as better-quality tenants. And when it is time to sell, the property will likely sell for that same 70% of what a similar property will sell for in a nicer area of town. The recommendation here is not necessarily to avoid investing in distressed areas of a town, but to make sure to consider the big picture and be prepared to work with tenants that the property will attract.

Be cautious when buying a rental property surrounded by other rental properties. For example, don't buy a duplex that is on a street filled with other duplexes. If the other investors let their property get run down, or let their tenants do car repairs in the front yard, your property will suffer. You are better off buying a duplex that is surrounded by single family homes where owners are more likely to maintain their property.

You should figure out what sections of town are attracting tenants, and why. Perhaps a certain part of town is becoming more popular because a new major employer has moved into that part of town. Or maybe freeway access or traffic patterns have changed, making certain areas more accessible. Maybe an older section has been revitalized, attracting new residents from other parts of town. Maybe a college or university has expanded, attracting additional students to that particular area. Maybe gas prices have skyrocketed, causing tenants to move away from the outlying areas to the downtown areas where they work.

Is Now the Right Time to Invest?

The best time to own rental property is when vacancy rates are decreasing and rents are on the rise (lower vacancy rates and higher rents result in higher values). And the best time to sell is before a downturn in the rental market (before values drop). Unfortunately, there is no crystal ball for predicting what will happen to the rental market. But you can do some research to make a well-educated guess. To help predict what the future holds, get input from an expert, like a qualified real estate agent or property manager. Here are some things to consider:

- *Unemployment trends.* During periods of increased unemployment, tenants tend to move in with relatives or double-up with other tenants, increasing the vacancy rate.

- *Mortgage interest rates.* When mortgage rates drop dramatically, tenants leave rental units to buy homes, increasing the vacancy rate.

- *Rental property construction.* A sudden surge of rental property construction quickly increases the vacancy rate. An area that has a small amount of vacant land to build rental properties has less risk than an area with ample available land.

- *Population changes.* Demographic data (population, average age, household income, etc.) can be found through local agencies or from sites on the Internet.

- *Diversified employment base.* If a particular industry or employer closes up shop or makes heavy lay-offs, the demand for rental units can disappear. It is less risky to invest in areas that have a diversified employment base.

- *Changes in income tax laws.* If tax laws change adversely for rental real estate, there will be fewer investors interested in investing in rental property, causing a decrease in values of rental property.

- *Vacancy rates and rental rates.* Vacancy rates are a function of *supply and demand.* If demand (the number of tenants) outpaces supply (the number of rental units), vacancy rates drop. If supply (the number of rental units) outpaces demand (the number of tenants), vacancy rates increase. And rental rates are a function of vacancy rates. A low vacancy rate (less than 5%, perhaps) puts landlords in a favorable position, able to increase rents. A high vacancy rate (over 10%, perhaps), puts landlords in an unfavorable position, probably forced to decrease rents. A marginal vacancy rate (between 5% and 10%, perhaps) often results in no dramatic changes in rental rates.

Monitoring vacancy rates and rents is a critical part of the process. Your real estate agent and property manager can let you know what's happening with vacancy rates and rents, as well as where they get their data. In many areas, local agencies and companies (such as real estate companies that specialize in rental real estate, universities and colleges, and Apartment House Associations) monitor trends and make the information available with periodic reports. Local newspapers often publish the data. And check the Internet. You can also conduct your own survey by visiting or calling a few large complexes, asking them how many units they have at their complex and how many units are currently vacant. Suppose, in your survey, there are 76 vacant units out of 1,824 units. The vacancy rate in your survey is: $76 \div 1{,}824 = .0417$, or 4.17%. Keep in mind that in some areas, vacancy rate changes are seasonal; in a small town with a university that attracts out-of-town students, the vacancy rate may spike during the summer months when students return to their hometowns.

If you conclude that something will adversely affect the rental market in the near future, it would be wise to wait before investing; you could instead buy when prices bottom out or invest in a different type of property.

How to Find Specific Properties to Invest in

Once you decide which type of property to invest in, which geographical area to invest in, and that the time is right to invest, you and/or your agent can start to look for specific properties. Let's assume you decide to invest in a residential rental property, with 8 to 24 units, and buildings no more than 30 years old. You want each unit to have it's own gas and electric meters so that tenants can pay for their own heat, lights, air-conditioning, and hot water. You would be okay with one-bedroom units, but would prefer two-bedroom units. For two-bedroom units you would prefer that each unit has two bathrooms, and would prefer that each unit have it's own laundry hookups. You want adequate off-street parking, and you want the property to be in a nice area of town, preferably one that is within 15 miles of the downtown business district and the local university.

Your real estate agent will have connections with sellers and other agents. Some agents belong to a Multiple Listing Service (MLS), in which agents share listings; some agents specializing in rental real estate do not belong to the MLS, but still share listing information with other agents through a networking system. Here is a suggestion: work with only one real estate agent. Loyalty to the agent breeds loyalty from the agent; you want to be the first person the agent calls about a newly listed property. If a property doesn't fit the bill, let the agent know as soon as possible, and why.

You can also find rental properties on the Internet (*www.loopnet.com* and *www.costar.com*). Most local real estate offices that specialize in rental real estate have their own website that shows available properties. And most local newspapers have ads showing rental property available for sale.

You can ask other members of your team (like your property manager, lawyer, income tax advisor, contractors, suppliers, lender, accountant, etc.) to let you know of any available properties.

If there don't seem to be any properties that fit the bill, you can do some bird-dogging of your own. You can call owners who have placed "for rent" ads in the paper or on the Internet, asking if they would be interested in selling their property. Or you can drive around and write down addresses of properties that might fit the bill. To find the owner's name and phone number, ask a tenant or resident manager at the property, or go to the county assessor's office for the contact information. For a property you find on your own, you might want to ask your real estate agent to help put the deal together; he or she may do it for a lower-than-normal commission since you found the property.

Finding Money

Mortgage lenders decide whether to make loans, and at what interest rate, based on the borrower's ability to make the payments, and the collateral. Collateral is the property that can be claimed by the lender in the event of default. When evaluating the borrower, lenders consider the borrower's credit history, income and expenses, job stability, and assets and liabilities. When evaluating the collateral, lenders get an appraisal (generally paid for by the borrower) to make sure that the loan amount does not exceed the value. The percent of the value that will be loaned is referred to as the loan-to-value (LTV) ratio. A borrower with good credit and ability to pay can get a lower interest rate than someone who is more of a risk. And a loan with a lower LTV ratio would be more attractive to a lender because there is less risk to the lender.

The basic type of loan is called a conventional loan. An FHA loan must meet Federal Housing Administration (FHA) guidelines; payments are made to the lending institution, *not* to the FHA. A VA loan must be approved by the Veterans Administration (VA). The borrower must be a qualified veteran. Payments are made to the lending institution, *not* to the VA.

Loans are much easier to get on 1- to 4-unit properties (single family homes, condos, duplexes, triplexes, and fourplexes) than they are on properties of 5 units and more. On 1- to 4-unit properties, the LTV ratio will often be in the range of 80%. Higher LTV ratios are available if the owner will be an occupant of one of the units; in fact, if the buyer will be an occupant the LTV ratio can be as high as 97% for an FHA loan, and as high as 100% for a VA loan. For 5 units and up, the LTV ratio is often about 70% to 80%, but is sometimes less, depending on the borrower's ability to pay, value of collateral, leases in place, and projected cash flow.

Repayment Variations

Many mortgage loans have an interest rate that remains fixed for the entire loan; these loans are referred to as fixed-rate loans. Most fixed-rate loans have monthly payments spread over either 15 years or 30 years, but some are for 10 years, 20 years, or 40 years. The monthly payment on a 15-year $200,000 mortgage loan at 7% interest is $1,797.66.

With an adjustable-rate mortgage (ARM), the interest rate changes at set intervals (like each year). ARMS often start out with a rate lower than that of fixed-rate loans. The interest rate is tied to an index (such as the 1-year T-bill rate). Payments change to reflect the new rate. Most ARMS provide for a maximum interest rate change each year (annual cap) and during the life of the loan (lifetime cap). ARMS work well for borrowers when rates drop, but can be costly when rates rise. The Appendix shows how to calculate payments on an ARM with each interest rate change.

A balloon payment pays off a loan with one large payment. For example, a monthly payment could be calculated using a 30-year term but the borrower may be required to pay the lender whatever balance is still unpaid at the end of 7 years; the required final payment is called a balloon payment. The Appendix shows how to calculate a balloon payment. Some loans on rental properties, especially larger properties, require a balloon payment.

With an interest-only mortgage, the borrower pays interest only (no principal) for the first few years. The monthly interest-only payment on that same $200,000 7% loan would be: $200,000 \times 7\% \div 12 = \$1,166.67$. A borrower has an easier time qualifying because qualification is based on a lower payment. But the loan balance stays the same and when the loan stops being interest-only, the monthly payment jumps considerably.

With a negative amortization loan, the monthly payment starts out less than what is required to cover interest. This makes qualifying for the loan easier. The disadvantage is that the payment is not enough to cover the interest so the loan balance *increases*. And when the negative amortization period ends, the monthly payment jumps considerably.

With a graduated equity mortgage (GEM), monthly payments increase at set intervals. With a 15-year GEM, monthly payments on a $200,000 7% mortgage loan may be $1,500 for the first 3 years, $1,700 for the next 3 years, and then

$2,029.69 for the remaining 9 years. GEMs may work out well on a rental property if rents are increasing enough to cover the increased monthly payments.

<table>
<tr><td>TIP</td><td>can rates increase dramatically?</td></tr>
</table>

You may wonder if mortgage rates really change much. People in the early-1980s were caught by surprise when mortgage rates skyrocketed to 20%! People with ARMs or people who had to get a new loan were forced to pay the increased rate. Be careful, especially with ARMs and balloon payments.

Loan Charges

People getting a mortgage loan may be flabbergasted at how many fees they must pay to get the loan. An origination fee is usually charged, often about 1% of the loan amount. A borrower can pay points to buy down the interest rate; for example, a lender may offer a 5.75% rate with no points or a 5.25% rate with $1^1/_2$ points. Each point represents 1% of the loan amount; $1^1/_2$ points on a $200,000 loan would be $3,000 ($200,000 $\times$ 1.5% = $3,000). Some loans require the borrower to provide mortgage insurance, which insures the lender for an agreed-upon sum in the event the loan is not repaid. Mortgage insurance is generally not required if the LTV ratio is 80% or less. Depending on the type of loan, the mortgage insurance may be paid up-front, monthly, or both. Lenders often charge additional fees, such as processing fees, mortgage broker fees, or application fees.

Borrowers also pay fees to third parties, such as a document preparation fee, credit report fee, appraisal fee, closing fee, and recording fees. Typically, a seller provides a buyer with a policy of title insurance (that insures the buyer against defects in title), and the buyer (borrower) provides the lender with a separate policy, called a lender's policy.

In addition, there are a few other charges at closing. The buyer (borrower) must pay for hazard insurance, which provides reimbursement for losses arising from damage to the property (such as from fire). If the lender requires an escrow account, the borrower must make an initial deposit into the account so that when the upcoming property tax or insurance payment is due, sufficient funds will be in the account. For rental properties, there may be some adjustments between the buyer and seller, such as the seller remitting tenant security deposits or prepaid rent to the buyer, or the buyer reimbursing the seller for expenses the seller has prepaid.

Loan charges are like interest, except they are paid in advance, thereby increasing the *real* interest rate. The *real* interest rate is called the annual percentage rate (APR). The APR on a particular 6% mortgage loan might be 6.53% after considering the loan charges. We may want to instead get a 6.125% loan with lower loan charges and a resulting APR of 6.41%. Being able to calculate and compare APRs is a valuable tool when deciding which mortgage loan to get. The Appendix shows how to calculate an APR for a mortgage loan.

Some lenders offer a *no-cost* or *low-cost loan*, which means the lender waives part or all of the loan charges. This may sound like a great deal, but the lender needs to earn a certain yield. They do so by charging a higher interest rate. For a borrower who projects paying off a loan in a few years, a no-cost or low-cost loan may be a good choice because even though the borrower pays a higher rate for a few years, he or she saves the up-front loan charges. To protect themselves when this happens, some lenders require that the borrower pay a prepayment penalty if the loan is paid off within a specified number of years.

When getting a loan, make sure you understand all of the terms: interest rate, monthly payment, loan charges, late fees provisions, if there is a due-on-sale clause (requiring you to pay the loan off when you sell the property), prepayment penalty, etc.

TIP — **good faith estimate**

Not all mortgage lenders charge the same fees. When searching for a mortgage loan, check around with a few lenders to determine what fees they charge. Be sure to get a good faith estimate, which shows the interest rate, as well as the dollar amount of each loan charge.

Finding a Lender

Not all lenders make loans on rental property. Your real estate agent will likely have a working relationship with lenders who make loans on rental property. Your tax advisor, lawyer, and property manager may also have recommendations. You could also check with your local bank or credit union; if they don't make loans on rental property, ask who does.

Working with a mortgage broker may be a good choice. Mortgage brokers are *not* lenders; they place loans with a lender, acting as a middle man. Mortgage brokers are paid by charging an origination fee and/or by being compensated by the lender.

You may be tempted to search for a mortgage loan on the Internet. Often, promises made for loans on the Internet fall apart, so don't put too much faith in what you are led to believe.

Other Options

Suppose you are trying to buy a rental property for $400,000 and can get a mortgage loan for 75% of the price. You will need $100,000 ($400,000 × 25%). If you really want to do the deal but don't have $100,000, you do have options. You could talk to the seller about seller financing. You might pay the seller $70,000 down, and pay the $330,000 balance over 20 years with 7% interest. Maybe the seller doesn't really need the money and would prefer earning interest from you instead of having to figure out what to do with the money. And the seller may prefer to take his or her money gradually, allowing the profit from the sale (capital gain) to be reported gradually, as received, instead of all at once.

Instead of putting up $100,000 of your money, you could get three partners. Each of you would own 25% of the property. Each would put up 25% of the money ($25,000), report 25% of the income, and deduct 25% of the expenses.

You could look for a smaller property. For example, you could consider buying a $200,000 duplex instead of a larger $400,000 property. Chances are, you could borrow 80%, requiring a down payment of $40,000 instead of the $100,000 on the $400,000 property. If you want to live in one side of the duplex, you might need even less down payment.

You could delay buying a rental property until you have accumulated more money for a down payment. Saving money may mean getting an extra job or cutting back on expenditures.

If you own your home and are thinking of buying another home (or a duplex), you could keep your present home as a rental; keep the loan on your current home (assuming the loan provisions do not prevent you from doing so) and get a higher LTV ratio loan on the new property. Or you could use a home-equity loan. Suppose you own the home you live in, with a value of $350,000 and a first mortgage of $150,000. Many lenders will loan up to 80% of the value. In your case, the maximum combined loan amount would be $280,000 ($350,000 × 80%). Since you already owe $150,000, you could get a home-equity loan of $130,000. You will be given a checkbook; to borrow money, you write a check. You will be charged interest on the amount borrowed, not on the $130,000 credit limit. Most home-equity loans are ARMs. In many cases lenders pay for the appraisal, recording, and title fees.

For many stocks, you can borrow up to 50% of their value at reasonable interest rates. For whole life insurance policies, part of the premium is for life insurance and part is for savings. The savings portion, known as the cash value, grows over time. You may be able to withdraw the cash value or borrow against it. You could also borrow against a retirement plan if the plan allows it; before doing so, determine the required repayment period and the income tax consequences.

Many beginning investors are so anxious to get into a deal that they sacrifice common sense and get into a risky situation. The above ideas can be great solutions in certain situations, but can lead to financial disaster in other situations. Here are a few things to remember:

- Home-equity loans are fairly easy to get but must be repaid. Make sure the cash flows from the rental property will cover all expenses, including the payments on the home-equity loan. And make sure there is some cushion in the cash flows in case rents drop or vacancy rates increase. The last thing you want is to lose your home.

- Borrowing on stocks and bonds can be risky. For example, if you borrow 50% on the value of your stocks and the stock values drop, you will be required to repay part of the loan amount so that the new balance will not exceed 50% of the updated stock values.

- Borrowing against a retirement plan or against the cash value of a life insurance policy may be using the last resort you have in case of an emergency (like unexpected medical bills or a job loss); you will no longer be able to rely on those resources.

The bottom line is this: don't live on the edge when it comes to real estate investing. Things can change quickly. Before getting into any real estate investment, make sure you have adequate cash or other assets in case things change for the worse.

Partners & Forms of Ownership

Getting partners can be beneficial when investing in rental real estate. Having partners means less down payment for each person, less risk in case rents drop or vacancy rates increase, and less cash needed from each person for a renovation or upgrade of the property.

But there can be disagreements on who will do the day-to-day management of the property, what to do with excess cash flow, whether to make major improvements, what to do if one partner doesn't contribute his or her share of needed cash or needs to sell early, and deciding when the entire group should sell. If you get partners, be sure to agree on these things, in writing, up front.

Having partners with different skills can be valuable. A partner who is a real estate agent can be helpful in locating properties. A partner who is a lawyer can be helpful in dealing with tenant issues. A builder as a partner can be helpful for properties that require upgrading. And a property manager as a partner can answer the question of who will do the property management.

There are several ways to invest in rental property with people we know. Here's a quick breakdown:

Simple Joint Venture

Basics

With a simple joint venture, each investor takes title to his or her share of the property separately. If the investors take title as joint tenants, when one of the investors dies, his or her share goes to the surviving joint tenant(s). If the investors take title as tenants in common, when one of the investors dies, his or her share does *not* go to the survivors; it goes to his or her heirs. Suppose that Nelda wants to own 40% of a property and Jack and Jill Berry, a married couple, want to own the other 60%. Nelda could take title to her 40% as a tenant in common with the Berrys, who could take their 60% as joint tenants with their spouse, but as tenants in common with Nelda. Because laws differ from state to state, get legal advice before deciding how to take title.

Number of owners

Two or more.

Income taxes

Investors report their share of income and expenses on Schedule E and any gain from the sale on Form 4797 and Schedule D of their individual income tax return.

Personal liability

Investors are personally liable for the debts.

Cash distributions

Distributions of cash are not taxable.

General Partnership

Basics

Investors create a formal general partnership under state law. A partnership agreement spells out each partner's duties and rights; partners do not necessarily share profits equally. Title to the property is held under the name of the partnership.

Number of owners

Two or more.

Income taxes

The partnership reports income and expenses on a partnership return, but pays no tax with the return. The partnership gives each partner a Schedule K-1, showing the partner's share of profit or loss; this amount is reported on Schedule E of the partner's individual income tax return.

Personal liability   Each partner is personally liable for the debts of the partnership; creditors can collect 100% of the debt from any or all partners.

Cash distributions   Distributions of cash are not taxed.

Limited Partnership

Basics   A limited partnership requires special documentation with the state, showing who are general partners (these people run the business and make decisions) and who are limited partners (these people contribute money but are not involved in making any decisions).

Number of owners   Two or more.

Income taxes   A limited partnership handles income taxes just like a general partnership. However, if there is a loss for a particular year, the limited partners are generally not allowed to deduct their share of the loss; instead the loss is used to offset future income.

Personal liability   General partners are personally liable for the debts of the partnership; limited partners are not personally liable.

Cash distributions   Distributions of cash are not taxed.

Corporation

Basics   A corporation, formed under state law, is a separate entity, like a person: able to buy assets, borrow money, and perform other business activities. The corporation issues shares of stock to investors (called stockholders) who then become owners of the corporation.

Number of owners   One or more.

Income taxes   The income and expenses of the corporation are reported on a *corporate income tax return* and income taxes are paid by the corporation. For corporations with no more than 35 stockholders, the corporation can elect with the IRS to be treated as an S Corporation; the corporation files a tax return for informational purposes and provides each stockholder with a Schedule K-1, showing the stockholders' share of profit or loss. Each stockholder then reports that amount on his or her individual income tax return.

Personal liability   Individual stockholders are generally not personally liable for debts of the corporation beyond their personal contribution, except in the case of fraud. Because of the limited liability on debts, corporations may have a hard time borrowing money unless individuals (like one or more of the stockholders) agree to be personally liable.

Cash distributions   Distributions of cash (called dividends) must be reported by the stockholders. This is a form of *double taxation*: the corporation pays tax on any profits and whatever is left after paying taxes, if sent to stockholders, is taxed again. This double taxation also applies to distribution of sales proceeds; the corporation pays tax on any gain and the dividends sent to stockholders are taxed again. Corporate dividends may be taxed at lower rates than ordinary income; they are taxed at the same rates as capital gains (see Step 5 of the book). Distributions of cash (dividends) for an S Corporation are, under most conditions, tax-free.

Limited Liability Company

Basics   A limited liability company (LLC) is a special type of ownership, created under state law, that limits the personal liability of its owners.

Number of owners   One or more. Owners are referred to as members.

Income taxes   Before doing business, an LLC must get an Employer Identification Number (EIN) and select how it wishes to be taxed. If the LLC has only one owner, it must be taxed like a sole proprietorship, reporting the income and expenses on Schedule C of their personal income tax return. If the LLC has more than one owner, it can elect to be taxed as either a corporation or partnership.

Personal liability   Owners are not personally liable for the debts of the LLC beyond their personal contribution, except in the case of fraud. As with corporations, LLCs may have a hard time borrowing money unless individuals agree to be personally liable.

Cash distributions   Distributions of cash are treated according to how the LLC elected to be taxed.

TIP   **get professional advice**

When organizing the purchase of rental property with partners or setting up a business entity, be sure to get help from a qualified attorney and tax advisor. Laws that govern forms of ownership are complicated and vary from state to state. People who bring investors into a project must comply with federal and state securities regulations. Keep in mind that tax laws change frequently. Make sure you get qualified advice so that you can select the best form of ownership for your personal situation.

Alternatively, we can own rental real estate with people we don't know.

REITs

Real estate investment trusts (REITs) are corporations that, for the most part, own rental real estate. REITs that invest primarily in rental property (like apartment buildings, offices, shopping centers, hotels, and warehouse buildings) are known as equity REITs; a few REITs, referred to as mortgage REITs, make mortgage loans.

Equity REITs have managers or affiliates who select properties to invest in, find tenants, manage the properties, and decide when to sell properties. Investors are along for the ride, with no decisions to make. So, REITs can be a good way for people to invest in rental real estate without having to endure the headaches associated with direct ownership. And it is much easier to sell a share of stock in a REIT than it is to sell a directly owned rental property.

REITs have a few drawbacks. First, because REITs provide services beyond what a regular property management company does, the fees are greater. Second, the REIT managers may do a poor job of selecting properties, selecting tenants, managing the property, and deciding when to sell; individual investors have no say. And, in some cases, affiliate companies hired by the REIT have ownership ties with the REIT and are paid fees that are higher than market rates; inquire about a relationship between the REIT and its affiliates.

Some REITs are traded on major stock exchanges and must meet SEC regulations. Other REITs, known as private REITS, are not subject to those same requirements, and can make changes that adversely affect investors. Some private REITs require investors to keep their money invested for a certain period of time.

Because REITs are corporations, they must file a corporate income tax return. If the REIT meets certain IRS requirements, the REIT can deduct dividends paid from its taxable income. (The IRS requires REITs to distribute at least 95% of their net income to stockholders.) A REIT that distributes 100% of its taxable income therefore will have no federal income tax liability. The investor-stockholders must pay tax on the dividends they receive.

Rather than invest in a single company, investors can invest in REIT mutual funds; these funds invest in a variety of individual REITs. This results in more diversification than investing in a single REIT. Of course, the mutual fund company will add some management fees on top of the fees of the individual REITs.

TICs

Ownership in tenants-in-common (TIC) property is similar to that of a simple joint venture. The difference is a *sponsor* puts together the group of investors. Each investor receives title to an undivided interest in the property. TIC properties are often high-quality properties: office buildings, shopping centers, or large apartment complexes.

Before investing in a TIC property, here are a few things to consider. First, TIC properties often require a minimum investment (in some cases as much as $1,000,000) and investors must submit financial information for approval. Second, each investor has a vote equal to his or her percentage of ownership; a typical investor might own a measly 2%, providing little say in what happens. Third, to get a loan on the property or to sell the property all of the investors (not just a *majority* of the investors) must agree. Next, TIC properties may be overpriced. In some cases, properties have been recently purchased by the sponsor and marked up dramatically to TIC investors. In addition, the price of the property includes a lot of front-end costs: marketing and administrative services, fees to financial advisors and real estate agents who refer investors, and advisory and consulting fees. Be sure to ask if the property was recently purchased and for how much. And ask who is receiving fees and how much. Finally, many TIC sponsors own the property management company and the advisory company that provide ongoing assistance; the fees are sometimes higher than market rates. Ask about ongoing fees.

 Moving forward. After assembling our team of experts, deciding on a form of ownership, and having a system to find available properties, we get to move to Step 3, where we will separate the contenders from the pretenders!

Eliminate the Duds

We'll Explore

- Price Per Unit
- Price Per Square Foot
- Gross Rent Multiplier
- Is It Worth Pursuing?

M any beginning investors make the mistake of spending countless hours investigating each and every property they hear about. This results in a lot of wasted time. A better approach is to first determine which properties are worth pursuing, and then to explore the *worthwhile* opportunities. Which brings us to Step 3: methods we can use to quickly eliminate overpriced properties.

Price Per Unit

One simple approach to see if a property is worth considering is to figure the *price per unit*, and compare that with the price per unit for similar sold properties. The first step is to determine what similar properties are selling for per unit. If you are thinking about buying a residential apartment complex, with 8 to 24 units, in a particular region of town, you should find sales of similar properties in that area.

You may wonder, How do I find the sales information? Here are some ideas. You can check with owners of rental property to see what sales they know about. Ask your real estate agent. Or you can ask property management companies, real estate appraisers, title insurance companies, or the county assessor's office.

To find the price per unit of an 18-unit complex that sold for $1,480,000, we divide the price ($1,480,000) by the number of units (18), getting $82,222 per unit. Suppose you find eight recent sales that are similar in size and location:

Sale #	Address	Sales Price	# Units	Price Per Unit
1	512 Center St	$1,480,000	18	$82,222
2	1225 Club Ave	$850,000	10	$85,000
3	418 Ventura St	$1,857,000	24	$77,375
4	777 Green Ave	$1,300,000	16	$81,250
5	1383 Park Place	$1,000,000	12	$83,333
6	1075 Boardwalk	$1,050,000	15	$70,000
7	714 Jordan Blvd	$890,000	10	$89,000
8	1520 Ventura St	$705,000	8	$88,125

Make an allowance if one or two of the properties are different from the rest. For example, if the Boardwalk property consists of one-bedroom units and all of the others are two-bedroom units, that might explain the unusually low unit price of the Boardwalk property. If we ignore the Boardwalk sale, the average price per unit is about $83,800 (rounded to the nearest hundred):

$$\frac{\$82,222 + \$85,000 + \$77,375 + \$81,250 + \$83,333 + \$89,000 + \$88,125}{7} =$$

$$\frac{\$586,305}{7} = \$83,757.86 \approx \textbf{\$83,800}$$

We could conclude that buyers of similar apartment complexes are paying between $77,375 per unit and $89,000 per unit, with the average being about $83,800 per unit.

Now, let's suppose we hear about a 14-unit two-bedroom complex that is priced at $1,475,000. The price per unit is

$$\frac{\$1,475,000}{14 \text{ units}} = \textbf{\$105,357.14}$$

The asking price of $105,357 per unit far exceeds the $83,300 average price per unit of recent sales. Chances are, the 14-unit complex is overpriced.

A price per unit should *not* be the sole indicator of whether a property is a good buy. A price per unit ignores several factors, including: (1) location, (2) age, condition, and quality of construction, (3) size of units, (4) floor plan and features, (5) parking and other amenities, and (6) rental income and expenses.

Select sales that are similar to the property being considered. The sold properties should be as similar as possible in location, age, condition, size of the units, parking, etc.

Price Per Square Foot

Next, let's use the same eight sales to see what similar properties are selling for *per square foot*.

Sale #	Address	Sales Price	Livable Sq Ft	Price Per Sq Ft
1	512 Center St	$1,480,000	13,500	$109.63
2	1225 Club Ave	$850,000	7,800	$108.97
3	418 Ventura St	$1,857,000	19,200	$96.72
4	777 Green Ave	$1,300,000	11,600	$112.07
5	1383 Park Place	$1,000,000	10,200	$98.04
6	1075 Boardwalk	$1,050,000	10,000	$105.00
7	714 Jordan Blvd	$890,000	8,700	$102.30
8	1520 Ventura St	$705,000	7,200	$97.92

Buyers of similar apartment complexes paid between $96.72 per square foot and $112.07 per square foot, with the average being about $103.83 per square foot.

Now, consider that same 14-unit complex, priced at $1,475,000 with 11,200 sq ft. The price per square foot is

$$\frac{\$1,475,000}{11,200 \text{ sq ft}} = \textbf{\$131.70}$$

The asking price of $131.70 per square foot far exceeds the $103.83 average price per square foot found in recent sales, indicating the 14-unit complex may be a real "stinker."

Just as with the price per unit, a price per square foot should not be the sole indicator of whether a property is a good buy. Unlike a price per unit, price per square foot *does* consider the size of the units, but it ignores: (1) location, (2) age, condition, and quality of construction, (3) floor plan and features, (4) the amount of space devoted to common areas (like hallways, central laundry, etc.), (5) parking and other amenities, and (6) rental income and expenses.

Select sales that are similar to the property being evaluated. The sold properties should be as similar as possible in location, age, condition, parking, etc.

Gross Rent Multiplier

When tenants search for an apartment to rent, they consider a variety of factors, including location, age and condition of the building, size of the units, floor plan, special features, parking, landscaping, and other factors. The rent they agree to pay is a result of all of the benefits they receive. They are willing to pay more rent for a property in a nice location, in nice condition, with a good floor plan and good parking than they would for an inferior property. In other words, the rent tenants pay does *not* ignore most of the factors ignored by the cost per unit and the cost per square foot. As a result, many real estate investors use rents as an indicator of whether a property is fairly priced. The relationship between price and gross rent is called a gross rent multiplier (GRM):

$$\text{Gross Rent Multiplier} = \frac{\text{Price}}{\text{Gross Rent}}$$

"Gross" rent is rent before deducting anything for vacancies and expenses. When working with GRMs, some people prefer to use the annual gross rent; others prefer to use a monthly gross rent. We will use a monthly number. Let's use the same eight sales to determine the GRM in the market:

Sale #	Address	Sales Price	Monthly Rent	GRM
1	512 Center St	$1,480,000	$13,300	111.28
2	1225 Club Ave	$850,000	$8,150	104.29
3	418 Ventura St	$1,857,000	$19,500	95.23
4	777 Green Ave	$1,300,000	$12,200	106.56
5	1383 Park Place	$1,000,000	$8,950	111.73
6	1075 Boardwalk	$1,050,000	$9,750	107.69
7	714 Jordan Blvd	$890,000	$9,000	98.89
8	1520 Ventura St	$705,000	$6,700	105.22

Buyers of similar apartment complexes pay between 95.23 times the monthly rent and 111.73 times the monthly rent, with the average being about 105.11 times the monthly rent. In other words, buyers are paying $105.11 to get $1 back each month (in gross rent). Buyers prefer low GRMs because they would rather pay less for each dollar of monthly rent.

Now, let's look at that same 14-unit complex, priced at $1,475,000 with $11,070 of monthly rent. The GRM is

$$\text{Gross Rent Multiplier} = \frac{\text{Price}}{\text{Gross Rent}} = \frac{\$1,475,000}{\$11,070} = \mathbf{133.24}$$

It is no surprise that the GRM of this property far exceeds the GRM found in the market.

TIP　**areas of caution when using Gross Rent Multipliers**

Gross Rent Multipliers can be a good indicator of whether a property is priced right. But here is something to keep in mind: GRMs ignore expenses. As a result, it is important when comparing GRMs to use properties that have similar expense ratios.

An expense ratio is found by dividing expenses by rents. Suppose, for example, Property A and Property B each have 12 units and produce monthly rent of $10,200 (12 units × $850). If Property A has monthly expenses of $3,500, the expense ratio is 34.3% ($3,500 expenses ÷ $10,200 rents = .343 = 34.3%). If Property B has monthly expenses of $4,500, the expense ratio is 44.1% ($4,500 expenses ÷ $10,200 rents = .441 = 44.1%). A buyer would be willing to pay a higher price for Property A than for Property B because the bottom line, after expenses, is greater for Property A.

(cont. on next page)

Keep in mind that quality of tenants and utility costs dramatically affect expense ratios. A property in a distressed area will likely attract a lower quality of tenants, resulting in higher management fees, repairs, cleaning expense, and unpaid rent. That, in turn, results in a higher expense ratio than a property in a nice area of town. Similarly, a landlord who pays inside utilities will have a higher expense ratio than a landlord who does not pay inside utilities.

The bottom line is this: Don't make the mistake of using the same GRM for all properties. If you are thinking of buying a rental property in a certain area and want to use GRMs to see if a property is priced right, use GRMs from sold properties in the same area of town and with similar expense ratios.

Is It Worth Pursuing?

Let's summarize your findings on the newly available 14-unit complex, and compare the results to comparable sales.

	Available 14-unit Complex	Average, Comparable Sales
Price Per Unit	$\frac{\$1,475,000}{14 \text{ units}} = \$105,357$	$83,800
Price Per Sq Ft	$\frac{\$1,475,000}{11,200 \text{ sq ft}} = \$131.70$	$103.83
GRM	$\frac{\$1,475,000}{\$11,070 \text{ Mo Rent}} = 133.24$	105.11

Each indicator for the 14-unit complex far exceeds the indicators from recent sales. You should not waste any more time exploring this property; instead, go golfing or do something worthwhile!

Now, suppose you hear about a 12-unit apartment complex at 1100 Park Place that has just become available, at a price of $1,050,000. The property is in a nice area, is 15 years old, and is in good condition. Each unit has two bedrooms, one bath, separate utility meters (so tenants pay their own lights, heat, and air-conditioning), and individual laundry hookups. The property has 12 covered parking stalls plus 12 uncovered off-street parking stalls. The building contains 10,200 square feet. Rents are as follows: 4 units @ $820, 2 units @ $835, and 6 units @ $860—resulting in total monthly rent of $10,110. Let's calculate the price per unit, price per square foot, and GRM for the Park Place property, and then compare the results to comparable sales.

	Park Place Property	Average, Comparable Sales
Price Per Unit	$\frac{\$1,050,000}{12 \text{ units}} = \$87,500$	$83,800
Price Per Sq Ft	$\frac{\$1,050,000}{10,200 \text{ sq ft}} = \$102.94$	$103.83
GRM	$\frac{\$1,050,000}{\$10,110 \text{ Mo Rent}} = 103.86$	105.11

Based on what similar properties are selling for, the Park Place property is priced okay and worth pursuing.

 Moving forward. We will continue pursuing the Park Place property in Step 4!

Estimate Net Operating Income (NOI)

We'll Explore

- Operating Statements
- Seller's Operating Statement: Historical Data
- Reconstructed Operating Statement: Projection for the Future
- Cap Rates

---

nvestors in rental real estate are interested in how much income, after expenses, a property will produce. That amount is called net operating income (NOI). We will estimate NOI for the Park Place property. Keep in mind that we use the same evaluation techniques for all types of rental properties (commercial and residential, large and small).

Operating Statements

Businesses prepare an operating statement (also called an income statement, or profit and loss statement) to show how the business is doing. The statement shows income and expenses of the business, and the resulting profit, or net income.

Operating statements are also used for rental real estate. An operating statement can be used to show how a property has performed in the past, or can be used to project income and expenses for the future.

Most real estate investors prefer to create a standardized operating statement that can save time and can serve as a checklist to help reduce the chance of forgetting to include something on the statement. The items included on standardized operating statements vary, depending on the type of property and the region of the country. For example, janitorial service may be an appropriate expense category for office buildings but not for residential rentals. A standardized statement used in Minnesota may have an expense category for snow removal, while a statement in Florida may not. Illustration 4-1, on page 44, is an example of a standardized operating statement, providing for income, some common expense categories, and the resulting net operating income (NOI).

Notice that the expenses on the operating statement do not include money spent for capital improvements. A capital improvement is a long-lasting asset, such as a carport built on the property or the installation of new kitchen cabinets. The expenses on the operating statement are limited to expenses of the property and do *not* include mortgage payments, mortgage interest, depreciation, and auto expense. While the owner must make a mortgage payment and can deduct interest, depreciation, and auto expense on his or her federal income tax return, those items are expenses of the *owner*, not expenses of the *property*. To illustrate why we do *not* include expenses of an owner on an operating statement, suppose you are evaluating two properties that are for sale. The owner of each property has provided income and expense figures for the past year. For Property 1, the mortgage is paid off (so there is no interest expense), the owner has completely depreciated the improvements, and the owner lives next door to the property (so no auto expense). Here is the resulting NOI for each property, assuming (incorrectly) that expenses of the owner are used in calculating NOI:

Property 1		Property 2	
Annual income	$60,000	Annual income	$180,000
Less operating expenses	–18,000	Less operating expenses	– 55,000
Less interest expense	0	Less interest expense	– 48,000
Less depreciation expense	0	Less depreciation expense	– 34,000
Less auto expense	0	Less auto expense	– 1,000
Net operating income (NOI)	$42,000	Net operating income (NOI)	$ 42,000

These properties appear to have the same NOI but upon closer inspection, we see that for Property 2, the owner's expenses have been included and greatly reduce the actual NOI. Without including expenses of the *owner*, the NOI for Property 2 would be a whopping $125,000 ($180,000 - $55,000), which is about three times the NOI of Property 1. Because Property 2 produces about three times as much profit (NOI) as Property 1, we can correctly conclude that Property 2 is worth approximately three times as much as Property 1.

Seller's Operating Statement: Historical Data

Let's return to the 12-unit apartment building, located at 1100 Park Place, that we discussed in Step 3. The building is 15 years old and contains 10,200 sq ft. The seller is asking $1,050,000. The property is in a nice area of town. Each unit has two bedrooms, one bathroom, and laundry hookups, as well as a gas furnace, gas water heater, air -conditioning, and individual gas and electric meters. Parking consists of 12 covered stalls plus 12 uncovered stalls. The seller has shared the previous year's information:

Rents deposited	$112,400
Property taxes	8,520
Total loan payments	68,770
Interest portion of loan payments	61,543
Depreciation	23,272
Insurance	975
Water & sewer	1,317
Gas (during vacant periods)	377
Electricity (for outside lights and vacancies)	1,411
Repairs and painting	3,188
Advertising	625
Accounting and legal	300
Supplies	244
Licenses and permits	600
Auto expense	665
Trash removal	1,440
Snow removal	700
Flowers, shrubs, fertilizer	215

Because we are going to evaluate many future properties, it would be wise to create a standardized operating statement to evaluate the properties. For the sake of illustration, let's assume that we create a standardized operating statement and plug in the numbers for the Park Place property (see Illustration 4-1). Remember that we do not include the expenses of the *owner* (mortgage payments, interest expense, depreciation expense, and auto expense). Don't fall into the trap of listing expenses simply because the seller provides the information.

Illustration 4-1 Seller's Operating Statement: 12-Units, 1100 Park Place

Location: 1100 Park Place   **OPERATING STATEMENT**
Type of Property: 12-unit apartment
Time Period: Past year – seller's statement   *Notes & Comments*

1. Scheduled Rental Income			
2. – Vacancy & Credit Losses @____%			
3. Effective Rental Income			
4. + Other Income			
5. Gross Operating Income		112,400	
Operating Expenses			
6. Property Taxes	8,520		
7. Property Insurance	975		
8. Off-site Management			
9. On-site Management			
10. Repairs & Painting	3,188		
11. Water & Sewer	1,317		
12. Gas	377		
13. Electricity	1,411		
14. Advertising	625		
15. Accounting & Legal	300		
16. Licenses & Permits	600		
17. Supplies	244		
18. Yard Care	215		
19. Trash Removal	1,440		
20. Snow Removal	700		
21. Cleaning, Interior			
22. Cleaning, Exterior			
23. _____			
24. _____			
25. Total Operating Expenses		19,912	17.72 % of Line 5
26. Net Operating Income (NOI)		92,488	

Reconstructed Operating Statement: Projection for the Future

The Seller's Operating Statement (Illustration 4-1) shows the seller's data. While your first thought may be to use the data of the Seller's Operating Statement for cash flow projections, there are two reasons why you should not. First, the information may not be complete or accurate. For example, the seller may have done his or her own repairs and management, had few repairs recently, or may be stretching the truth about the rents. Second, the numbers are *historical* and you want to know what the income and expenses will be in the *future*.

Upon further investigation, you discover that the seller has in fact done the management, painting, cleaning, yard care, and many of the repairs. Remember, an operating statement is the foundation of the entire evaluation process, so careful thought should be given to each income and expense item. We will reconstruct, line by line, an operating statement for the Park Place property, showing realistic rents and expenses for the upcoming 12 months; the result, a Reconstructed Operating Statement, appears as Illustration 4-2 on page 56. (*Suggestion*: You may want to photo copy Illustration 4-2 so you don't have to keep flipping pages.)

Line 1. Scheduled Rental Income. Scheduled rental income is the amount the property would produce if occupied 100% of the time at reasonable rents. A good starting place in establishing this amount is to get a rent roll, which shows—by unit—the tenant's name, current rent, security deposit, and length of stay. A past history on rents, say for the last 3 or 4 years, helps give perspective.

It is also important to compare rents for similar properties. Current rents for the Park Place property may be too high; if you buy based on being able to collect those high rents and those tenants move out you may have to reduce the rent to market levels to attract new tenants. If current rents for the Park Place property are too low, your projections should provide for increasing rents to market levels as soon as possible. Keep in mind that you cannot increase rents until leases expire and you may not want to increase rents all the way to market levels for good, long-term tenants (doing so may result in losing those good tenants).

To determine what similar properties are renting for, check advertisements in the newspaper or on the Internet, or talk to landlords, property management companies, real estate agents, or apartment associations. Make a *personal* visit to available units in the area to better understand the competition: rents, size of units, floor plans, condition of units, parking, laundry, and the type of tenants the competition attracts. You should be up front and let the owners or managers of those properties know that you are considering buying a property in the area and want to determine if the rents for that property are reasonable.

> *Conclusions on the Park Place property.* You get a past history of rents, as well as a rent roll. The rent roll shows four of the units are rented @ $820 each, two @ $835 each, and six @ $860 each. The rents vary, based on condition and location. After doing a market analysis, you have concluded that the current rents are fair.

Line 2. Vacancy & Credit Losses. Landlords lose rent when units are vacant. In addition to the loss from vacancy, landlords occasionally have tenants who do not pay the rent; this is referred to as a credit loss.

Vacancy and credit losses are often expressed as a percent of scheduled rental income. To project vacancy and credit losses, we can examine the past history of the property, as well as the past history of similar properties. Consider what the future looks like: (1) are new tenants moving into the area, (2) are tenants moving out of the area or out of rentals to buy homes, and (3) are new apartment units being built that will increase vacancy rates?

To determine vacancy rate trends, consult with landlords, property management companies, real estate agents, and apartment associations. Some universities monitor vacancy rates in their areas.

> *Conclusions on the Park Place property.* You determine the current vacancy rate for properties like this is about 4.5% and will likely remain at that level for the next year. To allow for some credit loss, in addition to vacancy, you allocate 5% for vacancy and credit loss.

Line 3. Effective Rental Income. Line 1 minus Line 2.

Line 4. Other Income. This line provides for other sources of income from the property, such as income from laundry and vending machines. Other income could also include application fees, move-in fees, late fees, bad-check fees, and early termination fees; many investors, in an effort to keep things simple, do not use income from these sources in their projections.

For commercial properties, tenants are generally required to pay their share of common area expenses (yard care, snow removal, outside utilities, property taxes, etc.). The fee is referred to as a CAM (Common Area Maintenance) fee. Some residential landlords bill their tenants for a share of utilities or other expenses. The lease agreement should spell out what the tenant must pay and how the amount is determined. In some cases, landlords hire companies, like Relms (*www.gorelms.com*) or Ista (*www.ista-na.com*), to assist in billing tenants for their share. For utilities, the tenant's share is often determined with submeters. You may wonder how landlords treat the amounts collected from tenants. Some landlords offset the expense items they are being reimbursed for; this has the effect of reducing the landlord's utility expense, property tax, etc. Other landlords treat the amount as "Other Income" on the Operating Statement.

> *Conclusions on the Park Place property.* You will not bill tenants for common area expenses and will not include miscellaneous items (like move-in fees) as other income.

Line 5. Gross Operating Income. Line 3 plus Line 4.

Line 6. Property Taxes. Local governments and independent taxing districts (such as schools and parks) get much of their revenue from property tax. Owners of rental property pay property tax on the land and buildings, just like homeowners pay property tax on their homes. In addition, some local governments charge personal property tax on the personal property (like ranges, refrigerators, and window coverings in the rental units).

Call the local tax collector to determine the last property tax bill and contact the county assessor to find the current assessed value. If you buy a property that is undervalued by the county assessor and the property value is increased after you buy it, the property tax bill can be a big shock.

Conclusions on the Park Place property. The seller told you that last year's property tax was $8,520. You call the local tax collector; they confirm the amount and tell you it is paid. You contact the county assessor's office to see if the value they are using is realistic. Based on your sales research of Step 3, the assessor's value appears to be a bit low. If the property were valued correctly, next year's property taxes will be about $10,200. There is no personal property tax.

Line 7. Property Insurance. Owners of rental property maintain insurance on the property in case of fire or some other occurrence. The seller of the Park Place property told you his last annual insurance premium was $975. But the property may be underinsured or may not have proper coverage. Most investors, when projecting insurance premiums, use the "prudent-man" approach, asking, What type of coverage would the prudent (sensible) person want? Perhaps the prudent person would want coverage that protects against vandalism and includes rent-loss coverage, which pays the landlord for rent lost during the fix-up period. The prudent person would definitely want liability coverage in case someone is injured on the property. The amount of liability coverage depends on the type and size of property, as well as the financial condition of the owner.

You may think that if you buy a rental property for, say $500,000, you will need $500,000 of fire coverage. But part of the purchase price is for land and land doesn't need to be insured, so you may not need $500,000 of fire coverage. Most lenders require coverage equal to the loan amount and may require certain types of coverage.

Once we know what coverage is needed we can call a few insurance agents to determine what the annual premium would be.

Conclusions on the Park Place property. You decide a prudent person would want $800,000 of coverage on the property and that you need coverage for vandalism, rent loss, and $1,000,000 liability. You call two insurance agents; the best quote is $1,120.

Line 8. Off-site Management. Property managers typically place ads for vacant units, arrange for painting and cleaning, select tenants, collect rents, make deposits, order repairs as needed, oversee the repair people, oversee the appearance of the property (landscaping, parking lot, hallways, etc.), pay bills, and prepare summaries for the owner.

Some investors who plan on doing their own property management may not allocate money for off-site management because they will not be paying anyone. I advise against not allocating an amount on the operating statement. Here's why. First, you may have a change of heart; if you later hire someone to do the property management your cash flow will be substantially less than what you had originally projected. Second, you may want to compare your rental property investment with another investment, like a corporate bond, that has no management headaches. If you compare the cash flows from each to determine which provides the greater return, you will be overlooking your significant time contribution as property manager. If you allocate a fee to yourself for property management, you would be justified in comparing the cash flow on the rental property with the cash flow on the corporate bond.

In figuring a dollar amount to allocate for off-site management, you can call a few property management companies to see what they would charge. Charges are often based as a percent of *gross operating income* (the amount collected and deposited), rather than as a percent of the *scheduled rental income*. You may have heard about property management companies who charge the same percent from property to property, such as 10%. Consider the property management fee on these two properties, using a 10% fee:

Property 1. New duplex. 1,800 sq ft per unit. Rent is $1,500 per unit.

2 units × $1,500 =	$ 3,000
Percent for management fee	× 10%
Monthly fee	$ 300

Property 2. Old, 10-unit studio apartments. Rent is $300 per unit.

10 units × $300 =	$ 3,000
Percent for management fee	× 10%
Monthly fee	$ 300

Using a 10% rate results in a $300 monthly management fee for each property, but the 10-unit property requires *much* more time and energy than the duplex. Using the same percent fee for all properties is not a valid approach. Typically, management fees on residential properties vary from about 6% to about 15% of gross operating income, depending on (1) the age and condition of the building (older buildings or ones with poor-quality construction require more time overseeing repairs), (2) the type of tenants the property attracts (some tenants take care of the property better than others, pay their rent more promptly, and are easier to deal with), and (3) turnover rate (the more frequently tenants move, the greater the management headache).

Conclusions on the Park Place property. You call around and decide that for the Park Place property, a management fee of 7.5% is reasonable.

Line 9. On-site Management. For rental properties that have several units, a tenant is sometimes hired to assist with on-site duties, such as showing vacant units; monitoring sprinkling systems, outside lights, parking, noise problems, etc.; mowing the lawn; weeding; shoveling snow from walkways; and keeping walkways and common areas swept and clean.

The on-site manager can be paid hourly or with a set monthly fee. For larger properties, the manager could be given free rent as part of the compensation. For smaller properties, the manager could be given a reduction in rent. Some owners treat the on-site manager as an employee, in which case the owner is responsible for withholding federal, state, and local taxes, as well as paying employer taxes and benefits. The on-site manager must, of course, report the income (even if in the form of a rent reduction) as wages. Some owners and on-site managers agree that the on-site manager is a self-employed person, in which case the on-site manager must pay self-employment FICA tax as well as income taxes on the money received (certain conditions must be met to satisfy self-employment guidelines). While the money paid to an on-site manager in the form of a rent reduction is subject to taxes, some owners and on-site managers incorrectly ignore the rent reduction and the resulting tax consequences. Be sure to check with your tax advisor in deciding which approach to use.

Conclusions on the Park Place property. The seller has been performing all of the duties of an on-site manager. You think it would be a good idea to select one of the tenants to be an on-site manager to perform all of the duties listed above. You will give the on-site manager a rent reduction of $400 a month. You elect to treat the on-site manager as an employee; you figure the employer taxes on the $400 salary would be $55, resulting in total on-site manager expense of $455 a month.

Line 10. Repairs & Painting. Repairs vary from year to year, making this amount difficult to estimate. The amount should include painting (inside and outside), plumbing repairs, electrical repairs, roof repairs, water heater repairs and replacement, and repairs to air conditioners, furnaces, sprinkling systems, drive-ways and parking areas, and all other building and equipment items.

Relying on previous expense data can be a mistake. For example, the seller of the Park Place property personally did many of the repairs. Even on a property in which the owner hires out repairs, the owner may have done considerable fix-up 3 years ago, alleviating the need for hefty repairs the last 2 years. And the owner may have postponed some repairs this last year in order to limit last year's repair expense. Relying solely on recent repair expenses as a means of estimating future expense can result in underestimating the amount.

Many investors estimate repair expense as a percent of scheduled rental income. The percent may vary from around 4% to 15%, depending on the age of the building, quality of construction, location, turnover ratio, tenant profile, etc. To get a good estimate, check with other landlords, property management companies, or apartment associations. If you do estimate repairs as a percent of scheduled rental income, don't use the same percent for each property. Another word of caution: if rents have recently dropped dramatically, the percent allocated to repairs will go up.

Some investors and lenders like to separate repairs into two lines items: Repairs and maintenance, and reserves for replacement. Where this is done, the repairs and maintenance category includes routine repair items and day-to-day maintenance; the reserves for replacement covers replacement of major components like the roof, heating equipment, and appliances. When investors and lenders separate repairs into two line items, the reserves for replacement (often referred to as capital reserves) are estimated at $250 to $350 per unit per year, depending on the condition of the property. Some lenders, especially on larger properties, require the owner to make deposits into an escrow account; the money in the account is used to pay for the replacement of major components. To keep things simple, we will combine "repairs" and "reserves for replacement" on one line.

> *Conclusions on the Park Place property.* The seller reported last year's re-pairs to be $3,188, which is 2.63% of scheduled rental income. But the seller did all of the painting and many of the repairs. You know some-one who owns several apartment buildings around town similar to the Park Place property who says your repairs will likely be between 6% and 8% of scheduled rents. The Park Place property attracts nice-qual-ity tenants and the building is only 15 years old, so that estimate sounds reasonable to you. You estimate repairs at 7% of scheduled rents.

Lines 11, 12, and 13. Utilities. Landlords generally pay water and sewer, plus electricity for outside lights. When there is a central laundry room available to all tenants, the landlord pays electricity for the laundry room, plus the electricity or gas to heat the water used in the laundry room. For buildings that do not have separate gas or electric meters for each unit, landlords pay for those utilities and may, or may not, ask tenants to reimburse them for a prorated share.

When using previous utility expenses to project the upcoming 12-month amount, use a full 12-month historical amount, not 1 month times 12. Also, use utility *billings* for a 12-month period, *not* amounts paid by the owner during the 12-month period. Here's why. Maybe the owner had huge November and December gas bills but, in an effort to keep the calendar-year amount low, didn't pay the bills until January. To verify the *billed* amounts, we can call the utility company; depending on the policy of the utility company, we may have to get the seller to give written permission to verify amounts.

Another thing to keep in mind is that the 12-month billing amounts are historical; we want to estimate for the *upcoming* 12 months, so an adjustment may be needed.

> *Conclusions on the Park Place property.* The seller reported water and sewer was $1,317, gas was $377, and electricity was $1,411. You call the utility companies and confirm that those were the amounts billed during the previous calendar year. You anticipate a 4% increase.

Line 14. Advertising. Landlords lose money for each day a unit is vacant. So landlords try to find good-quality tenants as soon as possible. In some cases, landlords maintain a waiting list or another tenant might refer a prospective tenant to the landlord. In most cases some kind of advertising is required.

When vacancy rates are high, advertising is required for longer periods of time, increasing the advertising budget. Some landlords advertise only with a sign on the property. Some advertise on the Internet. Others place ads in local newspapers. Most use a combination of methods.

> *Conclusions on the Park Place property.* You figure that the average tenant in a property like the Park Place property stays for about 18 months (or 1.5 years). Based on that, you anticipate about eight vacancies a year (12 units ÷ 1.5 years = 8). You figure for each vacancy, you will spend about $80 in advertising. You figure you will have to buy three lawn signs a year @ $20 each.

8 vacancies a year × $80 =	$ 640
3 lawn signs × $20	+ 60
Total estimated advertising	$ 700

Line 15. Accounting & Legal. Property management companies often provide an owner with a summary of income and expenses. Owners, especially of larger

properties, may hire an accounting firm to complete an audit or to prepare tax forms.

Legal expense includes paying an attorney to handle tenant disputes, evictions, and to update rental agreements. Legal expense also includes the cost of obtaining credit reports and background checks on prospective tenants. Some owners have prospective tenants pay an application fee to cover the credit report and background check. Many landlords don't like collecting fees from prospective tenants that they may end up not renting to.

Conclusions on the Park Place property. You anticipate needing to consult with an attorney from time to time. You will not require accounting assistance beyond the summaries provided by the off-site manager. And you have decided that you will pay for credit and background checks. You have a company that will provide a credit and background check on each applicant (provided you have written permission on the application form) at a cost of $25 per application. You have projected about eight vacancies each year, and you estimate you will have to order two credit reports, on average, for each vacancy (you will turn down some of the applicants). You will charge approved tenants a $50 move-in fee to help offset the credit report fees.

Estimated legal fees	$ 200
Plus: 16 credit reports × $25	+ 400
Subtotal	$ 600
Less: 8 move-in fees × $50	– 400
Net amount	$ 200

Line 16. Licenses & Permits. Rental properties produce income. As a result, owners in many areas must get a business license and a health license. Some areas charge a tax on the income the property produces.

Conclusions on the Park Place property. The seller reports that licenses and permits for the last year were $600. You call and confirm that the amount was, indeed, $600. The amount will be the same for the upcoming year.

Line 17. Supplies. This category includes things like keys, light bulbs, hoses, snow shovels, and cleaning supplies.

Conclusions on the Park Place property. The seller reports spending $244 on supplies last year. You conclude that amount is reasonable. Allowing for a slight increase in costs, you allocate $260 for supplies.

Line 18. Yard Care. Yard care includes lawn mowing and edging, fertilizing, weeding planter areas, pruning, replacing old or dead trees and shrubs, and planting flowers.

> *Conclusions on the Park Place property.* The on-site manager will perform many of the yard care duties, so much of the yard care expense is reflected in the on-site manager category. You will, however, incur the following additional expenses:
>
> | | |
> |---|---|
> | Fertilizing: 4 applications × $50 per application = | $ 200 |
> | Pruning, replacing shrubs, planting flowers | + 400 |
> | Total | $ 600 |

Line 19. Trash Removal. In some cases, the local government provides trash receptacles for trash removal. In most cases, private companies are paid to provide receptacles and pick up the trash on a regular basis.

> *Conclusions on the Park Place property.* The property has a trash bin, which is emptied twice a week by a private company. They currently charge $120 per month, but say their rates are scheduled to go up to $130 per month. They have been doing a good job, and after calling other companies you decide their rates are competitive. You allocate $130 per month for trash removal.

Line 20. Snow Removal. For areas that get snow, the on-site manager may shovel snow from sidewalks, but the owner typically has a commercial company plow the drives and parking areas. Snow removal companies charge a set amount per month (or season) or charge per "plowable" storm (a plowable storm is one in which the snow is a certain depth, like 2 inches, or one in which the snow will not melt within 24 hours).

> *Conclusions on the Park Place property.* The seller has been paying a company $700 per season, but says the company was not very dependable. You get recommendations on snow removal companies. You find a company who seems reliable and charges $100 per plowable storm. You project eight plowable storms per winter: 8 × $100 = $800.

Line 21. Cleaning, Interior. Tenants are supposed to leave the place clean when they leave, but not everyone's idea of "clean" is the same. If an apartment is not clean when prospective tenants look at it, the good prospects go elsewhere. So it is important to get the apartment clean before showing it. Efficient landlords send a cleaning person for every vacancy. Most landlords also clean the carpets at every vacancy.

Cleaning fees can be deducted from a tenant's security deposit, meaning theoretically that the landlord should not incur any cleaning expense. However, some tenants feel that the landlord is incurring unnecessary costs ("it wasn't that clean when we moved in") so they dispute the cleaning charges. As a result, some landlords pay for the first portion of cleaning (maybe the first $50 or first $100) and withhold the remainder from the security deposit.

> *Conclusions on the Park Place property.* You decide that you will pay the first $50 of cleaning when a tenant vacates. Based on eight vacancies a year, that results in $400.

Line 22. Cleaning, Exterior. When prospective tenants visit a property, they notice how clean the property is, inside and out. If the exterior light fixtures and window frames are dirty, for instance, the good-quality prospects will look elsewhere. And if existing tenants notice cobwebs and grime on the exterior of the building they live in, they may decide to find a cleaner place to live. Many landlords clean units when vacant, but fail to regularly clean the outside (light fixtures, windows and frames, doors and frames, mail boxes, railings, etc.). The parking lot also needs a thorough cleaning from time to time.

> *Conclusions on the Park Place property.* You decide you will pay to have the exterior cleaned twice a year. You estimate the cost to be $200 for each cleaning of the building plus $150 for each sweeping of the parking lot: $(2 \times \$200) + (2 \times \$150) = \$700$.

TIP | **don't be forgetful**

Some investors don't take the time to carefully prepare an operating statement or forget to include some expenses (like exterior cleaning and sweeping). Forgetting to include an expense on paper *doesn't* mean the expense won't happen.

Lines 23 and 24. These lines are reserved for other expenses. For instance, if a property requires pest control on a regular basis, we must allocate an amount for that. Or, for a property with a swimming pool, we must allocate an amount for pool maintenance.

Line 25. Total Operating Expenses. Add Lines 6 through 24.

Line 26. Net Operating Income (NOI). NOI is the amount of profit, *before making mortgage payments and before depreciation expense and income taxes.* NOI is found by subtracting Total Operating Expenses (Line 25) from Gross Operating Income (Line 5).

Finally!

Phew! Now we have an operating statement that accurately represents what we expect from the Park Place property for the upcoming 12 months (Illustration 4-2). Notice, total expenses are $42,965 (compared with the seller's total expenses of $19,912 in Illustration 4-1). Expenses are 35.41% of scheduled rental income ($42,965 ÷ $121,320 = .3541). Expenses for a residential rental property are often 30% to 40% of scheduled rental income and will seldom be under 25%. For older properties or for properties in which the landlord pays some inside utilities, the percent can be much higher.

You may be saying, Because the process of estimating individual expenses is so time-consuming, and because expenses are often 30% to 40% of scheduled rental income, why can't I just estimate Total Operating Expenses as one lump-sum? Here's why: carefully preparing an operating statement is the foundation of the entire evaluation process; if you create a shoddy operating statement, the entire evaluation process is meaningless!

TIP   **are expenses within an acceptable range?**

If you prepare an operating statement for a residential rental property, or someone gives you an operating statement for a property you are considering, and expenses are lower than the normal 30% to 40% range, there is likely something wrong!

Notice the NOI in Illustration 4-2 is $72,289. Keep in mind that the $72,289 NOI does not reflect mortgage payments, depreciation expense, and income taxes. We will consider those things, and more, in Step 7 of the book.

Illustration 4-2 Reconstructed Operating Statement: 12-Units, 1100 Park Place

Location: 1100 Park Place   **OPERATING STATEMENT**

Type of Property: 12-unit apartment

Time Period: Upcoming 12 months (projected)   *Notes & Comments*

1. Scheduled Rental Income		121,320	$4 \times \$820 = \quad \$\ 3,280$
2. − Vacancy & Credit Losses @ __5__ %		6,066	$2 \times \$835 = \quad 1,670$
3. Effective Rental Income		115,254	$6 \times \$860 = \quad 5,160$
4. + Other Income			Total: 12 $\$10,110$
5. Gross Operating Income		115,254	$\$10,110 \times 12$ months = $\$121,320$
Operating Expenses			
6. Property Taxes	10,200		
7. Property Insurance	1,120		
8. Off-site Management	8,644		$\$115,254 \times 7.5\%$
9. On-site Management	5,460		$\$455 \times 12$ mo
10. Repairs & Painting	8,492		$\$121,320 \times 7\%$
11. Water & Sewer	1,370		
12. Gas	392		
13. Electricity	1,467		
14. Advertising	700		
15. Accounting & Legal	200		
16. Licenses & Permits	600		
17. Supplies	260		
18. Yard Care	600		
19. Trash Removal	1,560		$\$130 \times 12$ mo
20. Snow Removal	800		
21. Cleaning, Interior	400		
22. Cleaning, Exterior	700		
23. _____	_____		
24. _____	_____		
25. Total Operating Expenses		42,965	35.41% of Line 1
26. Net Operating Income (NOI)		72,289	

Cap Rates

In Step 3 of the book, we explored ways to determine if a property is worth pursuing. We used a sales comparison approach, determining how much money other properties are selling for per unit, per square foot, and per dollar of gross rent. For example, if similar apartment buildings are selling for 110 times the monthly gross rent (a GRM of 110) and a property we are thinking of pursuing is priced at 140 times the monthly gross rent (a GRM of 140), that property is probably not worth pursuing.

Now let's look at another method of figuring out if a property is priced right. This method involves what is called a capitalization rate, commonly referred to as cap rate. A cap rate is found by dividing a property's NOI by its value:

$$\text{Cap Rate} = \frac{\text{NOI}}{\text{Value}}$$

To find a current cap rate for a specific type of property, we calculate the cap rate on similar sold properties. Start by projecting the upcoming 12 months' NOI for each sold property, using the same rationale used in projecting NOI for Illustration 4-2. Then for each sold property, determine the cap rate by dividing its projected NOI by the sales price. Let's find the cap rate on three recent sales:

Sale #	Projected NOI	Sales Price	Cap Rate
1	$92,720	$1,340,000	$\text{Cap Rate} = \dfrac{\text{NOI}}{\text{Value}} = \dfrac{\$92,720}{\$1,340,000} = .0692 = 6.92\%$
2	$70,140	$995,000	$\text{Cap Rate} = \dfrac{\text{NOI}}{\text{Value}} = \dfrac{\$70,140}{\$995,000} = .0705 = 7.05\%$
3	$99,585	$1,450,000	$\text{Cap Rate} = \dfrac{\text{NOI}}{\text{Value}} = \dfrac{\$99,585}{\$1,450,000} = .0687 = 6.87\%$

Based on these sales, it appears that buyers are satisfied with a cap rate between 6.87% and 7.05%, with an average cap rate of about 6.95%. In other words, for this type of property, buyers are okay with an NOI that is about 6.95% of the price.

Here are some things to keep in mind when using capitalization rates:

- When calculating NOI for a property, *personally* estimate income and expenses; don't use an NOI that someone else has calculated, because other people will likely not use the same approach for estimating income and expenses that you do.

- NOI should be for the *upcoming* 12 months, not the *previous* 12 months.

- When calculating or comparing cap rates, make sure the properties are similar. Cap rates vary for different types of property. For example, cap rates for retail shopping centers may be dramatically different from cap rates for apartment complexes. Similarly, cap rates for large apartment complexes can be dramatically different from cap rates for smaller apartment complexes. Also, cap rates can vary from one area of town to another area of town.

- When calculating a cap rate, use at least four decimal places in the resulting decimal number. For example, the cap rate on a $1,500,000 property with NOI of $97,200 is: $97,200 ÷ $1,500,000 = .06 (with two decimal places), indicating a cap rate of 6%. The cap rate, with four decimal places, is .0648, indicating a more precise cap rate of 6.48%. There is a dramatic difference between cap rates of 6% and 6.48%.

- Be cautious when other people tell you what the cap rate is (in a general market or for a certain property). The cap rate they report depends on how they calculate NOI. And they may have calculated NOI based on historical expenses, below-average expenses, or inflated rents.

Now, let's find the cap rate on the Park Place property, based on the projected NOI of $72,289 (from Illustration 4-2) and the asking price of $1,050,000:

$$\text{Cap Rate} = \frac{\text{NOI}}{\text{Asking Price}} = \frac{\$72,289}{\$1,050,000} = .0688 = 6.88\%$$

The 6.88% cap rate is within the range found in the marketplace, indicating that the property is reasonably priced. Buyers prefer high cap rates. If you can negotiate a price lower than the $1,050,000 asking price, the cap rate will be higher than the 6.88% we just calculated.

To find a price based on a desired cap rate, we divide the NOI by the desired cap rate. Let's find the price based on a cap rate of, say, 7.05%:

$$\text{Price} = \frac{\text{NOI}}{\text{Desired Cap Rate}} = \frac{\$72,289}{.0705} = \$1,025,375.89$$

If you can negotiate a price of about $1,025,000, the resulting cap rate would be 7.05%.

Cap rates are a good tool to use in deciding if a property is worth *pursuing*, but don't make the mistake of concluding that just because a property has a good cap rate it is worth *buying*. Cap rates have limitations; they ignore the effect of down payment, financing, appreciation, and income taxes.

Moving forward. We will use a more comprehensive indicator than a cap rate to decide whether to buy the Park Place property: we will calculate an Internal Rate of Return (IRR) on the projected after-tax cash flow. Come back for that exciting conclusion in Step 7. Before we calculate an IRR, we need to review federal income taxes (Step 5) and do some critical calculations (Step 6).

Get to Know Your Hidden Partner—The Tax Man

We'll Explore

- IRS Real Property Classifications
- Tax Brackets
- Depreciation (MACRS)
- Purchase/Loan Costs
- Passive Losses
- Paying Tax on the Gain
- Alternative Minimum Tax

W hen comparing rates of return between different types of investments, it makes sense to compare the *after-tax* rates of return. Rental real estate has several unique tax rules that affect the after-tax rate of return.

IRS Real Property Classifications

The Internal Revenue Service (IRS) has a different set of rules for each type of real estate.

Personal Residence

There are certain rules that apply to homeowners. For example, homeowners are allowed to deduct interest and property taxes as itemized deductions. Also, homeowners do not have to report the first $250,000 of gain when they sell their home, provided they have lived in the home for at least 2 of the last 5 years ($500,000 of gain if they are married filing jointly). See page 6 for more details.

Income-Producing Property

Other rules—relating to passive losses, depreciation, and reporting gain from a sale—apply to rental property.

Non-Income-Producing Investment Property

Certain rules apply to investment property that does not produce income (such as vacant land held for investment). If we own vacant land as an investment, we can deduct interest and property taxes as itemized deductions. When we sell the property, the gain may be taxed at lower rates.

Dealer Property

Dealer property is property that is purchased with the intent to resell. Vacant land that is purchased, subdivided into lots, and sold as individual lots would be considered dealer property. A home purchased, fixed up, and then flipped is a dealer property. Gains from dealer property are taxed as ordinary income (just like interest from a savings account, at the taxpayer's full tax rate) versus being taxed as long-term capital gain (with lower tax rates). As a result, investors do not like to have property classified as dealer property.

Suppose an investor bought a home, fixed it up, and leased it to a tenant, giving the tenant the option to purchase it at the end of 2 years. You may think that because the investor used the property as a rental property, it might avoid being classified as a dealer property, but because the intent was to sell it, the IRS would likely classify the property as a dealer property and the gain would be taxed as ordinary income. Suppose instead, the investor bought a home, fixed it up, and leased it to a tenant. Two years later, the investor had a change of heart and decided to sell the home, giving the tenant the right to buy it before placing it on the market. If the investor's original intent was to keep the property as a rental property, and the investor owned the property for a reasonable length of time (like over a year, but the longer the better), the property would likely qualify as an income-producing property and the gain would be taxed accordingly (at lower rates).

Tax Brackets

A tax bracket is the rate that is applied to the *highest dollar* of a person's taxable income. A person in a 28% tax bracket pays 28¢ in federal income tax for each additional dollar earned.

The IRS publishes tax rate schedules that show a person's tax bracket. (You can access these at *www.irs.gov*.) Here are the most recent tax rate schedules (2011) as of the writing of this book for single taxpayers and taxpayers who are married filing jointly.

Single		Married Filing Jointly	
2011 Taxable Income Between	Taxed At	2011 Taxable Income Between	Taxed At
$0 and $8,500	10%	$0 and $17,000	10%
$8,500 and $34,500	15%	$17,000 and $69,000	15%
$34,500 and $83,600	25%	$69,000 and $139,350	25%
$83,600 and $174,400	28%	$139,350 and $212,300	28%
$174,400 and $379,150	33%	$212,300 and $379,150	33%
Over $379,150	35%	Over $379,150	35%

Keep in mind that taxable income is what's left after deducting either itemized deductions (if we itemize deductions) or a standard deduction (if we do not itemize deductions), and after deducting for exemptions (one exemption for ourself, one for our spouse, and one for each dependant, such as children). For example, suppose a married couple filing jointly has income from wages and interest totaling $85,000. Taxpayers are allowed to make *adjustments to income* (for example, qualified contributions to an IRA account can be subtracted from total income). To keep it simple, let's assume they had no adjustments to income, so their *adjusted gross income* is $85,000. If they itemize deductions (such as medical expenses, interest paid on a home mortgage, property taxes, charitable contributions, etc.) totaling, say, $30,000, and have five exemptions of, say, $3,700 each (the exemption amount changes from year to year), their taxable income would be $36,500 ($85,000 - $30,000 itemized deductions - $18,500 exemptions), resulting in the following federal income tax:

First $17,000: $17,000 × 10% =	$ 1,700
Between $17,000 and $36,500: $19,500 × 15% =	+ 2,925
Total tax	$ 4,625

In this example, the couple is in a 15% tax bracket because their highest dollar of taxable income is taxed at 15%. This does *not* mean that they pay 15% of their taxable income as federal income tax; it means that for each *additional* dollar of taxable income, they must pay 15% to the IRS. To find the rate of tax for the *average dollar* of taxable income, we divide the actual tax by the taxable income:

$$\frac{\$4{,}625 \text{ tax}}{\$36{,}500 \text{ taxable income}} = .1267 = 12.67\%$$

So, even though they are in a 15% tax bracket, their tax is only 12.67% of their taxable income.

Knowing our tax bracket lets us know how much more tax we must pay for any additional income (the bad news) but also lets us know how much we will save from additional deductions (the good news).

Depreciation (MACRS)

As owners of rental property, we are allowed to deduct a certain amount each year on our income tax return because of the wear and tear of the buildings. The expense—depreciation expense—is calculated under the IRS's Modified Accelerated Cost Recovery System, commonly referred to as MACRS (pronounced "makers").

MACRS Provisions

Depreciation for income tax purposes is treated just like other expenses, and reduces taxable income. Depreciation, however, is not a cash outlay; it is a "paper entry," so it is possible to have positive cash flow from a rental property and still have a tax loss. Here are a few guidelines in claiming depreciation under MACRS:

- *The property must be owned.* We can depreciate a rental property we own. We cannot depreciate assets that are leased, such as laundry machines leased from a third party, or leased vehicles used in the operation of the property. For leased property, we would deduct the lease payments and the owner of the property (the lessor) would claim depreciation expense on the asset.

- *The property must be income-producing.* We could take depreciation on an apartment building, along with appliances in the units, since they produce income. *Note*: If an asset is used in conjunction with a rental property, but also for personal use, we must prorate how much of its use is for producing income, and how much of its use is for personal use. For example, if we use a vehicle to help show vacant units, meet repair people, etc., but also for personal use, we should keep a mileage record showing mileage for each type of use, and base the vehicle's depreciation on the percent of mileage devoted to the rental property.

- *Land cannot be depreciated.* Because land is presumed to never wear out, we cannot depreciate it. So, when we purchase a property we must allocate part of the purchase price for land and part for buildings (referred to as *improvements*). Naturally, taxpayers would prefer that most of the purchase price is for buildings because that will result in more depreciation, and the IRS would prefer that a larger portion of the purchase price is for land. So, how do we make a fair allocation? Some advisors recommend using an 80-20 split—that is, allocate 80% of the price for buildings and 20% for land. For some properties, this approach may represent a fair allocation, but for others it may not, so it is suggested that taxpayers base the allocation on a more formal approach, such as an appraisal, Market Opportunity Analysis (conducted by a qualified real estate agent), or county assessor's valuation. *Note*: In some cases, the total assessed value by a county assessor is different from the actual value (market value). To illustrate how an allocation is done, suppose you buy a 6-unit rental property for $800,000. And suppose that the county assessor has the land assessed at $150,000 and the improvements (buildings) at $570,000, resulting in a total assessed value of $720,000. The county assessor is saying the land accounts for approximately 21% of value ($150,000 ÷ $720,000 = .21 = 21%) and improvements account for approximately 79% of value. Using the county assessor's valuation, a taxpayer would allocate $168,000 to land ($800,000 × 21% = $168,000) and $632,000 to buildings ($800,000 × 79% = $632,000).

So how much depreciation can we take each year? Under current IRS guidelines, all building depreciation for income tax purposes must be straight-line depreciation—that is, we take the same amount for each full year. For residential income-producing property, we have two choices: 27.5-year life or 40-year life. For income-producing property that is not residential (referred to as "commercial" property), the two choices are 39-year or 40-year. (You may wonder how the IRS came up with those choices; only a few lobbyists may know the answer to that question!) A property is considered "residential" if tenants occupy the property at least 30 days and no substantial services are provided, like health care or maid service. A property that has some residential tenants and some nonresidential tenants is considered "residential" only if income from the residential portion is at least 80% of the total income.

MACRS for the year of acquisition and the year of sale assumes what is called mid-month convention; regardless of the actual date of purchase or date of sale, the taxpayer gets half a month's depreciation for the month purchased and half a month's depreciation for the month sold. Suppose you buy a residential rental property for $1,200,000 in May of Year 1 and sell it in October of Year 8. Based on an appraisal, you allocate 23% of the price to land and 77% to improvements, and elect to use a 27.5-year life. For Year 1, you would get 7.5 months of depreciation (half of May, plus all of June through December). For Year 8, you would get 9.5 months of depreciation (January through September, plus half of October). Here are the depreciation calculations:

Value of the improvements: $1,200,000 × 77% = $924,000
Depreciation for a full year: $924,000 ÷ 27.5 = $33,600
Monthly amount: $33,600 ÷ 12 = $2,800
Depreciation for Year 1: $2,800 per month × 7.5 months = $21,000
Depreciation for Year 8: $2,800 per month × 9.5 months = $26,600

For Year 1, you would claim $21,000 in depreciation; for Years 2 through 7 (each full year of ownership), you would claim $33,600 a year; for Year 8, you would claim $26,600. The total depreciation is a whopping $249,200.

Cost Segregation Method

Some tax advisors recommend that improvements be depreciated using what is called the cost segregation method. With the cost segregation method, taxpayers obtain a professionally prepared cost segregation study that separates the building components into different categories, each with a different depreciable life. In our example above, with $924,000 being allocated to improvements, a cost segregation study may conclude that certain components like carpet, heating and air-conditioning equipment, and lighting fixtures represent $100,000 of the $924,000 and have a depreciable life of, say, 7 years. Perhaps the roof constitutes $50,000 of the $924,000 and has a depreciable life of, say, 15 years. The remainder of the $924,000 ($774,000) represents the main building structure with a depreciable life of, say, 27.5 years. By using a cost segregation method, taxpayers get additional depreciation expense.

We will *not* rely on the cost segregation method in this book because a professionally prepared cost segregation study costs money. In addition, some tax advisors discourage use of the cost segregation method because it could invite an income tax audit. (*Note:* Some companies who prepare cost segregation studies do not stand behind their findings in the event of an audit; if you do elect to use the cost segregation method, be sure to select a company who will stand behind their findings.) Finally, when we take depreciation, it gives us a larger tax deduction in the year taken but results in a larger gain (and resulting tax on the gain) later when we sell the property. Because of the additional tax at the time of sale, the overall income tax benefits of using the cost segregation method are not as great as they may first appear.

Fix-Up Costs: Expense or Improvement?

Most investors spend money fixing up a property during ownership. For example, an investor may redo kitchens or bathrooms, replace windows, or add garages and fencing. One dilemma investors have is whether to treat fix-up costs as an expense (which are deducted in the year incurred) or as an improvement (which must be depreciated over a number of years). In most cases, investors prefer to treat fix-up costs as expenses, whereas the IRS would benefit from treating the fix-up costs as improvements. The general rule of thumb in deciding whether to treat something as an expense or an improvement is whether the item will significantly add to the life of the property. As an example, painting a rental unit or repairing a roof would likely qualify as an expense. But if the expenditures are part of a major renovation, the entire renovation cost should likely be treated as an improvement. A kitchen remodel, or an entire roof replacement should be treated as an improvement, even if not part of a major renovation. When fixing up a property, be sure to get sound advice from a tax advisor about what should be depreciated and what should be treated as an expense.

TIP   **details, details**

Depreciation is one of the most complicated subjects in tax accounting. We have covered the basic concepts of MACRS. Remember, tax laws change frequently. For up-to-date details on MACRS, consult with your tax advisor, contact the IRS, or refer to IRS Publication 946 at *www.irs.gov*.

Purchase/Loan Costs

Buyers of rental property generally incur some special costs at the time of purchase. A partial list is shown below, along with how the items are generally treated for income tax purposes.

Costs of Acquisition

These are costs incurred in buying the property (but not associated with getting a mortgage loan), such as getting a survey to determine the property lines, hiring a property inspector to determine the condition of the building and its

---

components, and paying a closing fee to a title company for handling the transaction. Costs of acquisition are added to the basis and depreciated along with the building improvements.

Operating Expenses

These include expenses of operating the property, like property tax prorations on the settlement statement, fire and liability insurance premiums paid at or before closing, and prepaid interest on the mortgage loan (shown on a settlement statement).

Rental Income

Often the closing takes place on a date other than the date rents are due from tenants. For example, a closing might occur on May 28 and tenants paid May rent to the seller on May 1. Assuming the buyer and seller are using the closing date (May 28) for pro-rations, the seller will pay 4 days of rent (May 28, 29, 30, 31) to the buyer; the buyer should treat this as rental income, just as though the money were received from the tenants.

Loan Costs

These include costs of obtaining a mortgage loan, such as an origination fee, "points," the cost of a lender's title policy, an appraisal fee, fees to record loan documents, credit report fees, and other fees that are necessary to get the loan. For a rental property, loan costs cannot be deducted in the year they are incurred, and they are not depreciated; instead, they are amortized over the life of the loan.

To illustrate, if loan costs total $10,500 on a 20-year loan, the investor (borrower) would deduct $525 a year ($10,500 ÷ 20 = $525). If the loan is paid off early (such as when the property is sold), whatever loan costs have not yet been deducted are written off in the year of sale.

Escrow Deposits

Lenders often require borrowers to establish an escrow account from which the lender pays annual property taxes and insurance. The escrow account is similar to a savings account belonging to the borrower, except in most cases it earns no interest. Where an escrow account is required, the lender generally requires the borrower to make an initial deposit to get the account started. Money paid into an escrow account is not deductible because the money still technically belongs to the borrower.

Passive Losses

Under current IRS guidelines, all real estate investment income is referred to as passive income or, in the case of a loss, passive loss. The guidelines do not allow taxpayers to deduct passive losses on their income tax return unless the taxpayer is an *active participant* in the property, in which case the taxpayer can deduct up to $25,000 of loss per year.

Active Participant

If a taxpayer who is an active participant has more than one rental property, gains are combined with losses, and the combined loss cannot exceed $25,000. (For a married person filing separately, the combined loss cannot exceed $12,500).

An active participant is an investor who has a say in how the property is run. An investor who personally manages his or her rental properties would, of course, be an active participant. Even if we hire a property manager to oversee the management, we can be an active participant if we have some say in how the property is managed, such as how much rent to charge, how long the leases are for, when to paint or install new carpet, etc. So, you are probably wondering, If that is the case, what type of investor *wouldn't* qualify as an active participant? Here are a few. Corporations cannot deduct passive losses. Investors who own less than 10% of the rental property cannot deduct passive losses. And a limited partner in a limited partnership cannot deduct passive losses.

In determining how much passive income or passive loss a property has, we first total rents collected during the year. Then we subtract operating expenses (repairs, utilities, property taxes, insurance, yard care, etc.), interest expense, and depreciation expense. (*Note*: While the *interest* portion of loan payments can be deducted, the *principal* portion cannot be deducted.)

If we are an active participant and have combined losses exceeding $25,000, we deduct $25,000 for that year and carry forward the remainder to future years. If we still have unused losses at the time we sell the property we can use those unused losses to offset any gain.

Suppose you own only one rental property: a 4-unit residential property. You are an active participant. During the year you collected rents totaling $50,000, paid operating expenses totaling $15,000, paid interest of $30,000, and claimed depreciation expense of $15,000. Your gain or loss for income tax purposes would be:

Rental income		$ 50,000
Less deductions:		
Operating expenses	$ 15,000	
Interest expense	30,000	
Depreciation (MACRS)	15,000	
Total deductions		− 60,000
Taxable loss		**($ 10,000)**

Since you are an active participant you can deduct the entire $10,000 loss on your income tax return.

Now suppose you own two rental properties. You are an active participant on both properties. Property A has a taxable gain of $10,000 and Property B has a tax loss of $45,000. The $45,000 loss on Property B is offset by the $10,000 gain on Property A, resulting in a combined loss of $35,000. Because of the passive loss rules, you can deduct only $25,000 of the loss this year. The unused $10,000 will be carried forward to the next year.

Fast forward 1 year. Property A now has a taxable gain of $15,000 and Property B has a tax loss of $28,000. The $28,000 loss on Property B is offset by the $15,000 gain on Property A, resulting in a combined loss of $13,000. You are allowed to add the unused loss of $10,000 from the previous year, meaning you can deduct $23,000 this year.

Under current tax law, there is a further limitation on passive losses. If adjusted gross income, before the passive loss deduction, exceeds $100,000 we lose $1 of passive loss deduction for each $2 that adjusted gross income exceeds $100,000. As a result, once adjusted gross income exceeds $150,000 we cannot deduct passive losses; all of the losses must be carried forward.

Fast forward again. Suppose for a certain year you have combined passive losses of $31,000. Your adjusted gross income, before the passive loss deduction, is $118,000.

Adjusted gross income	$ 118,000	
Base amount	− 100,000	
Excess adjusted gross income	$ 18,000	
Passive loss	$ 31,000	
Maximum amount deductible		$ 25,000
Less: $18,000 × 50%		− 9,000
Amount deductible this year		**$ 16,000**

Suspended loss: $31,000 − $16,000 = $15,000

Real Estate Professional

A real estate investor who qualifies as a real estate professional can deduct *all* losses (not just $25,000 per year) from rental properties. To qualify as a real estate professional, you must

- Spend more than 50% of your personal services or employment time in real estate activities, including real estate development, construction, management of rental properties, leasing, and brokerage. You will not qualify if the services are as an employee, unless you own at least 5% of the company you work for.

- Spend more than 750 hours per year in real estate activities.

- *Materially participate* in each rental property. Material participation requires you to be involved "in a regular, continuous, and substantial manner" and should not be confused with the less stringent *active participant* requirement for being able to deduct up to $25,000 of combined losses per year. If you have a property manager for a rental property, it will be difficult to meet the material participation rule for that property.

Meeting the above requirements may be difficult, especially for an investor who has a different full-time job. For example, an investor may devote, say, 900 hours per year in real estate activities (thereby meeting the 750 hours requirement) but may work 1,500 hours per year at another job (thereby *not* meeting the 50% requirement). If an investor's spouse doesn't have a regular job, the spouse may be the likely person to manage the rental properties and meet the qualifications as the real estate professional; be sure to consult a tax expert on this before making any sudden lifestyle changes.

To document the number of hours devoted to real estate activities, maintain a regular log showing dates, hours worked, and what was done. Keep in mind that a person may qualify as a real estate professional one year but not the next year. To claim a *real estate professional status*, mark the appropriate box on Schedule E of Form 1040.

A real estate professional may elect to group *all* rental real estate activities as one activity. This is an important step, so before doing so consult a tax expert to determine if combining all rental real estate activities is the right thing to do.

Paying Tax on the Gain

If we have a gain on the sale of rental property, we must report the gain to the IRS and pay income tax on that gain. This involves four separate calculations.

First, we determine the adjusted basis of the property. Second, we determine the gain from the sale. Next, we separate the gain into recapture and capital gain. Finally, we calculate the tax. Let's walk through it.

Determine the Adjusted Basis of the Property

To determine the gain from the sale of a property, we must know the cost, or basis, of the property. For example, if someone bought some vacant land for $100,000 and sold it for $150,000, the gain would be $50,000. The same is true for a rental property. The difference is, with a rental property investors often make improvements to the property (which increase the basis) and take depreciation on the improvements (which decreases the basis). The result is referred to as adjusted basis:

Adjusted Basis = Purchase Price + Acquisition Costs + Improvements – Depreciation

Acquisition costs include survey costs, inspection fees, appraisal fees not required by a lender, fees to a title company for closing the transaction, etc. Loan costs are *not* part of the acquisition costs; they are treated differently, as outlined earlier. And, remember, there is a difference between an *improvement* (adds substantially to the life of the buildings) and an *expense* (which is a maintenance item and is deducted in the year it is paid). Improvements, unlike expenses, are depreciated over time, as explained earlier.

Suppose you just sold a rental property that you bought 5 years ago. You purchased it for $550,000. You paid $700 to a property inspector to evaluate the buildings at the time you bought the property. Two years after buying the property you remodeled kitchens in the units, at a cost of $40,000. You have taken depreciation on the improvements (including the kitchen improvements) totaling $85,000. Your adjusted basis would be

Adjusted Basis = $550,000 (purchase price) + $700 (acquisition costs) + $40,000 (improvements) – $85,000 (depreciation) = **$505,700**

Be sure to keep good records so that when it is time to calculate the gain from a sale, you can determine your adjusted basis.

Determine the Gain from the Sale

In figuring the gain from the sale of a rental property, the IRS allows us to deduct selling expenses (real estate commission, title fees, etc.) and deduct our cost (adjusted basis) in the property.

Gain = Selling Price – Selling Expenses – Adjusted Basis

Let's continue the previous scenario. Suppose you sell the property for $700,000 and pay selling expenses totaling $44,000. Your gain from the sale is

$$\text{Gain} = \$700,000 \text{ (selling price)} - \$44,000 \text{ (selling expenses)}$$
$$- \$505,700 \text{ (adjusted basis)} = \mathbf{\$150,300}$$

Every time we take depreciation on a rental property, our adjusted basis (or book value) drops. And the lower the adjusted basis, the greater the gain when we sell. So, taking depreciation benefits us when we take the deduction but catches up to us later when we sell. But we have no choice in taking depreciation; the tax code makes us lower the adjusted basis by the amount of depreciation taken or *allowable*. So if we don't take depreciation, our basis drops as though we had.

Taking depreciation has some benefits. First, we save tax when we claim depreciation and pay tax later at the time we sell; this is like getting an interest-free loan from the IRS. Second, the tax rate on the gain may be lower than the tax rate that was applied to the depreciation deduction.

Separate the Gain into Recapture and Capital Gain

In the preceding example, part of the gain was a result of taking depreciation (as we took depreciation our adjusted basis dropped, thereby increasing the gain) and part was due to the property increasing in value (from $550,000 to $700,000). To calculate the federal income tax on the gain, we must separate the gain into two parts: the part of the gain that is a result of taking depreciation (referred to as the recapture portion of gain) and the remainder of the gain (referred to as capital gain). The reason we must separate the gain into two parts is that each part is taxed at a different rate. The recapture portion is the total depreciation taken or the total gain, whichever is less. The capital gain is the total gain less the recapture portion. In the preceding example, your total gain was $150,300.

$$\text{Recapture Portion} = \mathbf{\$85,000} \text{ (total depreciation)}$$
$$\text{Capital gain} = \$150,300 \text{ (total gain)} - \$85,000 \text{ (recapture portion)} = \mathbf{\$65,300}$$

Calculate the Tax

Assuming we have a gain from a sale, we must pay federal income tax on the gain. If the property was held 12 months or less the gain is taxed at the taxpayer's regular tax bracket rate. If the property was held for more than 12 months, the gain is taxed at lower rates: as of the writing of this book (2011), the portion of gain attributable to depreciation (the recapture portion) is taxed at the taxpayer's regular tax bracket or 25%, whichever is less; the remainder of the gain (the capital gain portion) is taxed at 0% for taxpayers in a 10% or 15% tax bracket and is taxed at 15% for taxpayers in higher tax brackets. (The 0% capital gain tax rate may be to encourage people in lower tax brackets to invest in real estate.) These rates are scheduled to change in 2013 unless the rates are extended; *be sure to check with a tax advisor or the IRS for up-to-date capital gain tax rates.*

Assuming you are in a 28% tax bracket and using 2011 tax rates, your federal income tax from the gain would be

	Gain		Tax Rate		Tax
Recapture portion of gain:	$ 85,000	×	25%	=	$ 21,250
Capital gain portion of gain:	65,300	×	15%	=	9,795
Totals	$ 150,300				**$ 31,045**

Your total tax is $31,045, which is approximately 20.7% of the gain. If the $150,300 gain were taxed at your tax bracket rate of 28%, the tax would have been $42,084. Because of the lower tax rates on gain, you saved $11,039.

In the U.S., most states have state income tax (tax rates vary from state to state). For those states, there would not only be federal income tax on the gain but also state income tax on the gain.

Installment Sale Method

In the preceding example, the tax on the gain was paid all at once, in the year the property was sold. There are a few ways to *defer* paying the tax. One method is called the installment sale method. An installment sale is one in which the seller provides financing to the buyer; the seller takes on the role of a traditional lender.

The seller receives part of the sales price in the year of sale and gets the remainder from the buyer in subsequent years. With an installment sale, the seller has the option to report the gain as the money is received, rather than all at once. When an election is made to use the installment sale method, the seller figures the percent of sales price that is gain; this percent is referred to as *gross profit percentage*. The amount of gain that must be reported in any one year is the principal received in that year multiplied by the gross profit percentage; installment sales are reported on Form 6252. Note that the *interest portion* of payments is not included in the calculations; instead, the interest portion is treated as interest income on the seller's income tax return. All of the gain is eventually reported—it is just reported gradually, over time.

Before deciding to use the installment sale method to report a sale, keep in mind that if tax rates increase on the gain from a sale, the higher rates will apply each year. Also keep in mind that if the seller has a mortgage loan on the property being sold, and if the loan has a due-on-sale clause (which most loans do), the seller cannot do seller financing without paying off the mortgage loan. This makes an installment sale impractical in many cases in which the seller has a large mortgage loan.

Tax-Deferred Exchange

Another way to postpone paying taxes on a gain is by doing a tax-deferred exchange, often referred to as a 1031 tax-deferred exchange, or a Starker Exchange (named for an investor who challenged and won a case against the IRS). The seller of a rental property can exchange his or her property for another property instead of selling the property outright. The most common ways to achieve the exchange are

- *A straight exchange*, in which two parties trade properties that have approximately the same value.

- *A three-party or multi-party exchange* that involves three or more parties exchanging properties.

- *A delayed exchange*, which allows a seller to sell one property, place the proceeds with an approved third party, and later (within a certain time frame) use the proceeds to buy a replacement property. This type of exchange is by far the most popular of the exchange methods.

To qualify for a 1031 tax-deferred exchange, the transaction must meet strict IRS guidelines, including these:

- The properties must be *like-kind* real estate. *Like-kind* does not mean that the properties must be exactly the same kind of property, but it does mean that property held for business, trade, or investment purposes must be traded for property held for business, trade, or investment purposes. It is okay to trade, for example, a small residential rental property for an office building, or an apartment complex for raw land. But it is not okay to trade a personal residence or a dealer property for an investment property.

- The replacement property must be equal to or greater in value and in equity. For example, if the relinquished property is valued at $1,500,000 with a loan balance of $500,000, then the replacement property must be purchased for at least $1,500,000 and the equity has to be at least $1,000,000. Any cash you receive or debt relief is considered *boot* and is taxable.

- An approved, neutral third party must be involved. This party, called a *facilitator*, *accommodator*, or *intermediary*, should be arranged prior to closing; an agreement should be signed with the facilitator, and the facilitator is required to hold the proceeds from the sale unless the replacement property closing occurs at the same time. The seller can select a place for the funds and the funds can earn interest, but the seller cannot have access to the funds.

- The seller must clearly identify possible replacement properties (in most cases, up to three possible properties). The notice identifying the properties must be presented in writing to the facilitator within 45 days from the close of the relinquished property.

- The taxpayer must purchase one or more of the identified properties; the closing of the replacement property must take place within 180 days of the close of the relinquished property.

IRS rules for 1031 tax-deferred exchanges are very strict. Before venturing into a 1031 tax-deferred exchange, seek advice from a tax professional. Any goofs along the way will likely result in a heavy tax burden.

There are a few things to consider before doing a 1031 tax-deferred exchange. First, remember that the tax from the gain is not *eliminated*, it is only *deferred*. Here's how it works. The basis of the acquired property is the adjusted basis of the relinquished property plus any cash (or boot) given for the new property. If the taxpayer has been depreciating the relinquished property, the adjusted basis will likely be substantially less than the value of the acquired property. While there are no limits to the number of times a taxpayer can use a 1031 tax-deferred exchange, once the last property acquired is sold without using a 1031 tax-deferred exchange, the gain will be calculated based on the adjusted basis of that property, likely resulting in a substantial gain. And the tax rates may end up being higher than they were at the time of the previous exchange(s). Keep in mind that if the taxpayer dies before selling the property, the heirs can receive a step-up in basis on the inherited property; they basically get to start over with a basis equal to the current fair market value and don't have to worry about the deferred tax.

Another thing to think about is that the 45-day and 180-day deadlines are, in most cases, not easy to meet. Investors often find themselves rushed; in an effort to postpone paying taxes on the gain they may end up overpaying for a replacement property.

Alternative Minimum Tax

If a taxpayer's tax return includes certain *tax preference items*, they may owe additional tax, known as Alternative Minimum Tax. One thing that can trigger alternative minimum tax is using a depreciation life of less than 40 years (such as using a 27.5-year life). Using a depreciation life of less than 40 years does not necessarily mean the taxpayer will owe extra tax, but it *may* result in owing extra tax. To find out if we owe extra tax, we complete IRS Form 6251. Some taxpayers, to minimize the possibility of owing alternative minimum tax, use the optional 40-year straight-line MACRS depreciation.

TIP   **exceptions and change**

We have covered a few basic income tax topics in this section of the book. Income taxes are complicated. For every rule, there are 10 exceptions, each with lots of details. And tax laws and rates constantly change.

*Always check with your tax advisor or the IRS before
planning or completing a real estate transaction*

 Moving forward. Now it's time to play another numbers game. In Step 6 we will review how to calculate a monthly payment on a mortgage loan, interest and unpaid balance on the same loan, and a rate of return on a contemplated investment in rental real estate.

Crunch Numbers Like a Pro

We'll Explore

- The Three Types of Financial Problems

- Solving Problems with a Financial Calculator

- Solving Problems with Excel

Crunching numbers is an important part of making good financial decisions (and making money). To evaluate a potential investment in rental property you'll need to calculate a monthly payment on a mortgage loan, annual interest and unpaid balance on that same loan, and an internal rate of return (IRR). The most efficient method is to use a financial calculator. A list of suitable calculators appears on page 82. Another option is to use Excel.

The Three Types of Financial Problems

We'll start with a time-value-of-money (TVM) problem, move to an amortization problem, and bring it home with a cash flow problem.

TVM Problems

Time-value-of-money (TVM) problems are based on the principle that money earns interest over time. The frequency of compounding affects how money grows. The period of time between interest calculations is referred to as the compounding period, or as just the period. For example, if interest is compounded semiannually (twice a year), the compounding period is 6 months, and there are 2 periods per year. With monthly compounding, the compounding period is 1 month, and there are 12 periods per year. TVM problems involve five variables:

N Total number of periods. Stated another way, N is the total number of times interest is calculated. If you leave $100 deposited for 10 years and earn interest of 5% compounded quarterly, the n-value is 40 (10 years $\times$ 4 periods per year = 40 periods).

i Interest rate per period. The annual interest rate divided by the number of periods per year. If you earn 5% compounded quarterly, the i-value is 1.25% (5 $\div$ 4 = 1.25).

PV Present value. A one-time amount that happens at the beginning of the first period.

PMT Periodic payment. An amount that happens once every period.

FV Future value. A one-time amount that happens at the end of the last period.

To solve a TVM problem, we must know at least three of the five variables. Assume you get a 25-year $300,000 mortgage loan at 6.75% interest. We will calculate the monthly payment later. For now, let's simply identify the variables.

N 300 (25 years $\times$ 12 periods per year = 300)
i 0.5625% (6.75 $\div$ 12 = 0.5625)
PV $300,000 (this is the amount that happens at the beginning of the first period)
PMT This is the unknown
FV There is no future value amount

If there were no interest being charged, the monthly payment would be $1,000 ($300,000 $\div$ 300 payments). Because the lender is charging interest, the monthly payment will be greater than $1,000. There is no practical way to find the exact amount using simple arithmetic. We will calculate the amount later using financial calculators and Excel: $2,072.73.

Some mortgage lenders require borrowers to maintain an escrow account, from which the lender pays property taxes and insurance. The principal and interest (PI) portion of the monthly payment, calculated later, is $2,072.73. If an escrow account is required, a tax and insurance (TI) payment is also required, equal to 1/12 of the annual property tax and insurance. Here is what the total

PITI payment would be, based on annual property tax of $4,500 and annual insurance of $500:

PI portion of payment	$ 2,072.73
TI portion of payment: ($4,500 + $500) ÷ 12	+ 416.67
Total PITI	**$ 2,489.40**

Amortization for Mortgage Loans

A loan paid off with a series of equal periodic payments is called an amortized loan. For installment loans (like a car loan), we calculate interest to the day the lender receives our payment. For most mortgage loans, we calculate interest *per period*, regardless of the day the lender receives our payment; so for monthly payments, we are charged 1/12 of a year's interest for each payment.

To figure how much of each mortgage payment is interest and how much is principal, we first calculate interest. To calculate interest we multiply the loan balance by the interest rate to get the *annual* amount of interest; we then divide by 12 to get the *monthly* amount. The remainder of the payment is principal and reduces the loan balance.

In the previous scenario, you just got a 25-year $300,000 mortgage loan at 6.75%. Assume you got the loan on April 1. Your first payment is due May 1. Let's calculate interest, principal, and remaining balance for the first two payments.

Payment #	Due Date	PI Payment	Interest	Principal	Balance
New loan	Apr 1	—	—	—	$300,000.00
1	May 1	$2,072.73	$1,687.50	$385.23	$299,614.77
2	Jun 1	$2,072.73	$1,685.33	$387.40	$299,227.37

Procedure for May 1 payment
Interest = $300,000 × 6.75% = $20,250.00; $20,250.00 ÷ 12 = **$1,687.50**
Principal = $2,072.73 – $1,687.50 = **$385.23**
Balance = $300,000 – $385.23 = **$299,614.77**

Procedure for June 1 payment
Interest = $299,614.77 × 6.75% = $20,224.00; $20,224.00 ÷ 12 = **$1,685.33**
Principal = $2,072.73 – $1,685.33 = **$387.40**
Balance = $299,614.77 – $387.40 = **$299,227.37**

Notice, interest *decreases* with each payment. That's because interest is charged on the unpaid balance and the balance is gradually decreasing. On the flip side, principal *increases* with each payment (because the interest portion is decreasing).

Cash Flow Problems

A cash flow problem is one in which the periodic payment (PMT) changes. Let's say your friend Wade opened a savings plan 3 years ago by depositing $10,000. At the end of Year 1 he deposited an additional $500. At the end of Year 2 he withdrew $300. This morning Wade went in to close the account so he could have enough cash to buy a duplex. After the interest was posted for the third year, Wade's balance turned out to be $12,540. Wade earned $2,340 interest ($12,840 total received – $10,500 total deposited). But the more important question is, What interest rate, compounded annually, did Wade earn on his savings plan?

One way to calculate the interest rate is by using trial and error, guessing rates until one works. I'm going to suggest trying a rate of 7.10844%. Using chain calculations, without rounding intermediate results, we get:

$10,000 + 7.10844% =	$ 10,710.84	Balance, Year 1, after interest is posted
+ $500 =	$ 11,210.84	Balance, Year 1, after $500 deposit
+ 7.10844% =	$ 12,007.76	Balance, Year 2, after interest is posted
– $300 =	$ 11,707.76	Balance, Year 2, after $300 withdrawal
+ 7.10844% =	**$ 12,540.00**	Balance, Year 3

The rate of 7.10844% works! Lucky guess on my part, huh? Note that we had to use at least five decimal places in the rate to end up with an exact balance of $12,540. As you might guess, a trial-and-error method can take *lots* of time. Fortunately we can find the answer quickly with financial calculators and Excel. We'll do that later.

Solving Problems with a Financial Calculator

Only certain calculators can solve the types of problems we will do:

HP 10B	HP 17BII	TI-83 PLUS
HP 10BII	HP 19BII	TI-84 PLUS
HP 10BII+	TI BAII PLUS	Casio 9750G PLUS
HP 12C	LeWORLD Fin. Calc.	

The three on the right are not ideal because they require far more keystrokes than the others. If you don't have access to one of these calculators, I recommend you get either the HP 10BII+ or the TI BAII PLUS; they sell for about $35 and are easy to use. You can even rent one for under $10; go to *webbertext.com* (click Get a Calculator). Or you can download a financial calculator application (preferably the HP 10BII+ or TI BAII PLUS) to a Smart phone.

Keystrokes for the HP 10BII+ and TI BAII PLUS appear in the book. For selected keystrokes for the other calculators, send an e-mail request to *info@getrichslowwebber.com*.

The Appendix shows some basic operations (including setting the decimal, percent calculations, and storing numbers). You may want to review those basic operations, on pages 165-169, before proceeding.

Special note: We have created several videos for the HP 10BII, HP 10BII+, and TI BAII PLUS. To access the videos, go to *getrichslowwebber.com* (click Calculator Videos).

Solving TVM Problems with a Financial Calculator

Financial calculators have a register for each of the five TVM variables: N, i, PV, PMT, and FV. We let the calculator know the value for each of the given variables, and the calculator uses built-in formulas to do the arithmetic and give us the answer. Using financial calculators to solve TVM problems does *not* alleviate the need for common sense; calculators are only a *tool* in solving problems.

The main keys we will be using are highlighted below. Notice, for the HP 10BII+, the TVM registers are located on the top row; the *i-register* is labeled "I/YR." For the TI BAII PLUS, the TVM registers are on the third row down; the *i-register* is labeled "I/Y."

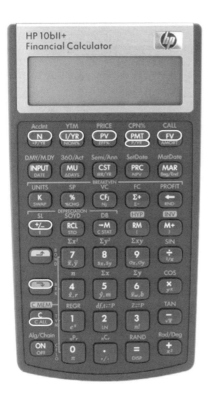

Note that we will let the *i-register* represent the interest rate *per period*. Doing this alleviates the need to change a "periods per year setting" from problem to problem. To let the *i-register* represent the interest rate per period, we must set the "periods per year" register to 1, and then leave it that way for life. Here's how:

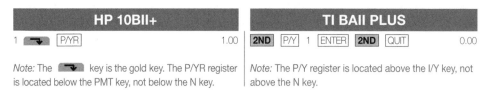

HP 10BII+	TI BAII PLUS
1 [⬇] [P/YR] 1.00	[2ND] [P/Y] 1 [ENTER] [2ND] [QUIT] 0.00
Note: The [⬇] key is the gold key. The P/YR register is located below the PMT key, not below the N key.	*Note:* The P/Y register is located above the I/Y key, not above the N key.

We can solve TVM problems using this three-step approach:

(1) Clear the TVM registers.

- For the HP 10BII+, press [⬇] [C ALL].
- For the TI BAII PLUS, press [2ND] [CLR TVM].

(2) Enter the given data.

- Enter dollar amounts *received* as positive numbers, and dollar amounts *paid* as negative numbers (example: 300 [+/−] [PMT]).
- Enter the periodic rate in the *i-register;* don't use the [%] key.

(3) Solve for the unknown.

- For the HP 10BII+, press the register representing the unknown.
- For the TI BAII PLUS, press [CPT] and then the register representing the unknown.

Now let's solve a problem (you're saying, It's about time, aren't you?). Assume you get a 25-year $300,000 mortgage loan at 6.75% interest. Let's calculate the monthly payment.

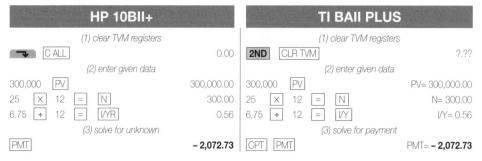

HP 10BII+					TI BAII PLUS				
(1) clear TVM registers					*(1) clear TVM registers*				
[⬇] [C ALL]				0.00	[2ND] [CLR TVM]				?.??
(2) enter given data					*(2) enter given data*				
300,000 [PV]				300,000.00	300,000 [PV]				PV= 300,000.00
25 [×] 12 [=] [N]				300.00	25 [×] 12 [=] [N]				N= 300.00
6.75 [÷] 12 [=] [I/YR]				0.56	6.75 [÷] 12 [=] [I/Y]				I/Y= 0.56
(3) solve for unknown					*(3) solve for payment*				
[PMT]				− 2,072.73	[CPT] [PMT]				PMT= − **2,072.73**

Notice, the $300,000 loan amount is entered as a positive amount because the lender *gives* you $300,000. The answer ($2,072.73) appears as a *negative* because you must *pay* that amount each month.

If you want more practice solving TVM problems, you're in luck! I strongly recommend doing additional problems now in the Appendix (pages 171-178).

Amortization with a Financial Calculator

The HP 10BII+ and TI BAII PLUS calculators have special amortization registers:

When interest is calculated in the business world, it is figured to the nearest penny (two decimal places). For our calculators to figure interest to the nearest penny for *each* interest calculation, we must have our decimal set at two places.

We can slice out any series of payments we want and the calculator will let us know the interest, principal, and ending balance for that series of payments.

For the HP 10BII+, we key in the beginning payment number, press INPUT , key in the ending payment number, followed by ➥ AMORT . Then, pressing = gives principal, next = gives interest, next = gives balance. Press = to go through the cycle again. If the next series is for the same number of payments, press ➥ AMORT .

For the TI BAII PLUS, press 2ND AMORT , then clear the worksheet by pressing 2ND CLR WORK . We provide beginning (P1) and ending (P2) payment numbers. Then, we scroll down (↓) to get balance, principal, and interest. If the next series is for the same number of payments, press CPT at the P1 prompt.

So, let's do some amortizing for that same $300,000 mortgage loan. We'll start by re-calculating the monthly payment. Then we'll calculate the interest, principal, and balance for each of the first 2 monthly payments, and then for the first 3 *calendar years* (because taxpayers can deduct interest paid during a *calendar-year* on income tax returns, calculating calendar-year interest is commonplace). We'll assume your first payment is due May 1.

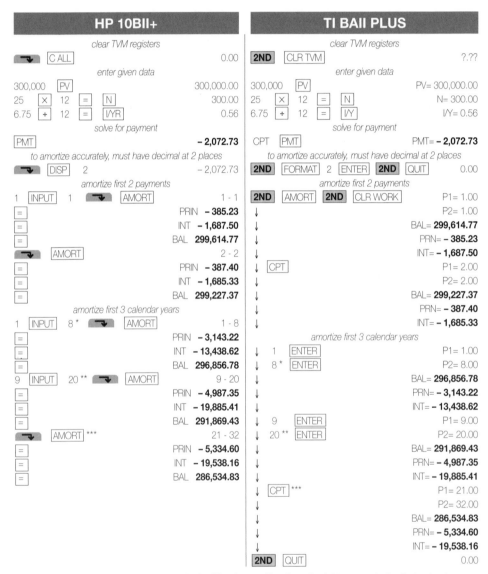

HP 10BII+		TI BAII PLUS	
clear TVM registers		*clear TVM registers*	
🔻 C ALL	0.00	2ND CLR TVM	?.??
enter given data		*enter given data*	
300,000 PV	300,000.00	300,000 PV	PV= 300,000.00
25 X 12 = N	300.00	25 X 12 = N	N= 300.00
6.75 ÷ 12 = I/YR	0.56	6.75 ÷ 12 = I/Y	I/Y= 0.56
solve for payment		*solve for payment*	
PMT	– 2,072.73	CPT PMT	PMT= – 2,072.73
to amortize accurately, must have decimal at 2 places		*to amortize accurately, must have decimal at 2 places*	
🔻 DISP 2	– 2,072.73	2ND FORMAT 2 ENTER 2ND QUIT	0.00
amortize first 2 payments		*amortize first 2 payments*	
1 INPUT 1 🔻 AMORT	1 - 1	2ND AMORT 2ND CLR WORK	P1= 1.00
=	PRIN – 385.23	↓	P2= 1.00
=	INT – 1,687.50	↓	BAL= 299,614.77
=	BAL 299,614.77	↓	PRN= – 385.23
🔻 AMORT	2 - 2	↓	INT= – 1,687.50
=	PRIN – 387.40	↓ CPT	P1= 2.00
=	INT – 1,685.33	↓	P2= 2.00
=	BAL 299,227.37	↓	BAL= 299,227.37
amortize first 3 calendar years		↓	PRN= – 387.40
1 INPUT 8 * 🔻 AMORT	1 - 8	↓	INT= – 1,685.33
=	PRIN – 3,143.22	*amortize first 3 calendar years*	
=	INT – 13,438.62	↓ 1 ENTER	P1= 1.00
=	BAL 296,856.78	↓ 8 * ENTER	P2= 8.00
9 INPUT 20 ** 🔻 AMORT	9 - 20	↓	BAL= 296,856.78
=	PRIN – 4,987.35	↓	PRN= – 3,143.22
=	INT – 19,885.41	↓	INT= – 13,438.62
=	BAL 291,869.43	↓ 9 ENTER	P1= 9.00
🔻 AMORT ***	21 - 32	↓ 20 ** ENTER	P2= 20.00
=	PRIN – 5,334.60	↓	BAL= 291,869.43
=	INT – 19,538.16	↓	PRN= – 4,987.35
=	BAL 286,534.83	↓	INT= – 19,885.41
		↓ CPT ***	P1= 21.00
		↓	P2= 32.00
		↓	BAL= 286,534.83
		↓	PRN= – 5,334.60
		↓	INT= – 19,538.16
		2ND QUIT	0.00

* Because your first monthly payment is due May 1 you will make only eight payments the first calendar year.
** For the second calendar year, the ending payment number is 20 (8 + 12 = 20), *not* 21 (9 + 12 = 21).
*** When amortizing for the third calendar year, we did not have to tell the calculator the beginning and ending payment numbers, since the previous year (second calendar year) was for the same increment of payments (12).

Doing Cash Flow Problems with a Financial Calculator

When payments change, we cannot use our TVM registers; that's because we can't enter more than one amount in the PMT register. Instead, we use a different set of registers, referred to as *cash flow registers*.

To solve a cash flow problem we first enter the cash flows:

> **For the HP 10BII+,** we enter cash flows in the CFj register; if cash flows happen more than once, enter the number of times in the Nj register.

> **For the TI BAII PLUS,** we use the cash flow worksheet CF to enter cash flows: CFo (initial cash flow), C01 (first periodic cash flow), F01 (frequency of first cash flow), C02 (second periodic cash flow), F02 (frequency of second cash flow), etc.

After entering the cash flows, we can solve for the interest rate (referred to as internal rate of return, or IRR) or the present value (referred to as net present value, or NPV).

For the HP 10BII+, to solve for IRR, press ⬛ IRR/YR . To solve for NPV, enter the periodic interest rate in I/YR , then press ⬛ NPV .

For the TI BAII PLUS, to solve for IRR, press IRR , then CPT . To solve for NPV, press NPV , key in the periodic rate, press ENTER , then ↓ , and finally press CPT .

As you will see, the cash flow registers are a piece of cake to use. Just as with the TVM registers, enter cash *received* as a positive number and cash *paid* as a negative number.

Let's say your friend Wade opened a savings plan 3 years ago by depositing $10,000. At the end of Year 1 he deposited an additional $500. At the end of Year 2 he withdrew $300. This morning Wade went in to close the account so he could have enough cash to buy a duplex. After the interest was posted for the third year, Wade's balance turned out to be $12,540. You wonder what interest rate, compounded annually, Wade earned on his savings plan. We cannot use the TVM registers because the payments change, so let's use the cash flow registers to find the interest rate (IRR) Wade earned.

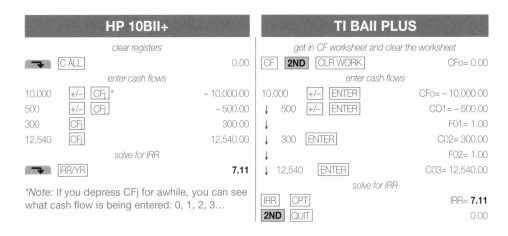

Wade earned 7.11% compounded annually. If you set your decimal at five places, you would get the more precise 7.10844%, the same answer we used earlier on page 82. As you can see, our cash flow registers must know what they are doing!

Calculating IRRs is extremely valuable when comparing investments. We can project cash flows from several investment choices and compare the projected IRRs to help decide which investment(s) to make.

We do only a few problems in this section of the book—those required to evaluate a potential investment. If you enjoy doing problems like these half as much as I do, you should dig deeper by reviewing pages 171-183 of the Appendix, which contain a variety of real-world applications: savings plans, sinking funds, yields on investments, APRs, ARMs, balloon payments, NPV, and more.

Solving Problems with Excel®

The Excel® spreadsheet program can be used to solve a variety of business applications. We will use Excel to solve the same problems we explored earlier. We'll start with a time-value-of-money (TVM) problem, then do an amortization problem, and finally solve a cash flow problem.

Solving TVM Problems with Excel

Excel relies on compound interest formulas to solve TVM problems. We provide the values for the TVM variables (n, i, PV, PMT, and FV) and the Excel program does the arithmetic. We can solve TVM problems using this three-step approach:

(1) **Select the Excel format that represents the unknown value:**

If solving for	Excel format
n	=NPER(i, PMT, PV, FV, Mode)
i	=RATE(n, PMT, PV, FV, Mode, Guess)
PV	=PV(i, n, PMT, FV, Mode)
PMT	=PMT(i, n, PV, FV, Mode)
FV	=FV(i, n, PMT, PV, Mode)

where n = total number of periods (such as 48 or 4*12); i = interest rate per period (such as 9%/12 or .09/12); **PV** = present value; **PMT** = periodic payment; **FV** = future value; **Guess** = estimated periodic rate; **Mode** = 0 if periodic payments start after one period has lapsed (*end* mode); Mode = 1 if periodic payments start immediately (*begin* mode). *Note*: We will use the word "Mode" in place of Excel's word "type."

(2) **Enter the given data.** In any cell on an Excel spreadsheet, type the format, substituting known values inside the parentheses. Don't use

dollar signs. Use commas only to separate values. Enter dollar amounts as positives if the money is received or negatives if the money is paid.

(3) To solve for the unknown, press ENTER. The answer appears. A negative value appears in parentheses.

Assume you get a 25-year $300,000 mortgage loan at 6.75% interest. Let's calculate the monthly payment.

(1) Select format for PMT	=PMT(i, n, PV, FV, Mode)
(2) Enter given data	=PMT(6.75%/12, 25*12, 300000, 0, 0)
(3) Press ENTER	**(2,072.73)**

Notice, the loan amount is entered as a positive amount because the lender *gives* you $300,000; and the amount is entered without a dollar sign and comma. The answer (2,072.73) appears in parentheses because you must *pay* that amount each month.

For more practice solving TVM problems, I recommend doing additional problems in the Appendix (pages 185-190).

Amortization with Excel

As of the printing of this book, Excel does not have an amortization program that is precise, unless we create an Excel spreadsheet that rounds the interest portion of each payment to the nearest penny. Almost all amortization programs on the Internet, including those that use an Excel spreadsheet, do *not* round the interest portion of each payment to the nearest penny, so results are not precise (setting the decimal at two places does not do the job; we must use the ROUND function in each interest calculation). We will use the =FV format to *approximate* an unpaid balance. To get *precise* results, create your own Excel spreadsheet that rounds the interest portion of each payment to the nearest penny. We have such an amortization spreadsheet on our website; feel free to give it a try.

We will now do some amortizing for that same $300,000 mortgage loan. We'll start by re-calculating the monthly payment. Then we'll calculate the interest, principal, and balance for each of the first 2 monthly payments, and then for the first 3 *calendar years* (because taxpayers can deduct interest paid during a *calendar-year* on income tax returns, calculating calendar-year interest is commonplace). We'll assume your first payment is due May 1.

Monthly payment:

Select format for PMT =PMT(*i*, *n*, PV, FV, Mode)
Enter given data =PMT(6.75%/12, 25*12, 300000, 0, 0)
Press ENTER **(2072.73)**

Interest, principal, and balance for each of the first 2 monthly payments:

With any calculator, not with Excel
Int, May 1 pmt $300,000 × 6.75% = $20,250.00; $20,250.00 ÷ 12 = **$1,687.50**
Prin, May 1 pmt $2,072.73 – $1,687.50 = **$385.23**
Bal $300,000 – $385.23 = **$299,614.77**
Int, Jun 1 pmt $299,614.77 × 6.75% = $20,224.00; $20,224.00 ÷ 12 = **$1,685.33**
Prin, Jun 1 pmt $2,072.73 – $1,685.33 = **$387.40**
Bal $299,614.77 – $387.40 = **$299,227.37**

Interest, principal, and balance for the first calendar year (payments 1-8):

Select format for FV =FV(*i*, *n*, PMT, PV, Mode)
Enter given data =FV(6.75%/12, 8, –2072.73, 300000, 0)
Press ENTER (BAL) **(296,856.80)**

With any calculator, not with Excel
Principal for Year 1 $300,000 – $296,856.80 = **$3,143.20**
Interest for Year 1 (8 × $2,072.73) – $3,143.20 principal = **$13,438.64**

Interest, principal, and balance for the second calendar year (payments 9-20):

Select format for FV =FV(*i*, *n*, PMT, PV, Mode)
Enter given data =FV(6.75%/12, 20, –2072.73, 300000, 0)
Press ENTER (BAL) **(291,869.45)**

With any calculator, not with Excel
Principal for Year 2 $296,856.80 – $291,869.45 = **$4,987.35**
Interest for Year 2 (12 × $2,072.73) – $4,987.35 principal = **$19,885.41**

Interest, principal, and balance for the third calendar year (payments 21-32):

Select format for FV =FV(*i*, *n*, PMT, PV, Mode)
Enter given data =FV(6.75%/12, 32, –2072.73, 300000, 0)
Press ENTER (BAL) **(286,534.85)**

With any calculator, not with Excel
Principal for Year 3 $291,869.45 – $286,534.85 = **$5,334.60**
Interest for Year 3 (12 × $2,072.73) – $5,334.60 principal = **$19,538.16**

Doing Cash Flow Problems Using Excel

A problem in which the periodic payment changes is known as a cash flow problem. For cash flow problems, we refer to the interest rate as an internal rate of return (IRR), and we refer to the present value as net present value (NPV). To solve a cash flow problem:

(1) **Enter cash flows.** Start with a clear Excel spreadsheet. Enter cash flows in Column A. Don't use dollar signs or commas. Enter dollar amounts as positives if the money is received or negatives if the money is paid. Enter the initial cash flow (the cash flow that occurs at the beginning of the first period) in Cell A1. Enter the remaining cash flows in the same column, in order, one at a time. If a cash flow repeats, copy the amount into cells below so that each cash flow shows up as a separate entry. If more than one cash flow occurs *at the same time*, combine before entering.

(2) **Select the format (IRR or NPV), and then enter the format values in Cell B1:**

- If solving for IRR, the format is: =IRR(A1:A?, Guess)
- If solving for NPV, the format is: =NPV(*i*, A2:A?)+A1

  where **A1** is the cell that contains the initial cash flow; **A2** is the cell that contains the cash flow that happens at the end of the first period (the second cash flow to appear in the list); **A?** is the cell that contains the last cash flow (we must type in the actual cell number, like A34); *i* = periodic rate; **Guess** is required when solving for IRR (we will base the guess on an annual rate of 12%).

(3) **Press ENTER.** The answer appears. (If you are solving for IRR and the answer does not appear as a percent, or does not have 2 decimal places in the percent, right-click on the cell, click Format Cells, highlight Percentage, adjust the decimal setting to 2 places, and then click OK.)

Let's say your friend Wade opened a savings plan 3 years ago by depositing $10,000. At the end of Year 1 he deposited an additional $500. At the end of Year 2 he withdrew $300. This morning Wade went in to close the account so he could have enough cash to buy a duplex. After the interest was posted for the third year, Wade's balance turned out to be $12,540. Wade earned $2,340 interest ($12,840 total received – $10,500 total deposited). But the more important question is, What interest rate, compounded annually, did Wade earn on his savings plan? Because the payments change, we cannot solve for *i*. Instead we solve for IRR:

(1) Enter the cash flows in Column A:

Cell A1:	−10000
Cell A2:	−500
Cell A3:	300
Cell A4:	12540

(2) In Cell B1, use the IRR format: =IRR(A1:A?, Guess). "A?" represents the last cell number, in this case A4. We will use a 12% rate for our "Guess."

In Cell B1, type: =IRR(A1:A4, 12%)

(3) Press ENTER. *The answer appears*: **7.11%**

(If the answer does not appear as a percent, or does not have 2 decimal places in the percent: right-click on the cell, click Format Cells, highlight Percentage, adjust the decimal setting to 2 places, and then click OK.)

Wade earned 7.11% compounded annually. If you set your decimal at five places, you would get the more precise 7.10844%, the same answer we used earlier on page 82.

Calculating IRRs is extremely valuable when comparing investments. We can project cash flows from several investment choices and compare the projected IRRs to help decide which investment(s) to make.

TIP   **are you a glutton for punishment?**

We do only a few problems in this section of the book—those required to evaluate a potential investment. You can dig deeper by reviewing pages 185-194 of the Appendix, which contain a variety of real-world applications: savings plans, sinking funds, yields on investments, APRs, ARMs, balloon payments, NPV, and more.

 Moving forward. Now that we can crunch numbers like a pro, it's time to determine whether the Park Place property is worth buying. On to Step 7!

Figure the Bottom Line: Cash Flows & Rate of Return

We'll Explore

- Figuring a Cash-on-Cash Return
- Projecting Cash Flow After Tax (CFAT) from the Operation
- Projecting Cash Flow After Tax (CFAT) from the Sale
- Calculating an After-Tax Rate of Return (IRR)

In Step 3 we determined that the Park Place property was worth pursuing. In Step 4 we estimated its Net Operating Income (NOI). In Step 5, we explored how the Tax Man affects an investment in rental property. In Step 6 we made some critical calculations: (1) a mortgage payment, (2) calendar-year interest, and (3) an IRR.

Now we will get our money's worth out of all this knowledge—by projecting the cash flow from the Park Place property, and the resulting rate of return!

Figuring a Cash-on-Cash Return

A simple way of evaluating cash flows is to calculate what is called a cash-on-cash return: the first year's projected cash flow divided by the amount of money invested.

Before we calculate a cash-on-cash return for the Park Place property, let's do a quick recap. In Step 3, we heard that the Park Place property was available for sale at a price of $1,050,000. In Step 4, we estimated the first year's NOI to be $72,289 (see Illustration 4-2 on page 56) and decided that a price of $1,025,000 is more realistic. Let's assume we can get a 30-year 6.5% mortgage loan of $765,000 (that's about 75% of the $1,025,000 price); the monthly payment is $4,835.32 (we will calculate the payment a bit later). We must pay loan costs of $12,000. Based on these assumptions, here's how we'd calculate the cash-on-cash return:

First year's projected cash flow:

Projected NOI	$ 72,289
Less annual debt service: 12 × $4,835.32	− 58,024 (rounded)
Projected cash flow	$ 14,265

Invested money:

Down payment: $1,025,000 price − $765,000 loan amount	$ 260,000
Add loan costs	+ 12,000
Total investment	$ 272,000

Cash-on-cash return: $14,265 ÷ $272,000 = .0524 = **5.24%**

To decide if a rate of return is acceptable, we can compare the rate with cash-on-cash returns from similar properties that are available for sale.

Most investors who figure a cash-on-cash return do so only on the first year's cash flow; some investors project cash flows for additional years (allowing for a change in rents, vacancy rates, and expenses from one year to the next) and calculate a cash-on-cash return for each of those years as well. For example, if the projected NOI for the Park Place property is $74,653 for Year 2 and $76,445 for Year 3, the cash-on-cash return for each of those years would be

Year 2: $74,653 NOI − $58,024 debt service = $16,629; $16,629 ÷ $272,000 = **6.11%**
Year 3: $76,445 NOI − $58,024 debt service = $18,421; $18,421 ÷ $272,000 = **6.77%**

TIP　　　　　**ignore what others say**

When other people tell you what the cash-on-cash return is on a certain property, ignore it. People calculate NOI differently. Some people, in an effort to maximize NOI, cheat on the numbers by understating expenses (such as showing no management fee or a minimal amount for repairs) or overstating rents (perhaps taking the position that current rents are too low, so they show rents at inflated amounts). When evaluating a property, always calculate your own NOI and the resulting cash-on-cash return.

Using a cash-on-cash return to evaluate an investment has limitations. First, a cash-on-cash return ignores income taxes, even though income tax benefits are a major reason people invest in rental real estate. A cash-on-cash return also ignores the fact that part of each mortgage payment is for principal. Finally, it ignores the effect that fix-up expenditures have on value and it does not reflect a sale of the property. So, a much better way to evaluate a contemplated investment is to project cash flows, after tax, over a specified period of time, like a 5-year holding period.

Projecting Cash Flow After Tax (CFAT) from the Operation

Because rental property has such unique income tax consequences, the cash flows we project will be *after-tax* cash flows. We will project the cash flow after tax (CFAT) from the *operation* of the property; then we will estimate the after-tax proceeds from a projected *sale* in 5 years. Based on these cash flows we can calculate a rate of return on the investment. These findings will help us decide whether to buy the Park Place property or walk away.

Keep in mind that the projected cash flows are based on some guesses. Some of the big guesses are what will happen to rents during ownership, what will happen to vacancy rates, what will happen to expenses, and what the property will sell for. If our guesses are wrong, the projected cash flows will be off. Some people argue that because the projections are based on guesses, it is not worth even making the projections. But almost all serious investors, including me, argue wholeheartedly that we are better off making decisions based on educated guesses, rather than making decisions blindly.

Our cash flow projections during ownership can be recorded on a *cash flow worksheet* like that of Illustration 7-1, on page 106. (*Suggestion*: You may want to photo copy that page so you don't have to keep flipping pages.) Please take a moment to look over the different parts of Illustration 7-1:

Top Portion. This section is used to record basic information (price, mortgage data, and depreciation data).

Net Operating Income (Lines 1-6). These lines are used to project NOI for each year of ownership.

Cash Flow Before Tax (Lines 7-9). This is the cash available to the owner before settling up with the IRS.

Tax Liability or Savings (Lines 10-19). This is the tax, or tax savings, as a result of owning the property.

Cash Flow After Tax (Lines 20-23). This is the cash that's left after settling up with the IRS.

In projecting cash flows from the Park Place property, we'll make these assumptions:

Purchase price. Assume a purchase price of $1,025,000; this is the value we estimated in Step 4 of the book.

Depreciation. Allocate 80% of the purchase price to buildings. Use a 27.5-year straight-line depreciation method. Assume you purchase the property in January and sell the property in December of Year 5.

Mortgage loan. Assume you can get a 30-year $765,000 mortgage loan at 6.5% interest. Loan costs = $12,000.

Income and expenses. For Year 1, use the income and expenses from the Reconstructed Operating Statement of Illustration 4-2 (page 56). For Year 1, rents total $121,320; assume that rents will increase 3% per year. For Year 1, vacancy and credit loss is 5%, or $6,066; for Years 2-5, assume vacancy and credit loss at 4.5%. For Year 1, operating expenses total $42,965; assume expenses will increase 4% each year.

Sale of the property. Assume you will sell the property at the end of Year 5. Establish the selling price based on a 7.3% cap rate and the sixth year NOI. Round the projected price to the nearest thousand dollars. Assume selling expenses of 6.4% (to cover real estate commissions, title insurance, etc.). *Note*: In Step 4, we found that buyers were paying prices that resulted in cap rates between 6.87% and 7.05%. High cap rates result in lower prices, so a buyer would prefer a 7.05% cap rate to a 6.87% cap rate. Our 7.3% cap rate allows some room for error.

Tax consequences. Assume that you are in a 28% tax bracket. Assume this will be your first real estate investment; you will be an active participant (able to deduct up to $25,000 in losses each year). Assume you will report the gain from the sale at the time of sale (rather than using a 1031 tax-deferred exchange or an installment sale method). Assume the capital gain tax rate in place at the time of sale is 15%; use a tax rate of 25% for the portion of gain attributable to depreciation.

When experienced investors do cash flow worksheets, they try to keep things simple. After all, the numbers are only estimates.

Most investors assume a purchase date of January 1, even if they are considering a purchase later in the year. And they assume they will sell the property 5 years later, on December 31. That way, they can include 5 full years of income and expenses in their evaluation.

Most investors include 12 months of interest expense in the first year even though, with a January 1 purchase, their first monthly payment wouldn't be made until February 1. In effect, they figure the payments could be made a bit early, so the February 1 payment would be made at the end of January and the January 1 payment of the following year would be made at the end of December. Make sense?

Investors record amounts on the worksheet rounded to the nearest dollar (except for the monthly mortgage payment, which is recorded to the nearest penny).

Let's get started by completing the top part of the worksheet.

Purchase Data	
Property 12 units @ 1100 Park Place	
Purchase Price	1,025,000
Down Payment	260,000
Amount Borrowed	765,000

Mortgage Data		
	1st Mortgage	2nd Mortgage
Loan Amount	765,000	
Interest Rate	6.5%	
Term (yrs)	30	
Monthly Pmt	4,835.32	
Loan Costs	12,000	

Depreciation Data	
Building %	80%
Building Value	820,000
MACRS Life	27.5 yr
Full-Yr Depreciation	29,818
Month of Purchase	January
Month of Sale	December

Notes:
1. Most of the information was given in the list of assumptions.
2. Down Payment = $1,025,000 purchase price – $765,000 loan amount = $260,000.
3. Monthly Pmt found with a financial calculator or with Excel; *see below.*
4. Building Value = $1,025,000 purchase price × 80% = $820,000.
5. Full-Yr Depreciation = $820,000 building value ÷ 27.5-yr life = $29,818 (rounded).

HP 10BII+				
calculate the monthly payment				
➥ C ALL				0.00
765,000 PV				765,000.00
30 × 12 = N				360.00
6.5 ÷ 12 = I/YR				0.54
PMT				**– 4,835.32**

TI BAII PLUS				
calculate the monthly payment				
2ND CLR TVM				?.??
765,000 PV				PV= 765,000.00
30 × 12 = N				N= 360.00
6.5 ÷ 12 = I/Y				I/Y= 0.54
CPT PMT				PMT= **– 4,835.32**

Note: If you get a wrong answer, make sure your P/YR register is set at 1 and you are not in "Begin" mode. Refer to Step 6 of the book for details.

EXCEL SOLUTION

Select format for PMT =PMT(*i, n*, PV, FV, Mode)

Enter given data =PMT(6.5%/12, 30*12, 765000, 0, 0)

Press ENTER **(4,835.32)**

Note: We entered the $765,000 loan amount as a positive number because the lender gives you $765,000 (don't enter $ sign or comma). The answer (4,835.32) appears in parentheses because you must pay that amount each month.

Now let's calculate Net Operating Income (NOI) for 6 years. You may wonder why, if we are projecting a sale of the property at the end of Year 5, we need to find NOI for Year 6. Here's the reason. We want to project a sales price at the end of Year 5 using a cap rate. Whenever we use a cap rate to estimate value, we always use the *upcoming* year's NOI; so if we are estimating a value at the end of Year 5, we must use the NOI for the upcoming (sixth) year. Remember to round amounts to the nearest dollar.

NET OPERATING INCOME						
	Year 1	Year 2	Year 3	Year 4	Year 5	Year 6
1. Scheduled Rent	121,320	124,960	128,708	132,570	136,547	140,643
2. – Vacancy	6,066	5,623	5,792	5,966	6,145	6,329
3. = Effective Income	115,254	119,337	122,916	126,604	130,402	134,314
4. – Operating Expenses	42,965	44,684	46,471	48,330	50,263	52,273
5. – Other Expenses						
6. = NOI	72,289	74,653	76,445	78,274	80,139	82,041

Notes

Line 1. $121,320 (given) + 3% = $124,960; + 3% = $128,708; etc. OR $121,320 × 1.03 = $124,960; × 1.03 = $128,708; etc.

Line 2. $121,320 × 5% = $6,066; $124,960 × 4.5% = $5,623; etc.

Line 3. $121,320 – $6,066 = $115,254; etc.

Line 4. $42,965 (given) + 4% = $44,684; + 4% = $46,471; etc. OR $42,965 × 1.04 = $44,684; × 1.04 = $46,471; etc.

Line 6. $115,254 – $42,965 = $72,289; etc.

Suggestion: To save time, calculate Lines 1 and 4 first, and then calculate Lines 2, 3, and 6. Also, if your calculator allows you to set the decimal at zero places, that will round numbers to the nearest dollar.

Notice in the worksheet, NOI is increasing gradually each year. You may wonder how NOI is able to increase if expenses are increasing 4% a year while rents are increasing only 3% a year. That's because the *dollar* amount of increase in rents is more than the *dollar* amount of increase in expenses. NOI is increasing at a fairly regular rate—about $1,800 to $1,900 a year, on average; the Year 2 increase is a bit more because the vacancy rate was greater for Year 1. If you notice a change in the trend, make sure there is a good reason for it; otherwise you may have made a goof in the arithmetic.

Assuming you deposit rents in a bank account, the amount you would deposit is Line 3 of the worksheet (Effective Income). After paying operating expenses you are left with NOI (Line 6). Next let's find what's left after making mortgage payments.

CASH FLOW BEFORE TAX					
	Year 1	Year 2	Year 3	Year 4	Year 5
7. – Annual Debt Service	58,024	58,024	58,024	58,024	58,024
8. –					
9. = CFBT (Line 6 – 7 – 8)	14,265	16,629	18,421	20,250	22,115

Notes
Line 7. $4,835.32 monthly payment × 12 months = $58,024 (rounded).
Line 9. $72,289 (NOI) – $58,024 = $14,265; $74,653 – $58,024 = $16,629; etc.

In the next section of the worksheet (Lines 10 through 19), we calculate federal income tax for each year. On Lines 1 through 6, we subtracted operating expenses from rental income; the result is NOI. At income tax time, the IRS lets us deduct a few more things: interest, depreciation, and a prorated portion of loan costs. If the result is a positive number (taxable gain), we must *pay* tax; we find the tax by multiplying the taxable gain by the tax rate. If the result is a negative number (tax loss), we *save* taxes; we find the tax savings by multiplying the tax loss by the tax rate.

TAX LIABILITY OR SAVINGS					
	Year 1	Year 2	Year 3	Year 4	Year 5
10. NOI (Line 6)	72,289	74,653	76,445	78,274	80,139
11. – Interest – 1st Mortgage	49,473	48,901	48,290	47,638	46,942
12. – Interest - 2nd Mortgage					
13. – Depreciation Bldgs	28,576	29,818	29,818	29,818	28,576
14. – Amortized Loan Costs	400	400	400	400	10,400
15. –					
16. –					
17. = Taxable Inc (or Loss)	(6,160)	(4,466)	(2,063)	418	(5,779)
18. If Loss, Amt Allowed	(6,160)	(4,466)	(2,063)		(5,779)
19. × 28 % Tax Rate =	Save 1,725	Save 1,250	Save 578	Pay 117	Save 1,618

Notes

Line 10. NOI, from Line 6.

Line 11. Most investors assume 12 monthly payments are made each year, including the first calendar year. When amortizing with a calculator, remember to set the decimal at two places. *Calculator keystrokes, as well as an Excel solution, are shown below.* Record interest to the nearest dollar.

Line 13. Depreciation for a full year (Years 2, 3, and 4) = $820,000 building value ÷ 27.5 yrs = $29,818. Depreciation for Year 1 and Year 5 are for 11.5 months, since the IRS allows only 1/2 month for the month purchased and month sold.

Line 14. Loan costs are spread over the life of the loan (30 years). The annual amount = $12,000 total loan costs ÷ 30 yrs = $400. Because we are projecting a sale in Year 5 and paying the loan off at that time, we can take whatever is left in Year 5 ($10,400).

Line 17. Taxable Income (or Loss). Year 1 = $72,289 – $49,473 – $28,576 – $400 = tax *loss* of $6,160. Same procedure for Years 2, 3, and 5. Year 4 = $78,274 – $47,638 – $29,818 – $400 = taxable *income* of $418.

Line 18. Remember, the loss is limited to $25,000.

Line 19. Year 1: $6,160 taxable loss × 28% tax bracket = $1,725 tax *savings*. Same procedure for Years 2, 3, and 5. Year 4: $418 taxable income × 28% tax bracket = tax *liability* of $117.

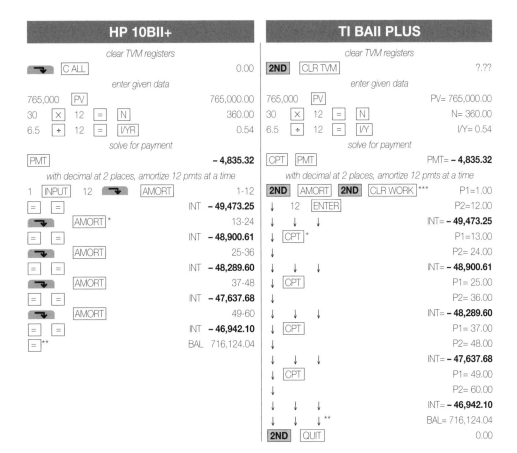

HP 10BII+		TI BAII PLUS	
clear TVM registers		*clear TVM registers*	
🔻 C ALL	0.00	**2ND** CLR TVM	?.??
enter given data		*enter given data*	
765,000 PV	765,000.00	765,000 PV	PV= 765,000.00
30 × 12 = N	360.00	30 × 12 = N	N= 360.00
6.5 ÷ 12 = I/YR	0.54	6.5 ÷ 12 = I/Y	I/Y= 0.54
solve for payment		*solve for payment*	
PMT	− 4,835.32	CPT PMT	PMT= − 4,835.32
with decimal at 2 places, amortize 12 pmts at a time		*with decimal at 2 places, amortize 12 pmts at a time*	
1 INPUT 12 🔻 AMORT	1-12	**2ND** AMORT **2ND** CLR WORK ***	P1=1.00
= =	INT − 49,473.25	↓ 12 ENTER	P2=12.00
🔻 AMORT *	13-24	↓ ↓ ↓	INT= − 49,473.25
= =	INT − 48,900.61	↓ CPT *	P1=13.00
🔻 AMORT	25-36	↓	P2= 24.00
= =	INT − 48,289.60	↓ ↓ ↓	INT= − 48,900.61
🔻 AMORT	37-48	↓ CPT	P1= 25.00
= =	INT − 47,637.68	↓	P2= 36.00
🔻 AMORT	49-60	↓ ↓ ↓	INT= − 48,289.60
= =	INT − 46,942.10	↓ CPT	P1= 37.00
= **	BAL 716,124.04	↓	P2= 48.00
		↓ ↓ ↓	INT= − 47,637.68
		↓ CPT	P1= 49.00
		↓	P2= 60.00
		↓ ↓ ↓	INT= − 46,942.10
		↓ ↓ ↓ **	BAL= 716,124.04
		2ND QUIT	0.00

   * When amortizing for the second calendar year, we don't have to tell the calculator the beginning and ending payment numbers, since the previous year was for the same increment of payments (12).
  ** We find the balance at the end of 5 years because we will need it later.
 *** The [CLR WORK] register of the TI calculator is located at the lower left; it is not the same as the [CLR TVM] register.

Interest for Year 1 (first 12 payments):

Select format for FV	=FV(i, n, PMT, PV, Mode)
Enter given data	=FV(6.5%/12, 12, –4835.32, 765000, 0)
Press ENTER (BAL)	(756,449.40)

With any calculator, not with Excel
Principal for Year 1 $765,000 – $756,449.40 = $8,550.60
Interest for Year 1   (12 × $4,835.32) – $8,550.60 principal = **$49,473.24**

Interest for Year 2 (payments 13-24):

Select format for FV	=FV(i, n, PMT, PV, Mode)
Enter given data	=FV(6.5%/12, 24, –4835.32, 765000, 0)
Press ENTER (BAL)	(747,326.16)

With any calculator, not with Excel
Principal for Year 2 $756,449.40 – $747,326.16 = $9,123.24
Interest for Year 2   (12 × $4,835.32) – $9,123.24 principal = **$48,900.60**

Interest for Year 3 (payments 25-36):

Select format for FV	=FV(i, n, PMT, PV, Mode)
Enter given data	=FV(6.5%/12, 36, -4835.32, 765000, 0)
Press ENTER (BAL)	(737,591.92)

With any calculator, not with Excel
Principal for Year 3 $747,326.16 – $737,591.92 = $9,734.24
Interest for Year 3   (12 × $4,835.32) – $9,734.24 principal = **$48,289.60**

Interest for Year 4 (payments 37-48):

Select format for FV	=FV(i, n, PMT, PV, Mode)
Enter given data	=FV(6.5%/12, 48, –4835.32, 765000, 0)
Press ENTER (BAL)	(727,205.75)

With any calculator, not with Excel
Principal for Year 4 $737,591.92 – $727,205.75 = $10,386.17
Interest for Year 4   (12 × $4,835.32) – $10,386.17 principal = **$47,637.67**

Interest for Year 5 (payments 49-60), and unpaid balance after payment 60:

Select format for FV	=FV(i, n, PMT, PV, Mode)
Enter given data	=FV(6.5%/12, 60, –4835.32, 765000, 0)
Press ENTER (BAL)	(716,124.00)

With any calculator, not with Excel
Principal for Year 5 $727,205.75 – $716,124.00 = $11,081.75
Interest for Year 5   (12 × $4,835.32) – $11,081.75 principal = **$46,942.09**

You may notice there is a slight difference in the results shown above, depending on whether you use a financial calculator or Excel. For example, Year 5 interest using a financial calculator is $46,942.10; with Excel, it is $46,942.09. And the unpaid balance after 60 payments is $716,124.04 with a financial calculator, and $716,124.00 with Excel. As of the writing of this book, Excel does not have an amortization program that is *precise*, unless we create an Excel spreadsheet that rounds the interest portion of each payment to the nearest penny (setting the decimal at two places does not do the job; we must use the ROUND function in each interest calculation). The Excel solution shown above is sufficiently accurate for our purposes.

We record the mortgage interest for each year on Line 11. Notice, interest decreases each year. That's because interest is figured on the unpaid balance, and as the balance decreases so does interest. We found the unpaid balance at the end of 5 years; we will need that amount later, when we calculate the cash flow from the sale.

We calculated the tax liability on Line 19. Notice there is a tax loss in Years 1, 2, 3, and 5, so you save money on your federal income tax. In Year 4 you had a taxable gain of $418, resulting in tax liability of $117. For years in which there is a tax savings, you do not actually receive a separate check from the IRS. For example, in Year 1, you do not receive a check for $1,725. Instead your $6,160 tax loss is combined with your other income (such as wages, interest income, etc.), so that your taxable income is $6,160 less than what it would be if you didn't own the Park Place property. By having $6,160 less taxable income, you save $1,725 on your federal income taxes. In Year 4, your taxable income will be $418 greater than it would if you didn't own the Park Place property, resulting in $117 more in federal income taxes.

Now we are ready to calculate cash flow after tax (CFAT). We start with CFBT (Line 9); that's what is left after collecting rents, paying expenses, and making the mortgage payments. We then add tax savings or subtract tax paid.

CASH FLOW AFTER TAX					
	Year 1	Year 2	Year 3	Year 4	Year 5
20. CFBT (Line 9)	14,265	16,629	18,421	20,250	22,115
21. + Tax Saved	Save 1,725	Save 1,250	Save 578		Save 1,618
22. – Tax Paid				Pay 117	
23. = CFAT	15,990	17,879	18,999	20,133	23,733

Notes

Line 20.   From Line 9.

Lines 21 & 22. From Line 19.

Line 23.   Year 1: $14,265 + $1,725 = $15,990. Same procedure for Years 2, 3, and 5.
                Year 4: $20,250 – $117 = $20,133.

See Illustration 7-1 for the entire completed Cash Flow Worksheet (During Ownership).

Illustration 7-1: Projected Cash Flow Worksheet (During Ownership)

Purchase Data		Mortgage Data			Depreciation Data	
Property 12 units @ 1100 Park Place			1st Mortgage	2nd Mortgage	Building %	80%
Purchase Price	1,025,000	Loan Amount	765,000		Building Value	820,000
Down Payment	260,000	Interest Rate	6.5%		MACRS Life	27.5 yr
Amount Borrowed	765,000	Term (yrs)	30		Full-Yr Depreciation	29,818
		Monthly Pmt	4,835.32		Month of Purchase	January
		Loan Costs	12,000		Month of Sale	December

NET OPERATING INCOME						
	Year 1	Year 2	Year 3	Year 4	Year 5	Year 6
1. Scheduled Rent	121,320	124,960	128,708	132,570	136,547	140,643
2. – Vacancy	6,066	5,623	5,792	5,966	6,145	6,329
3. = Effective Income	115,254	119,337	122,916	126,604	130,402	134,314
4. – Operating Expenses	42,965	44,684	46,471	48,330	50,263	52,273
5. – Other Expenses						
6. = NOI	72,289	74,653	76,445	78,274	80,139	82,041

CASH FLOW BEFORE TAX						
7. – Annual Debt Service	58,024	58,024	58,024	58,024	58,024	
8. –						
9. = CFBT (Line 6 – 7 – 8)	14,265	16,629	18,421	20,250	22,115	

TAX LIABILITY OR SAVINGS						
10. NOI (Line 6)	72,289	74,653	76,445	78,274	80,139	
11. – Interest – 1st Mortgage	49,473	48,901	48,290	47,638	46,942	
12. – Interest - 2nd Mortgage						
13. – Depreciation Bldgs	28,576	29,818	29,818	29,818	28,576	
14. – Amortized Loan Costs	400	400	400	400	10,400	
15. –						
16. –						
17. = Taxable Inc (or Loss)	(6,160)	(4,466)	(2,063)	418	(5,779)	
18. If Loss, Amt Allowed	(6,160)	(4,466)	(2,063)		(5,779)	
19. × 28 % Tax Rate =	Save 1,725	Save 1,250	Save 578	Pay 117	Save 1,618	

CASH FLOW AFTER TAX						
20. CFBT (Line 9)	14,265	16,629	18,421	20,250	22,115	
21. + Tax Saved	Save 1,725	Save 1,250	Save 578		Save 1,618	
22. – Tax Paid				Pay 117		
23. = CFAT	15,990	17,879	18,999	20,133	23,733	

Based on our projections, if you buy the Park Place property, your CFAT while you own the property will be $15,990 in Year 1, $17,879 in Year 2, $18,999 in Year 3, $20,133 in Year 4, and $23,733 in Year 5.

You may wonder what some of the blank lines of the cash flow worksheet are for. Line 5 (Other Expenses) is for additional operating expenses, other than those that occur from year to year. For example, you may have some extraordinary fix-up costs, like painting the exterior, in the first year. Line 8 is for capital improvement expenditures, like upgrading kitchens, heating or air-conditioning equipment, appliances, etc.; since these items cannot be treated as an expense for income tax purposes, the amount is not included on Line 5, but the amount still needs to appear as a cash expenditure. Lines 15 and 16 are for other tax-deductible items, like depreciation expense on improvements made after the initial purchase, or auto expense.

Projecting Cash Flow After Tax (CFAT) from the Sale

We have projected cash flow after tax from the *operation* of the Park Place property. Now we will project cash flow after tax from the *sale* of the property.

As part of our assumptions, we said you would sell the property at the end of Year 5. In Step 5 of the book, we explored the tax consequences of selling rental property. To recap: We must pay federal income tax on any gain from the sale. In figuring the gain, we are allowed to deduct selling expenses from the selling price, and we can subtract our cost in the property (called adjusted basis). Adjusted basis is the price we paid for the property plus any improvements, minus depreciation we take along the way. We save taxes when we take depreciation, but must pay extra taxes when we sell because as we take depreciation the adjusted basis drops, resulting in a larger gain from the sale. The part of the gain that is a result of depreciation (this part of the gain is referred to as the *recapture portion*) is taxed at a different rate than the remainder of the gain (called *capital gain*).

We will use a worksheet (Illustration 7-2) to project sales proceeds after tax. This worksheet is much easier to complete than the Worksheet During Ownership.

Illustration 7-2: Projected Sales Proceeds

ADJUSTED BASIS	
1. Original Basis	1,025,000
2. + Improvements	
3. – Depreciation	146,606
4. = Adjusted Basis	878,394

GAIN (AND RESULTING TAX)			
5. Selling Price _Yr 5_	1,124,000		
6. – Selling Expenses	71,936		
7. – Adjusted Basis (Line 4)	878,394	(B) Recapture	(C) Capital Gain
8. = Gain	173,670	146,606	27,064
9. – Suspended Losses			xxxxxxxx
10. = Reportable Gain	173,670	146,606	27,064
11. Tax Rate	xxxxxxxx	25%	15%
12. Tax	xxxxxxxx	36,652	4,060

CFAT FROM SALE	
13. Selling Price (Line 5)	1,124,000
14. – Selling Expenses (Line 6)	71,936
15. – Mortgage Balance	716,124
16. = Sales Proceeds Before Tax	335,940
17. – Recapture Tax (12B)	36,652
18. – Capital Gain Tax (12C)	4,060
19. = Sales Proceeds After Tax	295,228

Notes

Line 1.   This is the purchase price ($1,025,000)

Line 2.   We did not project any improvements during the 5-year holding period.

Line 3.   This is the total depreciation taken over the 5-year holding period (the total from Line 13 of the Worksheet During Ownership).

Line 4.   This is the adjusted basis (or book value): $1,025,000 – $146,606 = $878,394.

Line 5.   In the assumptions we made, we said to establish the selling price based on a 7.3% cap rate and the sixth year NOI (found on Line 6 of the Worksheet During Ownership). To find value, we divide the NOI by the cap rate: Value = $82,041 ÷ .073 = $1,123,849.32 ($1,124,000, rounded to the nearest thousand dollars).

Line 6.   We said to assume selling expenses of 6.4%: $1,124,000 × 6.4% = $71,936.

Line 8.   The gain is not the entire selling price ($1,124,000). The IRS lets us deduct the selling expenses and our cost in the property: Gain = $1,124,000 – $71,936 – $878,394 = $173,670. Part of the gain is because depreciation was taken; this is the recapture portion of the gain ($146,606, from Line 3). The remainder of the gain is called capital gain: $173,670 – $146,606 = $27,064.

Line 9.   This line is for losses we could not deduct during ownership, in which case we could use the losses to offset the gain.

Line 10. Since there are no Suspended Losses, this is the same as Line 8.

Line 11. We said to assume a 25% tax rate for recapture and a 15% tax rate for capital gains.

Line 12. Tax on the recapture portion of gain = $146,606 × 25% = $36,652. Tax on capital gain = $27,064 × 15% = $4,060.

Line 15. The mortgage balance is $716,124 (rounded) after making 60 payments (the balance started at $765,000). We found the unpaid balance while calculating interest for Line 11 of the Worksheet During Ownership.

Line 16. Imagine you are at a title company who is handling the sale of the property at the end of Year 5. They will not write you a check for the selling price ($1,124,000). They will deduct your selling expenses ($71,936) and they will pay off your mortgage loan ($716,124), writing you a check for what's left over: $335,940.

Line 19. You left the title company on December 31 of Year 5 with a check for $335,940. A few months later you complete your federal income tax return; because of the sale of the Park Place property you owe some additional taxes ($36,652 + $4,060), leaving you with $295,228 after settling up with the IRS.

Let's take a moment to look at the big picture of the sale. Based on the assumptions, you will buy the property for $1,025,000 and sell it for a bit more: $1,124,000. You must report the sale to the IRS; in calculating the gain, the IRS allows you to deduct your selling expenses and your cost in the property, so your gain is $173,670. A title company handles the sale at the end of Year 5 and writes you a check for $335,940 ($1,124,000 selling price – $71,936 selling expenses – $716,124 mortgage balance). Shortly thereafter you must report the gain on the sale, and as a result must pay an additional $40,712 to the IRS; that leaves you with $295,228.

You were asked to assume a 25% tax rate on the recapture portion of gain, and a 15% tax rate on capital gain. That's because these are the rates in place (for a 28% tax bracket) at the time the book was written. *When doing projections for a contemplated investment, make sure to check with the IRS or a tax expert for current rates and rules, because they may have changed.*

Calculating an After-Tax Rate of Return (IRR)

Now let's calculate the projected rate of return from the Park Place property (if you do end up buying it).

In Step 6, we calculated an internal rate of return (IRR). When calculating an IRR, we do not focus on *prices*; instead we focus on *cash*. For the Park Place property, your initial investment is the down payment ($260,000) plus the loan costs ($12,000). The annual cash flows are the cash flows after tax (CFAT) found on Line 23 of the Worksheet During Ownership; we will assume those cash flows occur at the end of each year. Remember, in Year 5, you receive a cash flow from the operation *plus* a cash flow from the sale (Line 19 from the Sales Proceeds). Here's a summary of the projected cash flows:

Initial investment: $260,000 + $12,000 =	($ 272,000)
Year 1:	$ 15,990
Year 2:	$ 17,879
Year 3:	$ 18,999
Year 4:	$ 20,133
Year 5: $23,733 + $295,228 =	$ 318,961

If you buy the property, you will take $272,000 out of your pocket and will be able to put a total of $391,962 back in your pocket ($15,990 + $17,879 + $18,999 + $20,133 + $318,961); that's a profit of $119,962, but doesn't tell you what interest rate you would earn on your money. We can use a financial calculator or Excel to determine the rate of return (IRR). Keystrokes for the HP 10BII+ and the TI BAII PLUS are shown below, followed by an Excel solution.

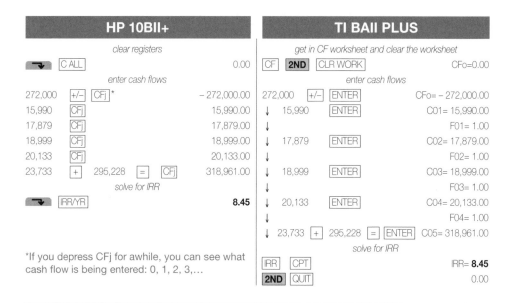

EXCEL SOLUTION

Enter the cash flows in Column A.

Cell A1:	− 272000
Cell A2:	15990
Cell A3:	17879
Cell A4:	18999
Cell A5:	20133
Cell A6:	318961

In Cell B1, use the IRR format: =IRR(A1:A?, Guess). "A?" represents the last cell number, in this case A6. We will use a 12% rate for our "Guess."

In Cell B1, type: =IRR(A1:A6, 12%)

Press ENTER. *The answer appears*: **8.45%.**

If the answer does not appear as a percent or does not have 2 decimal places in the percent: right-click on the cell, click Format Cells, highlight Percentage, adjust the decimal setting to 2 places, and then click OK.

Based on your projections, you will earn 8.45%, compounded annually, on your invested money.

TIP   **real-life considerations**

Here are a few things to keep in mind when projecting cash flows for an actual contemplated investment:

- Take your time figuring NOI; estimating income, vacancy, and expenses is the foundation of the entire cash flow projections. Make sure rental rates are reasonable, based on what is happening in your area.

- Be conservative in your guesses. For example, if you think rents will go down during the first few years, or vacancy rates will increase, show that in your projections.

- Remember that the cash flow projections and resulting IRR are only as good as your guesses (rents, vacancy, expenses, and sales price). Make your guesses carefully.

- Tax laws and rates change often. When doing cash flow projections for a contemplated investment, be sure to check with the IRS or a tax expert about current tax laws and rates.

- To save time, you might want to create your own cash flow spreadsheet. As of the printing of this book, we are making arrangement to have a cash flow spreadsheet available for a nominal fee; visit *getrichslowwebber.com*.

 Moving forward. So, is the IRR of 8.45% good news or bad news? Should you buy the property or walk away from the deal? We'll figure that out in Step 8.

Buy It or Walk Away:
Decision Time

We'll Explore

- Does It Meet Investment Criteria?
- Make an Offer
- Due-Diligence
- Modify CFAT and IRR Projections
- Modify Offer, if Necessary, or Walk Away

In Step 7, we projected cash flows and the resulting rate of return from the Park Place property. Now, it's decision time! If a rental property meets our investment criteria, we may want to make an offer, subject to certain things (such as a thorough inspection, financing, appraisal, etc.). Based on our findings, we can buy the property as outlined in the offer, get the seller to modify some terms of the offer, or walk away from the deal.

Does It Meet Investment Criteria?

Let's use the 8 Investment Criteria of Step 1 to compare the Park Place property with an alternative investment—a AAA-rated (quite safe) corporate bond paying 6.5% interest and maturing in 20 years.

1. **Management.** The corporate bond wins easily. There are minimal management headaches with the bond, but lots of personal involvement required

with a rental property.

2. **Liquidity.** The corporate bond wins again. If you need to generate cash quickly (for a business opportunity, medical emergency, etc.), you can do so by selling the bond, but cannot realistically sell the rental property overnight.

3. **Cash flow.** The rental property produces annual after-tax cash flow of about $16,000 to $24,000. If you invested $272,000 in the corporate bond, you would receive an interest check of $17,680 ($272,000 $\times$ 6.5% = $17,680) each year, before tax. Based on your 28% tax bracket you would end up, after taxes, with $12,730. The Park Place property edges out the corporate bond on this one.

4. **Appreciation.** The corporate bond is a fixed-return investment; that is, you know exactly what your return will be. (The bond, if held until maturity, will give you your $272,000 back plus interest checks of $17,680 each year— no more, and no less. The bond may go up in value in the interim if interest rates drop [because buyers will pay a premium for your bond that pays 6.5%], but if you hold it for the entire 20 years, there will be no bonus money.) The Park Place property, on the other hand, can go up in value. Because the rental property has the *potential* to increase in value (and historically, rental real estate values *have* increased considerably over time), the rental property wins on this one.

5. **Tax consequences.** The interest from the corporate bond is fully taxable. With the real estate, you get some tax shelter (like from depreciation and lower tax rates on the gain). The real estate is a big winner on this one.

6. **Risk.** There is considerable risk with rental real estate. For example, you could experience an increase in vacancy rates and a decrease in rental rates. With the bond, the company could go broke, in which case bondholders would be treated just like other creditors of the company, getting back less than they are owed. Also, bond values can drop considerably if interest rates on newly issued bonds increase; investors would prefer to buy a newly issued bond instead of yours unless you are willing to drop your price. This would not affect you if you held the bond until it matures, but would affect you if you needed to sell the bond before it matures. The majority of investors would probably agree that there is less risk with corporate bonds (depending on the bond) than with rental real estate. So, let's give the bond an edge on this one.

7. **Leverage.** Bond investors can often use bonds as collateral to borrow up to 50% of the value of the bonds. With rental real estate, investors can generally borrow up to 75% of value. So, let's give the rental property an edge here.

8. **Rate of return.** Based on our projections on the Park Place property, you would earn 8.45% on your money. With the corporate bond you would earn 6.5%.

But remember that the 8.45% is *after-tax* and the 6.5% is a *before-tax* rate. Your after-tax rate on the corporate bond (based on your 28% tax bracket) is

Before tax rate	6.50
Portion to IRS: 6.5 × 28%	−1.82
Remainder (after-tax)	**4.68**

Your after-tax rate of return on the corporate bond is 4.68%, compared with the after-tax rate of 8.45% on the Park Place property. That's a dramatic difference. Here's another way of looking at this: You would have to earn 11.74% on a corporate bond to get an after-tax return of 8.45% (11.74 − 28%[11.74] = 8.45). The rental property is a huge winner on this one!

Final score: Park Place, 5; corporate bond, 3. You may conclude that you should go with the Park Place property. But if you are like most investors, you do not place the same emphasis on each of the 8 Investment Criteria; perhaps you are more risk-averse or more interested in rate of return. And for some criteria it might be fairly even, while for other criteria, one investment is a big winner. Most investors, then, simply follow their gut when their analysis doesn't clearly indicate a winner.

Let's assume that you decide the Park Place property is a better alternative for you than other types of investments (like corporate bonds or corporate stocks). Does that mean you should jump on this opportunity? Maybe, but what if there are other rental properties that are better than the Park Place property? Before deciding on the Park Place property, project cash flows (and resulting IRRs) on numerous rental properties to help distinguish between good and bad cash flows and good and bad IRRs. *Here's the bottom line:* before investing in a rental property, first compare that investment with alternative choices (like corporate bonds). If you decide that rental real estate is the best choice, select the best rental real estate available.

Make an Offer

So you've decided the Park Place property meets your investment needs and is the best available choice. Now what? It's time to muster up the courage to make an offer.

That first real estate deal can be a bit scary. Buying a rental property is a major decision. By taking certain steps, the fear of the unknown can be minimized. You have already taken lots of steps investigating the Park Place property. You have assembled a team of experts to help along the way. Your real estate agent can guide you through the process of buying a property.

You have a lender lined up. You've projected income and expenses, cash flow after tax, and even projected a rate of return on the investment. You have compared the property with other possible investments and the Park Place property passed the test.

You may have seen inside one or two of the units of the Park Place property, but you probably haven't yet seen inside all of the units. And you probably haven't done a thorough inspection of the buildings, reviewed the seller's records, reviewed leases, etc. Your projected cash flows up to this point are based on what you *expect* to find. Your agreement with the seller should give you the right to inspect lots of things and void the agreement if the results of your investigations are unsatisfactory. This gives you one last chance to walk away.

Some investors hesitate walking away from a deal they have spent so much time and energy on; they make the mistake of getting emotionally attached to the property. Remember, if the numbers don't work out on paper, things likely won't work out once the property is owned.

Which Type of Form to Use to Make an Offer

Your offer should be in writing; that's because verbal agreements to buy or sell real estate are generally not enforceable. Each state has unique laws regarding buying and selling real estate; make sure your offer conforms to the laws of the state where the property is located. Your real estate agent will likely have state-approved forms to use, and the agent will help prepare the offer.

If you are not working with a real estate agent on a transaction, don't make the mistake of handwriting your offer; chances are it won't conform to state law and customs, or may not include important provisions that could put you at risk. Blank forms are available at many office supply stores and on the Internet, but those forms may not conform to the state laws and customs. In many states, title companies provide forms to buyers and sellers. If you use one of these forms, have the agreement reviewed by your attorney before presenting the offer to the seller. Or you can have your attorney prepare the offer. Chances are, your attorney has a boiler-plate form so the fee can be fairly reasonable; get a quote in advance.

Earnest Money Deposit

You will be required to submit an earnest money deposit as part of your offer. The earnest money shows the seller that you are serious about buying the property. The amount of the earnest money is negotiable, but is often about 1% to 2% of the price; the larger the earnest money, the more serious you appear. The offer should spell out who is to hold the earnest money and, if the earnest money is a check, when the check is to be deposited (such as once the seller accepts the offer). It is best to have a third party (such as a real estate agent's office, an attorney, or title company) hold the earnest money.

Items to Request from the Seller

Your offer to buy rental property should include a request for the seller to provide:

- A statement disclosing what problems, if any, the seller knows about the property; this form, in many states, is referred to as a seller disclosure statement.
- A rent roll showing, by unit, the name of the tenant, rent, security deposit, and expiration of the lease.
- Copies of all leases and tenant applications (together with credit reports and background checks).
- Income and expense records on the property for a given period of time (like the last 24 months).
- A copy of income tax forms for the last 2 years, showing rental income and expenses reported to the IRS.
- Service agreements with suppliers (landscape companies, trash removal companies, etc.).
- A preliminary title report from a title company indicating how title is vested, mortgage loans against the property, and any other items (such as easements, judgments, and liens) that affect the property.
- Copies of any studies or reports previously done on the property, such as surveys, site plans, environmental reports, soils studies, zoning violation notices, etc.

Contingencies to Include in an Offer

Your offer should spell out any contingencies. Most buyers of rental property list these:

- Buyer's satisfactory review of the documents provided by the seller (seller disclosure statement, rent roll, leases, tenant applications, income and expense records, service agreements, preliminary title report, studies/reports on the property, etc.).
- Satisfactory financing.

- A satisfactory appraisal. Where financing is required, the lender will require an appraisal.

- A satisfactory physical inspection of the property (including an inspection of the inside of each unit, as well as an inspection of all of the building components).

- Satisfactory review of any other issues affecting the property (such as zoning issues, soils studies, survey problems, etc.).

Your offer should state that if you are not satisfied with any of the contingency items, you have the option, for a certain period of time (known as the due diligence period), to declare the agreement *null and void* and get back your earnest money. If you do not declare the agreement null and void by the end of the due diligence period, and then fail to close the transaction, the seller, in most states, has several options: (1) keep the earnest money as *liquidated damages* and call the deal off, (2) require you to complete the transaction (called *specific performance*), or (3) sell the property to another buyer and sue you for any amount lost as a result of substituting buyers. Some pre-printed offers contain language that specifies the only option the seller has is Option 1.

The due diligence period is a very critical part of the process. During the due diligence period we can learn more about a property and the amount of income the property can produce. Later, we will explore specific things to be done during the due diligence period.

Other Things to Include in an Offer

While the following is not meant to be a complete list of additional things to include in an offer on a rental property, here are a few things you shouldn't forget to include:

- A description of the property. Identify the property by address or by legal description so that there is no confusion about which property is being purchased. For rental properties, state how many rental units are included. Spell out what *personal property* is being included, such as: 12 ranges, 12 refrigerators, and all window coverings currently on the premises; also any other personal property on the premises belonging to the seller that is incidental to the operation of the property. We don't want the seller suggesting later that the appliances and other personal property are not included in the sale.

- Price, earnest money deposit, and remainder of down payment at closing.

- A statement that the seller cannot make any changes to the property, modify any existing leases, or enter into any new leases without the buyer's written permission. For example, we don't want the seller to extend a lease for 5 years at a reduced rent for his favorite tenant(s).

- A requirement for the seller to provide you with a policy of title insurance, in the amount of the purchase price. A *policy of title insurance* is different from a *preliminary title report*. A preliminary title report merely *shows* the status of the title to the property, whereas a policy of title insurance *guarantees* you that title is good and that the property is free of any liens (other than the ones excluded in the policy, such as your new mortgage loan).

- The type of deed that will be used to transfer title from the seller to you. The three most common choices are Warranty Deed, Special Warranty Deed, and Quit Claim Deed. With a Warranty Deed, the seller "warrants" (guarantees) that title is good. With a Special Warranty Deed, the seller says he or she has done nothing to blemish the title but is not responsible for things that happened before. With a Quit Claim Deed, the seller simply gives you whatever the seller has, without guarantees of any kind. Insist on a Warranty Deed.

- How your name is to appear on the deed. For example, if you want to take title with a spouse as *joint tenants*, make that clear in the offer. (*See Step 2 of the book for a discussion on forms of ownership.*)

- The date the due diligence period ends, the date of closing, etc. Also specify the date that rents, property taxes, etc., will be prorated; for rental properties the proration date is often the closing date.

- A statement that the seller will transfer tenant deposits to you at closing.

Presenting the Offer and Negotiating with the Seller

Most buyers make an initial offer at a price less than what they are ultimately willing to pay, realizing that the seller may not accept the original offer and instead make a counteroffer at a higher price.

If an offer is subject to financing, include a letter from the lender stating what has been done so far with respect to getting the financing. There are two common types of letters lenders provide: (1) A *pre-qualification letter* stating that, based on the verbal information provided to the lender, the borrower should be able to get the loan needed; and (2) a *pre-approval letter* stating that, based on the written application submitted to the lender, the buyer should be able to get the loan needed. A letter from the lender is designed to help alleviate fear on the part of the seller that the buyer may not be able to get the loan; as you can see, a *pre-approval letter* will serve this purpose better than a *pre-qualification letter*.

In some areas it is customary for buyers, if they elect, to present a letter of intent before preparing a formal offer. A letter of intent spells out the main points the buyer and seller need to agree upon; it also states that neither party is bound by the letter of intent until both parties execute a formal agreement of sale. One drawback of a letter of intent is that since it is not binding, the seller can work a deal with another buyer; in some cases, sellers use a letter of intent to "shop" for a higher price from other buyers.

Present the offer directly to the seller, rather than fax or e-mail the offer. By presenting the offer in person (or through your real estate agent), you have a better chance of figuring out how the seller really feels about the offer, how motivated the seller is to sell, what the most important factors are to the seller, and what, if anything, the seller hates about the offer.

Some sellers are fixated on getting a certain price, and the projected cash flows may not justify paying that price. To make the deal work, you might be able to pay that price if the seller will make concessions. For example, you could ask the seller to pay some of the loan costs charged by the lender. Or you could have the seller give some money for certain repairs or improvements to the property. Or the seller could provide *seller financing* with an interest rate below the prevailing rate, with no loan costs.

Let's assume you make an offer of $1,000,000 for the Park Place property, subject to getting financing, and you ask the seller to pay $5,000 of your loan costs. The offer includes all of the provisions we discussed earlier. The seller makes a counteroffer at a price of $1,040,000; the seller will pay the $5,000 of loan costs. You then make a counteroffer to the seller of $1,025,000 with the seller to pay $5,000 of loan costs; the seller accepts.

Now the fun starts: the due diligence period.

Due Diligence

The projected cash flows on the Park Place property, up to the point of making an offer, are based on what you already know about the property. The offer the seller just signed gives you a period of time, known as the *due diligence period*, to dig in deeper. During the due diligence period, if you find things you do not like, you can walk away from the deal. You made the offer subject to satisfactory review of documents, financing, appraisal, physical inspection, and other issues. Let's explore some things to focus on during the due diligence period.

Review of Documents Provided by the Seller

The seller disclosure statement reveals problems the seller knows about the property; it should address structural issues, plumbing, electrical, heating/air-conditioning, roofing, surface drainage, environmental issues, and more. Review the disclosure statement carefully. Some things mentioned may be unimportant but others can be significant issues. If you discover things you were unaware of that are costly to remedy, you may want to ask the seller to fix it or give you some money to fix it. (We'll discuss the options the seller has later.)

The rent roll shows, by unit, the name of the tenant, rent, security deposit, and expiration of the lease. Make sure the rent roll matches the information you were provided before making the offer. Some sellers, in an effort to make the property look more appealing, show rents for vacant units as though they are rented (likely at an inflated rent), instead of disclosing that the units are vacant; this is highly misleading, but it happens. You can discover this when matching leases to unit numbers and when doing a physical inspection of each unit.

In reviewing leases, make sure that all occupied units have a signed lease. Pay attention to the name(s) on each lease, rental rate, security deposit, pets, expiration date, and other terms of the lease. When doing an inspection of the inside of the units, confirm the rent, security deposit, ownership of appliances, names of all occupants, and pets. Ask tenants if there are any verbal agreements with the landlord not mentioned in the lease, and if they know of any problems with the property. Almost all buyers of commercial rental property, and some buyers of residential rental property, get a confirmation *in writing* from each tenant, verifying the details mentioned; the written confirmation is called an estoppel certificate.

Review the applications filled out by the tenants before they moved in, as well as the credit reports and background checks. The information may help you determine the overall quality of current tenants, which may, in turn, help you decide whether to follow through in buying the property.

In your offer, you asked the seller to provide records showing income and expenses of the property. Take time to figure out the seller's system of recording rental receipts and disbursements. Pay special attention to which tenants paid their rent promptly and which did not. Make sure the total rents collected are in line with what should have been collected; if the actual rents were too low, figure out why (high vacancy rate, tenants did not pay their rent, poor management, bad economy, etc.). Determine whether the expenses over the last few years are in line with what you projected; if not, figure out why. Compare what you find in the seller's records with what the seller reported on his or her income tax return; if there are differences, figure out why.

Review the service agreements currently in place: laundry equipment, pest control, trash removal, alarm systems, cable or satellite TV, landscaping, on-site property management, off-site property management, etc. Some of these agreements may be long-term contracts, and unless the provider agrees to cancel or change the terms, you may be bound by what is in the agreement. Take the time to review each agreement with a representative from the company providing the service; you may be pleasantly surprised, in some cases, to find that the current service provider offers better service or a better price than you thought you could get.

Review the preliminary title report, paying close attention to how title is currently vested, mortgage loans and other liens currently against the property, easements, and other things that affect the property. If you have questions, ask the title company, your real estate agent, and your attorney. If there are problems with the title that the seller cannot remedy, walk away from the deal before wasting more time and energy; better to find out now with a preliminary title report than to find out later after paying to get a physical inspection, appraisal, etc. Remember, a preliminary title report and a policy of title insurance do *not* address boundary line discrepancies; if you suspect part of the Park Place improvements (fences, buildings, etc.) are on a neighbor's property, or part of a neighbor's improvements are on the Park Place property, get a survey from a qualified engineer. If there is a problem that cannot be remedied, you can walk away from the deal.

Review any studies and reports the seller provides, such as surveys, site plans, environmental reports, soils studies, flood zone maps, zoning violation notices, etc. If you suspect any problems in these areas and the seller has no study or report to give you, investigate on your own. For example, if you suspect that the buildings may not conform to current zoning regulations, investigate with the appropriate agency. If you suspect there is a boundary line problem, get a survey. It's better to discover a problem now, rather than after you become the owner.

Obtaining Financing

Some buyers make the mistake of using the following wording on a financing contingency: "subject to obtaining financing." Let's say a buyer needs a 30-year loan of $800,000 and is hoping for an interest rate of 6.5%, with loan costs not exceeding $15,000. Let's say the lender gives the buyer a commitment for a 15-year loan of $650,000 at 8% interest, with loan costs of $30,000. Since the buyer *can* obtain financing, the buyer would not be allowed to walk away from the deal because of the financing contingency. Fortunately, you made your offer "subject to obtaining financing *that is satisfactory to the buyer*." Much better wording.

Getting a mortgage loan on a personal residence can be a lengthy process; getting a loan on a rental property can be even more time-consuming. Many buyers lose out on a deal because they fail to get approval of financing before the due diligence period ends. Here are a few suggestions:

- The lender you selected as part of your team in Step 2 should have lots of experience making loans on rental property. Develop a relationship with your lender long before making any offers. Let the lender educate you on the process of getting a loan. Determine the parameters for a loan on rental property: loan-to-value (LTV) ratio, length of the loan, interest rate, loan costs, requirements when the property is sold, etc. For some loans, especially those on larger properties, the lender may require special inspections, such as an inspection by a structural engineer or an environmental testing company. Find out in advance what will be required. If something is not acceptable, find another lender. You don't want to be searching for a lender *after* you have made an offer on a property!

- Complete an application with the lender before starting the search for properties to buy. That way, the lender can do their preliminary work and be ready to issue a pre-approval letter when you need it for a specific property.

- Ask the lender how many days will be needed to get the financing approved, and how many days after the approval before you get the money. Then, multiply each by 2.3! Just kidding, but allow plenty of cushion when establishing expiration dates in an offer: date to obtain an appraisal, date to obtain financing commitment, end of due diligence period, date to close the transaction.

- As soon as you have a signed offer, let the lender know. Immediately get the lender whatever documents are needed to keep the process moving forward.

- You must provide the lender with a lender's policy of title insurance. This is similar to the policy of title insurance the seller provides to you, but is a separate policy that insures the lender. Many title companies provide a lender's policy at a reduced rate, since it is a secondary policy. If you don't want to use the same title company the seller is using, you can, in most states, select your own title company to provide the lender's policy.

- Check in regularly with the lender. Find out who the backup person is at the lender's office in case your main contact is not available. Keep informed on the status of the application, the appraisal, the underwriting department, etc. Let the seller know what's happening. If it's okay with your lender, you may want to let the seller check directly with the lender so the seller can be assured of the progress.

- If the loan process is taking longer than allowed for in the offer, ask the seller for an extension. Chances are, unless the seller has another buyer waiting in the wings, the seller will grant an extension as long as you are doing your part to get the financing. If the seller does agree to provide an extension of time, get it in writing. Some buyers include a provision in the offer that allows the buyer to extend the financing deadline for a specified period of time; typically the buyer agrees to increase the earnest money deposit if they elect to extend the financing deadline.

- When you get the loan commitment, make sure it's for what was promised: loan amount, term, interest rate, and loan costs.

Appraisal

You made the offer subject to obtaining a professional appraisal that is satisfactory to you. Since you are getting a mortgage loan, the lender will order the appraisal. You must either pay the lender in advance for the appraisal or the lender will ask to be reimbursed later.

For buyers who are paying cash for a property or for transactions in which the seller is providing the financing to the buyer, the buyer is not required to get an appraisal. Even when not required, most buyers get an appraisal to make sure they are not overpaying for the property.

In selecting an appraiser, some people rely on recommendations; some select an appraiser based on having a certain national affiliation (such as MAI, SRA, SRPA, or IFA).

Getting an appraisal can be a bottleneck in the due diligence period. Help make arrangements for the appraiser to see as much of the property as he or she wants to see, and as quickly as possible. And help by providing rent rolls, income and expense records, etc., to the appraiser.

Remember, an appraisal is only that appraiser's *estimate* of value. If you were to hire several appraisers to appraise the same property, the value estimates would likely all be different, maybe by as much as 5% to 10%, or even more, depending on the type of property. An appraisal showing a value slightly less than the agreed-upon price is generally not a reason to cancel a deal. Experienced investors often rely as much on their own opinion of value as they do on an estimate of value by an appraiser. A low appraisal can, however, result in a lower-than-anticipated loan amount.

Physical Inspection

You made the offer subject to satisfactory results from a physical inspection of the property, including the inside of each unit, the exterior of the buildings and grounds, and all of the building components.

Don't pinch pennies by forgoing a physical inspection by a trained professional; doing so could result in finding serious problems with the property after you are the owner! The inspector you selected as part of your team should have lots of experience inspecting rental properties, and be affiliated with a local or national organization of inspectors. Ask what he or she charges, and what he or she looks at (and doesn't look at) during the inspection.

Be there when the inspection is done. Accompany the inspector into each unit; doing so provides a chance to verify that the units are occupied, see the condition of each unit, see how each tenant maintains their unit, meet tenants, and verify what is on the rent roll. Make notes of your findings in each unit. Ask the inspector to point out things that are defective, how serious each defect is, and the best remedies. Finally, review the inspection report carefully and ask the inspector about anything you don't understand.

The best news from an inspection is that there are no serious problems. An inspection will likely uncover some minor problems, like leaky faucets or bad light switches. Chances are, you can live with a few of those things. But if you uncover some serious problems that are costly to remedy or that can't be remedied, you will need to figure out what to do.

Findings During the Due Diligence Period

You made your offer subject to satisfactory review of documents, financing, appraisal, physical inspection, and review of any other issues affecting the property. The following list shows the main things, good and bad, that you discovered during the due diligence period:

- The units have nice floor plans and the rooms are spacious.

- All of the units are occupied and the rents are as stated on the rent roll: four units @ $820, two @ $835, and six @ $860. The six units at $860 have newer carpet and paint; the other six units will need new carpet and paint when they become vacant.

- The quality of tenants is somewhat below what it could be with better management.

- The *seller disclosure statement* reported a roof leak about 6 months ago; the seller said the roof was repaired. The physical inspection supports what the seller said and indicates that the roof should, with regular maintenance, last another 10 to 12 years.

- The seller's records indicate that income and expenses are in line with what the seller provided before you made the offer.

- You discover that all of the service agreements are month-to-month, allowing you to either continue with the current providers or find new providers.

- The preliminary title report indicates that title to the property is vested in the seller's name and the only lien on the property is the seller's current mortgage loan, which will be paid off at closing.

- The appraisal came in at a value of $1,010,000 (just under the $1,025,000 price you agreed upon).

- You received a financing commitment. Because the appraisal came in lower than expected, the loan amount will be a bit less than what you planned on: $1,010,000 × 75% = $757,500 (instead of at least $765,000 you had hoped for). The lender did agree to the 30-year term and 6.5% interest (resulting in a monthly payment of $4,787.92), with loan costs totaling $12,000.

- The physical inspection shows a few minor repairs are needed. The inspection did, however, reveal one notable problem: The kitchen floors in three of the units are uneven, crowning in the center and dropping off an inch or two on each side. This defect could be a concern and annoyance to tenants. The inspector identified the cause: the floor joist running under the center of the floor is, for those three units, a double joist; while the other joists have settled a bit over time, the double joist has not, causing the crowning. The best remedy would be to pull up the flooring material (including the plywood underlay), shave the double joist, and relay new flooring material. You confirm with an engineer that shaving the double joist will not affect the integrity of the floor system. The cost is approximately $2,200 per unit; you would delay the work until the tenants move.

Modify CFAT and IRR Projections

Now that you have completed your due diligence you could (1) go ahead with the offer the way it is and close the transaction, (2) declare the agreement null and void and walk away from the deal, or (3) ask the seller to modify something in the original offer (in which case, the seller does not have to agree with your requests).

Your original cash flow projections (shown as Illustration 7-1 and 7-2 on pages 106 and 108) and resulting IRR are based on *what you knew about the property before making an offer*. Now that you have completed your due diligence, you have a much better understanding of the property and it's cash flow potential. Suppose you decide that if you proceed to buy the property you will ask the seller to help defray the cost of fixing the uneven floors. After all, that is something you were unaware of at the time you made the offer and it will take a substantial amount of money to correct. Hopefully the seller will realize that if you don't do the deal, other buyers will have the same concern.

Before approaching the seller you decide to modify the projected CFAT and IRR to determine if the property is still worth buying. Here are the factors that will affect your cash flow, based on what you *now* know:

- The loan amount will be reduced to $757,500, meaning you will need a slightly larger down payment. The monthly payment (PI) will be $4,787.92.

- In your original cash flow projections you assumed you would pay $12,000 in loan costs. In the offer, the seller agreed to pay the first $5,000 of loan costs, meaning you would pay only $7,000.

- Six of the units will need new carpet and paint. You estimate it will cost $3,500 per unit. You would upgrade the units as they become vacant: you project three units in Year 1, and three units in Year 2. Once the units are fixed up, you project you can increase the rent $40 per month per unit.

- Assume you will fix the uneven floors as the units become vacant: one unit in Year 1, and two units in Year 2, at a cost of $2,200 per unit. Assume the seller will give you $5,000 at closing to defray the projected $6,600 cost of fixing the uneven floors.

- As a result of what you discovered from the physical inspection, you project $1,500 of extra repairs in Year 1 (in addition to carpet, paint, and fixing floors).

Illustration 8-1 shows the modified cash flow projection during ownership. Some of the key differences are circled. Notice, the down payment is now $267,500 ($1,025,000 price – $757, 500 loan amount). Loan costs are $7,000 ($12,000 total – $5,000 paid by the seller). On Line 5 (Other Expenses), for Year 1 you will incur the following additional expenses: $1,500 for minor repairs, $10,500 to carpet and paint three units (3 × $3,500 = $10,500), $2,200 to fix uneven floors for one unit, less a $5,000 credit from the seller, resulting in $9,200. For Year 2, you will pay $10,500 to carpet and paint another three units (3 × $3,500 = $10,500), plus $4,400 to fix uneven floors for two more units (2 × $2.200 = $4,400), for a total of $14,900.

On Line 1 (Scheduled Rent), rent for Year 2 will be $121,320 (Year 1) + 3% = $124,960. Plus you will get an additional $1,440 rent because of the new carpet and paint in three units (3 units × 40 per month × 12 months = $1,440 per year): $124,960 + $1,440 = $126,400. Rent for Year 3 will be $126,400 (Year 2) + 3% = $130,192. Plus you will get an additional $1,440 rent because of the new carpet and paint in the other three units: $130,192 + $1,440 = $131,632. For Years 4, 5, and 6, we add 3% each year.

For Line 7 (Annual Debt Service), we multiply the new monthly payment ($4,787.92) by 12, getting $57,455. For Line 11 (Interest), we find interest using a financial calculator (using the procedure of page 103) or Excel (using the procedure of page 104); the unpaid balance at the end of Year 5 is $709,103. For Line 14 (Amortized Loan Costs), we spread the $7,000 loan costs over the life of the loan (30 years), resulting in $233 a year; since you will sell the property (and pay the loan off) at the end of Year 5, you can deduct the remainder of loan costs in Year 5.

Illustration 8-2 shows the modified sales proceeds. Some of the key differences are circled. Notice, the selling price at the end of Year 5 is: $85,092 NOI Year 6 ÷ .073 cap rate = $1,166,000 (rounded).

Illustration 8-1: Projected Cash Flow Worksheet, Modified (During Ownership)

Purchase Data		Mortgage Data			Depreciation Data	
Property 12 units @ 1100 Park Place			1st Mortgage	2nd Mortgage	Building %	80%
Purchase Price	1,025,000	Loan Amount	757,500		Building Value	820,000
Down Payment	267,500	Interest Rate	6.5%		MACRS Life	27.5 yr
Amount Borrowed	757,500	Term (yrs)	30		Full-Yr Depreciation	29,818
		Monthly Pmt	4,787.92		Month of Purchase	January
		Loan Costs	7,000		Month of Sale	December

NET OPERATING INCOME						
	Year 1	Year 2	Year 3	Year 4	Year 5	Year 6
1. Scheduled Rent	121,320	126,400	131,632	135,581	139,648	143,838
2. – Vacancy	6,066	5,688	5,923	6,101	6,284	6,473
3. = Effective Income	115,254	120,712	125,709	129,480	133,364	137,365
4. – Operating Expenses	42,965	44,684	46,471	48,330	50,263	52,273
5. – Other Expenses	9,200	14,900				
6. = NOI	63,089	61,128	79,238	81,150	83,101	85,092

CASH FLOW BEFORE TAX						
7. – Annual Debt Service	57,455	57,455	57,455	57,455	57,455	
8. –						
9. = CFBT (Line 6 – 7 – 8)	5,634	3,673	21,783	23,695	25,646	

TAX LIABILITY OR SAVINGS						
10. NOI (Line 6)	63,089	61,128	79,238	81,150	83,101	
11. – Interest – 1st Mortgage	48,988	48,421	47,816	47,171	46,482	
12. – Interest – 2nd Mortgage						
13. – Depreciation Bldgs	28,576	29,818	29,818	29,818	28,576	
14. – Amortized Loan Costs	233	233	233	233	6,068	
15. –						
16. –						
17. = Taxable Inc (or Loss)	(14,708)	(17,344)	1,371	3,928	1,975	
18. If Loss, Amt Allowed	(14,708)	(17,344)				
19. × 28% Tax Rate =	Save 4,118	Save 4,856	Pay 384	Pay 1,100	Pay 553	

CASH FLOW AFTER TAX						
20. CFBT (Line 9)	5,634	3,673	21,783	23,695	25,646	
21. + Tax Saved	Save 4,118	Save 4,856				
22. – Tax Paid			Pay 384	Pay 1,100	Pay 553	
23. = CFAT	9,752	8,529	21,399	22,595	25,093	

Illustration 8-2: Projected Sales Proceeds, Modified

ADJUSTED BASIS	
1. Original Basis	1,025,000
2. + Improvements	
3. – Depreciation	146,606
4. = Adjusted Basis	878,394

GAIN (AND RESULTING TAX)			
5. Selling Price _Yr 5_	1,166,000		
6. – Selling Expenses	74,624		
7. – Adjusted Basis (Line 4)	878,394	(B) Recapture	(C) Capital Gain
8. = Gain	212,982	146,606	66,376
9. – Suspended Losses			xxxxxxxx
10. = Reportable Gain	212,982	146,606	66,376
11. Tax Rate	xxxxxxxx	25%	15%
12. Tax	xxxxxxxx	36,652	9,956

CFAT FROM SALE	
13. Selling Price (Line 5)	1,166,000
14. – Selling Expenses (Line 6)	74,624
15. – Mortgage Balance	709,103
16. = Sales Proceeds Before Tax	382,273
17. – Recapture Tax (12B)	36,652
18. – Capital Gain Tax (12C)	9,956
19. = Sales Proceeds After Tax	335,665

Here are a few key differences between your original cash flow projections (before you made the original offer) and the modified cash flow projections (after doing the due diligence):

	Initial Projections	Modified Projections
Price	1,025,000	1,025,000
Initial investment (down payment + loan costs)	272,000	274,500
Cash flow after tax from operations		
Year 1	15,990	9,752
Year 2	17,879	8,529
Year 3	18,999	21,399
Year 4	20,133	22,595
Year 5	23,733	25,093
NOI, Year 6	82,041	85,092
Selling Price, Year 5	1,124,000	1,166,000
Sales Proceeds After Tax	295,228	335,665

Here's a summary of the modified after-tax cash flows:

Initial investment: $267,500 down + $7,000 loan costs	(274,500)
Year 1:	9,752
Year 2:	8,529
Year 3:	21,399
Year 4:	22,595
Year 5: $25,093 (from operations) + $335,665 (from sale)	360,758

Based on these changes in after-tax cash flows, let's calculate the new IRR:

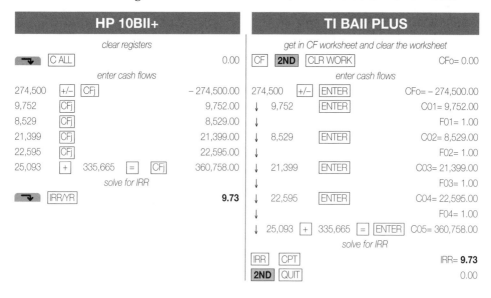

HP 10BII+				TI BAII PLUS			
clear registers				*get in CF worksheet and clear the worksheet*			
⬇	C ALL		0.00	CF	2ND	CLR WORK	CFo= 0.00
enter cash flows				*enter cash flows*			
274,500	+/− CFj		− 274,500.00	274,500	+/− ENTER		CFo= − 274,500.00
9,752	CFj		9,752.00	↓ 9,752	ENTER		C01= 9,752.00
8,529	CFj		8,529.00	↓			F01= 1.00
21,399	CFj		21,399.00	↓ 8,529	ENTER		C02= 8,529.00
22,595	CFj		22,595.00	↓			F02= 1.00
25,093	+ 335,665 = CFj		360,758.00	↓ 21,399	ENTER		C03= 21,399.00
solve for IRR				↓			F03= 1.00
⬇	IRR/YR		**9.73**	↓ 22,595	ENTER		C04= 22,595.00
				↓			F04= 1.00
				↓ 25,093 + 335,665 = ENTER			C05= 360,758.00
				solve for IRR			
				IRR CPT			IRR= **9.73**
				2ND QUIT			0.00

EXCEL SOLUTION

Enter the cash flows in Column A.

Cell A1:	− 274500
Cell A2:	9752
Cell A3:	8529
Cell A4:	21399
Cell A5:	22595
Cell A6:	360758

In Cell B1, use the IRR format: =IRR(A1:A?, Guess). "A?" represents the last cell number, in this case A6. We will use a 12% rate for our "Guess."

In Cell B1, type: =IRR(A1:A6, 12%)

Press ENTER. *The answer appears*: **9.73%**.

If the answer does not appear as a percent or does not have 2 decimal places in the percent: right-click on the cell, click Format Cells, high-light Percentage, adjust the decimal setting to 2 places, and then click OK.

The projected IRR, based on your *original* projections (before you made the offer) was 8.45%; the IRR based on your *modified* projections is 9.73%.

You may think the 9.73% rate of return is not that fabulous. But suppose you continued to earn that same after-tax rate for a 35-year period of time. Your original $274,500 of cash would grow to over $7,000,000—a pretty nice sum for retirement! (If you're curious, you can confirm this with your calculator or with Excel: PV = negative $274,500; N = 35; i = 9.73%; solve for FV→ $7,078,326.98.)

Modify Offer, if Necessary, or Walk Away

To help convince the seller to go along with your request of $5,000 to defray the cost of fixing the floors, you provide the seller with a copy of the inspection report, which reveals the deferred maintenance items as well as the uneven floors. You also let the seller see the appraisal report, with a value estimate of $1,010,000 (less than the $1,025,000 agreed-upon price). You let the seller know that you (and your lender) are ready to close the transaction quickly.

The seller is not required to accept what you are asking. The seller's options are hopefully spelled out in the offer; the options vary from state to state. Here's how it works in many states:

1. If the buyer provides written objections to the seller, the buyer and seller have a certain number of days to agree in writing how to resolve the buyer's objections.

2. If the buyer and seller have not agreed in writing by that deadline, the buyer has the option to cancel the agreement by providing written notice to the seller within a certain number of days after the expiration of the response period.

3. If the buyer does not cancel the agreement, the parties will close the transaction as they originally agreed.

Let's suppose the seller thinks it over and decides that what you are asking is fair. After all, you are willing to pay the $1,500 for deferred maintenance items and are willing to pay part of the cost to fix the uneven floors ($6,600 – $5,000 seller's share = $1,600). And you are able to close the transaction quickly. If the seller does not agree and the deal fails, the seller would have to start over with another buyer; that buyer might have trouble with financing and would likely have the same objections after doing a physical inspection. So the seller agrees to your request. You schedule a closing and then become the proud owner of the Park Place property! Hopefully, your actual cash flows will closely match your projected cash flows.

 Moving forward. You are a landlord. Now what? On to Step 9!

STEP 9

Help the Money Tree Thrive: Effective Landlording

We'll Explore

- Follow-Up Items After the Closing

- Getting Good Tenants

- Keeping the Property in Good Condition

- Record Keeping

- Maximizing Rent

- Controlling Expenses

- Management Options

Congratulations! You have become a LANDLORD! You get to collect rents, keep the place in good condition, pay the bills, and record the income and expenses. When you have a vacancy, you must get the unit ready to rent and find a new tenant.

Some investors enjoy being a property manager. Others prefer to let a property management company have all of that fun! Think of this step as either what you can do as your own property manager to help things go smoothly or, if you hire a property management company, what to expect of the property manager.

Follow-Up Items After the Closing

You just purchased the Park Place property. Now what? Here are a few things you should do right after becoming the owner:

- If you have not yet purchased an insurance policy, get adequate insurance, including fire coverage, liability coverage, and rent loss coverage.

- Sign up for services: water, sewer, electricity, gas, trash, snow removal, landscaping services, pest control, etc. For electricity and gas, sign up for common areas (like outside lights and laundry room), and also sign a *landlord agreement* with each utility company that automatically transfers utilities into your name while a unit is vacant; doing so will allow vacant units to have electricity and heat during periods of vacancy.

- If the seller is providing you with a policy of title insurance, make sure you receive the policy; once it arrives, read it and call the title company with any concerns.

- Open a checking account for the rental property; don't use your *personal* account.

- Mail or deliver a written notice to tenants, letting them know you are now the owner. The notice should include: (1) the amount of the security deposit that has been transferred to you, (2) confirmation of the rental amount, (3) where to mail or deliver rent, and (4) your contact information along with an invitation to get in touch with concerns or requests for maintenance.

- If you did not meet the tenants during the inspection process, schedule a time for a personal visit. Your visit may alleviate fears they have about having a new landlord.

Getting Good Tenants

Most landlords would probably agree that, by far, the most critical part of being a landlord is this:

Select Good Tenants

It's better to have a unit that is vacant than to have a unit occupied by a bad tenant. We want tenants who pay their rent promptly, take care of the property, stay for a long time, and are easy to get along with. Here are a few things that will help us attract good tenants:

- Keep the exterior of the property in good condition. If a property looks run down, dirty, or neglected, it will not attract good tenants.

- Get rid of bad tenants. A tenant who doesn't respect the property or the rights of other tenants will drive good tenants away.

- Don't show a unit to prospective tenants until the unit is fixed up and clean. A unit in poor condition will attract only poor-quality tenants.

- Set the rent at the right amount. If you ask too much rent, you won't get qualified applicants. If you set rent too low, you will be overwhelmed with applicants.

Tenant Application

Showing units can be time-consuming. To eliminate unnecessary showings, do a *pre-interview* when prospects call. Ask for their name, how many people will be occupying the property, where they work, where they live, why they are moving, if they have pets, if they smoke, if they have good credit, etc. If the caller appears to have no chance of being accepted as a tenant, let the person know.

Once a prospective tenant has seen the property and wants to rent it, have the person complete an application form. A generic form appears in the Appendix. In general, the application should ask for the following information: (1) a list of everyone who will live in the apartment, their date of birth, social security number, and driver's license number; (2) employer's name, supervisor's name, phone number, date employment started, work hours per week, salary or rate of pay, position; (3) present residence, showing address, length of stay, rent, landlord's name and phone number, reason for moving; (4) references; (5) vehicles, including year, make and model, color, license plate number; (6) contact information (e-mail address, cell phone number); (7) pets; (8) whether they smoke. The applicant should sign and date the application form, warranting that the information is correct, giving you permission to verify information on the application, and allowing sources to divulge information to you.

Some landlords give prospective tenants an application form and let them return the completed form later. This is a bad idea; it allows bad prospects some time to get friends to pose as an employer or landlord. Instead, have applicants complete the application in your presence.

Interview

Carefully go over the application with the prospective tenant, filling in additional bits of information. (You may want to tell the applicant that you will be asking *lots* of questions to insure that you understand everything on the application.) Ask each adult applicant to show you his or her driver's license (or other official photo ID). You want to know that applicants are who they say they are; bad tenants have been known to use the identities of other people so they can get approved. Compare the address on the driver's license with the current address shown on the application; clarify any discrepancies. If you approve the application, put a photocopy of the ID in the tenant file.

To minimize the chance of selecting someone who will move into your property, then move right back out, ask certain questions. Determine how long the applicant has lived in your area. If they have moved to your area recently, find out why they moved to your area, if they like it (including the climate), if they have relatives in the area, and how long they will likely stay. If an applicant is moving out of a parent's place and has never rented before, keep in mind that the person may not adapt well to being on his or her own and may move back with parents after a short time. If the applicants have not lived together before, keep in mind that they may not get along and you may lose one or more of them as tenants. While it is against the law to ask about a person's marital status, many applicants volunteer the information; if the person is recently separated from a spouse, try to ascertain the likelihood of a reconciliation. While a reconciliation may be good for them, it won't be good for you when they vacate your property to move back to their spouse.

When considering the person's source of income, make sure you understand what kind of business they are in, what they do for the company, how long they have been employed, how much they earn, how often they are paid, and what hours of the day they work. If their current employment is for less than 2 years, get similar information about their previous employment. If the person is self-employed, get a copy of the person's income tax return for the previous year (or two), showing self-employment income.

When reviewing where they currently live, confirm the address, how long they have occupied the property, and the amount of rent. Ask who lives with them; if they have a roommate, ask who pays the rent and utilities for the group.

Ask if rent has ever been paid late, and if they have ever received a complaint from the landlord or neighbors. Ask why they are moving, and if they have let their landlord know they will be moving.

Be sure to ask where they lived before they moved into their current residence. Get the address, rent, dates moved in and out, why they moved, landlord's name and phone number, etc. Here's why we want to know this. In some cases, a tenant is being evicted from their current place and the landlord will give a glowing report; they want them out of their place. By going back one or two previous landlords, you have a better chance of determining if they have been a good tenant.

When reviewing references, get at least one who is a relative (relatives are often better sources of tracking someone down later, if the need arises).

When reviewing vehicles, pay attention to the age of the vehicle; older vehicles generally require more repairs, which leaves less money to pay the rent. Consider whether the applicant has more vehicles than your property can accommodate, and if the vehicles are in running condition (after all, you don't want beat-up vehicles sitting around on your property). Accompany the applicant to his or her vehicle after the interview; the condition of the vehicle and it's interior cleanliness can be a good indicator of how well the person will take care of your property.

If the person has a pet, ask for a description: weight, color, breed, gender, age, pet's name. Here are a few general conclusions about pets: large dogs generally do more damage than small dogs; younger pets are generally more unpredictable than older pets; pet odors are difficult to get rid of, especially those from pet urine; male cats generally leave more pet odor than female cats do (male cats often mark their territory); some pets make a lot of noise, disturbing neighbors.

If the person smokes, determine how often, and if the person is willing to smoke outdoors. Make sure all of the adult applicants have signed the application. Let them know you will be ordering a credit report and background check on each applicant. Ask if the reports will disclose anything bad; by doing so, you give them a chance to reveal, in advance, any problems they have had.

Review key elements of the lease to make sure you and the tenant are on the same page: dollar amount of rent, date rent starts, due date each month, date lease ends, security deposit, total amount due at lease signing, and utilities that are paid by tenant. No sense wasting time processing an application that won't work.

By the time you finish the interview you will likely have more of your handwriting than the prospective tenant's on the application form. If you don't have a clear picture of who the applicant really is, continue asking questions until you have a clear picture. Your goal is to figure out if they will pay their rent promptly, take care of the property, stay for a long time, and be easy to get along with. Thank the applicant for allowing you to ask so many questions, and invite them to ask any questions they have.

Verification Process

The written rental application and the interview responses may, or may not, be accurate. Once the interview is over, you can begin verifying the information.

A good starting place is to order a credit report and background check on each adult applicant. If you don't know how to get the reports, ask your real estate agent, other landlords, management companies, or your bank or credit union. Or check on the Internet. Compare prices. Many landlords require applicants to pay an application fee to cover the cost of the reports. The credit reporting agency will require a copy of the rental application, giving them permission to provide the reports to you. Review the credit report carefully; if there's something you don't understand, ask the credit reporting agency for an explanation. Compare the addresses found in the credit report with those provided on the rental application; investigate any discrepancies.

When confirming employment, verify that the phone number is really for the employer. Applicants have been known to provide a phone number that is for a friend, not their employer. When talking to the employer, explain that their employee has filled out an application to *rent* from you; otherwise the employer may think the employee is applying for a new job. Some employers may not tell you everything you want to know; ask them to verify as much as they can. In addition to verifying what the applicant has told you, try to determine if the employee shows up for work on time, does a good job, gets along with other employees, and appears to have a good future with the company.

When talking to the applicant's landlords, confirm what you have been told and ask if the tenant caused any problems with other tenants, left the property in good condition, ever paid rent late, gave proper notice when moving, etc.

Some applicants may provide you with a letter from their previous landlord, a letter from their employer, or even a copy of their credit report. Keep in mind that the documents may not be authentic; for example, a letter from a landlord could be signed by the applicant's friend. If you can't verify the authenticity of a document, don't rely on it.

Call the personal references to see what they have to say about the applicant. If the applicant has a pet, make an appointment to visit the tenant's current residence and see the pet; determine if there are any odors or damage from the pet. If the applicant does not live in your town and you cannot check out their previous place, call the landlord to see if the pet caused any problems or left any odors. If you have any unanswered questions along the way, call the applicant to get more information. Some landlords like to drop by the tenant's current residence, unannounced, to ask the questions. While there, they casually take a look to see how the tenant takes care of the place, if there are any undisclosed pets, etc.

You may be saying, This is pretty boring stuff! I tend to agree. But the process is instrumental in selecting good tenants.

In cases where the applicant has no credit history you can ask for the tenant to provide a co-signer on the lease; the co-signer guarantees that if the tenant does not pay rent, does any damage to the property, or fails to abide by any of the terms of the lease, the co-signer will pay you any amounts owed. Be sure to have the co-signer complete an application; process the co-signer (including getting a credit report) just as if the co-signer were the actual tenant. Keep in mind that an out-of-state co-signer may be difficult to collect from. Some landlords require a co-signer for *marginal* tenants as well as for those with no credit history. But don't accept a bad applicant, even with a good co-signer; you don't want to have to argue later with the co-signer about how much is owed.

Once the verification process is complete, you must decide if you want to approve the applicant. You may discover, like many other landlords, that you turn down more applicants than you approve. Here's a bit of sound advice:

If you don't feel confident that the applicant will make a good tenant, say no!

It can be gut-wrenching to say "No" to an applicant. If something on an application has not checked out, simply tell the applicant that the information didn't check out; it's not a good idea to explain exactly "what" didn't check out if doing so will get a source in trouble. If the person's credit is bad, that is reason enough to say no. Don't make the mistake of renting to a bad or marginal applicant because you feel guilty about saying no; you are much better off saying, "Sorry, but based on the information, I can't get the application approved." Make sure to abide by anti-discrimination laws, as well as state and local laws that affect tenant selection. To minimize the chance of a discrimination claim against you, keep copies of all rental applications, along with your notes, for a few years; that way, you have evidence of the criteria used in tenant selection.

If you are careful in selecting tenants, you may not have to deal with "bad apples." But what happens if you inherit a bad tenant when you buy a property, or goof by selecting a bad tenant? If a tenant does not pay rent or violates other terms of the lease agreement, you must ask the tenant to remedy the situation or move. If the tenant doesn't comply, you may be forced to evict the tenant. When evicting a tenant, be sure to follow the laws in your area; consult with your attorney each step of the way. Never change locks, turn off utilities, or move (or sell) the tenant's property.

Signing the Lease

A lease agreement should, of course, be in writing. Most landlords use a standard form, filling in the blanks with the tenant's name, location of the property, dollar amount of rent, when the lease starts and ends, etc. Lease agreements are available from apartment associations, at office supply stores, on the Internet, and from other landlords who are willing to share what they use. *Make sure the lease agreement you decide to use, including each of the provisions, conforms to state and local laws, and have your attorney review the agreement before you use it.* Here are some key provisions every lease agreement should contain:

- The date the lease is being signed, the date rent starts, the date the lease ends, the due date for rent each month, what constitutes payment date, and how rent is to be paid. Also, what happens when the lease term is up.

- How late fees and bad-check fees are determined.

- Who will pay for heat, lights, air-conditioning, glass breakage, replacing light bulbs/furnace filters/smoke detector batteries, yard care, snow removal, water, sewer, trash, etc.

- What off-street parking, if any, is reserved for the tenant.

- Whether smoking is permitted and, if so, exactly where on the premises.

- Which, if any, pets are permitted.

- A "use and occupancy" clause, indicating that the property can be used only as a private dwelling and the occupants are limited to those on the rental application.

- Agreement to not remodel, paint, or make any changes without landlord's written permission.

- Agreement to not disturb neighbors, either with noise, odors, parking interference, litter, etc. No vehicle repairs may be performed on the property, and no vehicles may be parked in non-running condition.

- Agreement to take care of the property, including items of personal property belonging to the landlord. And agreement to reimburse the landlord for any damage.

- Request to promptly notify landlord of any needed repairs.

- Required notice when the tenant is going to move. What happens if a tenant moves without giving proper notice or moves before the lease is up.

- Your right to show the unit to prospective tenants, buyers, lenders, and inspectors with adequate notice. And the right to enter in the case of an emergency.

- What happens if the tenant does not pay rent or breaks any terms of the lease, including reimbursement for attorney fees.

Suppose you are preparing a lease agreement for a tenant who will move into the Park Place property on August 18. The rent is $900 a month. Rent for each of your tenants is due on the first day of each month. You will have the tenant pay a portion of August rent, all of September rent, and a security deposit of $800. August has 31 days; the tenant will pay rent for 14 of those days (31 days – 17 days = 14 days). Rent per day (referred to as the *rent per-diem*) is: $900 ÷ 31 days = $29.03. Here is the total amount you will collect from the tenant at the lease signing:

Rent for August: 14 days @ $29.03 =	$ 406.42
Rent for September	900.00
Security Deposit	800.00
Total Amount Due	**$ 2,106.42**

Before the tenant comes to sign the lease, review the basic terms again: monthly rent, date rent commences, how long the lease is for, security deposit, amount of money to bring to the lease signing (with a breakdown of what it is for), and any special terms of the lease. Let the tenant know that the initial money must be paid in cash, by cashier's check, or with a money order—not with a personal check. Then, when the tenant comes to sign the lease, make it a practice to carefully go over all of the terms of the lease before having the tenant sign it. All adult tenants, along with you as the landlord, must sign the lease agreement; sign two copies—one for you and one for the tenant. Be sure to have tenants sign any necessary addendums and disclosures, including disclosures for lead-based paint, mold, etc. Disclose these hazards in advance so you don't surprise the tenant at the lease signing.

Use an inspection sheet to document the condition of the property before the tenant moves in, and again when the tenant moves out. That way, if the tenant does any damage, you have evidence of the change in condition. Be sure to have the tenant sign the inspection sheet *before* moving in. The inspection sheet should indicate any defects and what will be done, if anything, to correct the defects (see the Appendix for a sample inspection sheet). And always re-key a unit when a new tenant moves in.

Keeping the Property in Good Condition

Some landlords figure they can maximize profits by skimping on upkeep. To protect tenants from landlords who refuse to maintain their properties, most states have laws that require landlords to maintain their properties in "habitable" condition. Doing just enough to keep a property "habitable" is counter-productive. By taking this approach, the property will attract poor-quality tenants, who may not pay their rent and may not take care of the property. While it helps to find people who will not overcharge for their services, it is a mistake to avoid maintaining the property. If we want to keep the property occupied by *good-quality tenants*, we must provide a *good-quality property*. Chances are, you can drive around in your area and find some rental properties that are well-maintained, some that are marginal, and some that are downright shabby. The quality of tenants will likely be consistent with the quality of the property.

Keeping the Exterior in Good Condition

Do regular inspections of the exterior. Because it is easy to overlook flaws that you see on a regular basis, consider hiring someone (like a property manager, real estate agent, or designer) to occasionally accompany you on the inspection. You might end up deciding to do something dramatic, like paint the exterior with a new color, replace windows or doors, or upgrade the landscaping. Or you might decide to make some minor changes, like update the light fixtures or mailboxes. You can get ideas by driving around and taking photos of features, colors, etc. that you like on other properties.

Select a good landscaper. You can find one by asking around or by inquiring at properties that have nice landscaping. A well-maintained yard tells tenants that you care about the property. Fertilize lawns to keep them green and weed-free. Keep planter areas weeded, trees and plants pruned, and lawns edged. Plant nice flowers each year.

Consider having one of your tenants serve as an on-site manager. The on-site manager can assist you in keeping the property looking nice, and can be your eyes and ears to alert you of any problems.

Hire someone to periodically clean the exterior of the buildings: exterior of windows, window frames, doors, door frames, mailboxes, light fixtures, railings, hallways, etc. You have probably seen properties where these items look grimy; tenants and prospective tenants likely want to look elsewhere. If you don't take the time to clean the exteriors on a *regular* basis (like two or three times a year), your property will become one of those grimy properties. And hire someone on a regular basis (like two or three times a year) to professionally clean the driveways and parking areas. Otherwise those areas can start looking nasty with bits of gravel and other debris.

Keeping the Interior in Good Condition

A vacancy provides a good opportunity to make sure things are functioning correctly. Make sure electrical outlets, light fixtures, and switches are working, and check for water leaks or drips. Don't let problems slide; doing so can result in bigger problems. Replace batteries for smoke detectors and carbon monoxide detectors. Consider hiring someone to give you ideas on upgrading the unit. You might end up making dramatic changes, like removing a wall between a kitchen and living room (open spaces are very popular these days), painting with a contemporary color, remodeling the kitchen, or changing floor coverings, doors, or moldings. (If you're thinking about removing a wall, be sure to consult an engineer or architect first so you don't compromise the structural integrity of the building.) Or you might make some minor changes, like upgrading the window coverings, light fixtures, plumbing fixtures, knobs, door hinges, light fixtures, electrical switches, or cover plates. These things are relatively inexpensive and can give your unit a contemporary look. Don't use a mixture of styles—be consistent throughout. Replace appliances when needed; you may be able to sell the old items to recoup some of the cost.

Once you rent a unit and sign a lease, do an inspection of the unit with your new tenant. If the inspection results in things you as the landlord must correct, get those things fixed right away; doing so not only helps keep the property in good condition, it also lets your new tenant know that you are a responsible landlord.

Investing in rental property is a *people business*. Our tenants are our customers, and it is important to keep our customers happy. If a tenant calls with a request to get something fixed, listen carefully. Then, follow through quickly in getting the problem fixed. Some landlords provide a written guarantee to tenants, agreeing that if a necessary repair isn't made within a certain number of days, the landlord will refund rent for each day the problem goes unfixed. Whatever approach you use, make sure your tenants know you care.

TIP   **uncover hidden value**

Most rental properties have the potential for improvement. One way to make "bonus" money from a rental property is to make improvements to the property that will increase the value more than the cost of the improvements. In fact, this is one thing seasoned investors look for in a property: the potential to uncover that "hidden" value.

Record Keeping

Some basic record-keeping procedures help minimize headaches. A good starting point is to have a separate checking account for your rental property. Don't use your *personal* account for rental property deposits and expenditures. Doing so will be confusing, especially at income tax time. When opening a checking account, some landlords use a three-checks-to-a-page method; the stubs provide space to record details of each check and deposit. Some use a small checkbook with a check register; if that's what you use, show the details of each check and deposit in the register.

Many landlords with more than one rental property have only one checking account for all properties. This requires having a method for separating income and expenses *by property*, as well as a way to determine how much of the money in the checking account belongs to each property. One way to accomplish this is to create a spreadsheet with a column for each property and report income and expenses in the appropriate column; the spreadsheet can be hand-drawn or done on a computer.

If you pay for things with a credit card, it may be wise to have a separate credit card just for your rental properties. If you buy things for your rental property by paying cash, keep the receipts as proof to the IRS.

Have a method for showing which tenants have paid rent. You may want to use a spreadsheet program, with unit numbers on the left and a column for each month. When rent is paid, enter the date of deposit and amount paid; once rent is fully paid for that month, color or shade the cell. You can then tell at a glance which tenants have not paid their rent.

Landlords must report income and expenses to the IRS each year. That means we must determine how much income we collect each year, and expense amounts, by category, we pay each year. For an *individual* income tax return, the income and expenses are reported on Schedule E of Form 1040. The expense categories used by the IRS on Schedule E are: (1) advertising, (2) auto and travel, (3) cleaning and maintenance, (4) commissions, (5) insurance, (6) legal and other professional fees, (7) management fees, (8) mortgage interest paid to banks, etc., (9) other interest, (10) repairs, (11) supplies, (12) taxes, (13) utilities, (14) other (list). In addition, we can deduct depreciation expense (see Step 5 of the book). If you can't figure out an efficient system for recording income and expenses, ask your accountant to help create a system.

Many landlords, especially those with lots of rental units, use computerized rental property software that can write checks, prepare and post deposits, maintain tenant files, provide summary reports by property, offer reminders for lease expirations, and more. To find a good software package, visit large rental properties to see what they use; they may even take the time to show you the highlights of their system. Or you can search on the Internet.

Maximizing Rent

Investors of rental properties want to maximize cash flow. Let's explore some procedures that will help.

Rent Collection

Most landlords have all rents due on the first day of each month; that makes it easy to determine who is late with rent. Have provisions in your lease for late fees and bad-check fees. For example, you may require a late fee of $30 if rent is not paid by the 5th of the month, plus $5 per day after the 5th. With that provision, if a tenant pays rent on the 8th, he or she would owe a late fee of $45 ($30 + 3 days @ $5). Don't be tempted to alter from what is owed on late fees and bad-check fees; if you do you will be encouraging tenants to be repeat offenders and you could be accused of discrimination by tenants you do not cut slack to.

Some landlords have a provision in their lease that gives tenants a modest discount if they pay rent *early* (before the 1st). Offering a discount (like $10) can result in almost all tenants paying early; this makes your job easier and gets money in your account earlier. It also results in tenants feeling lucky to have such a nice landlord, meaning they might stay longer and refer family and friends.

Your lease should spell out what constitutes the payment date. Suppose your lease states that for mailed checks, the postmark date is what counts. Suppose a tenant writes a check on March 5, puts the check in the mail with a postmark of March 6, and you get it on March 8. You would calculate late fees based on the rent being paid on March 6.

Contact tenants who are late with their rent and make arrangements for payment; remind them how late fees are figured. Once a tenant is over 10 days late, you may want to give a notice to pay rent or vacate; your attorney can provide advice and the required forms. In some cases the notice should come directly from your attorney.

In most areas, long-term leases, such as 6 months or a year, are common. Residential leases can be longer than a year, but leases over 2 years are rare. In some cases, such as a tenant getting a job in a different area, the tenant moves before their lease is up. Some landlords require the tenant to pay rent until the lease expires. Many landlords re-rent the unit and charge the tenant only for advertising and lost rent. Some leases provide for the tenant to pay an early termination fee (like, perhaps, 3/4 of a month's rent), and the landlord takes the risk of finding a new tenant.

To protect your privacy and that of your family, avoid giving tenants your home address. Rather than having tenants mail rent payments to your home address, have them deliver or mail the rent to an office or use a post office box. And don't list your home address in phone directories.

Some landlords visit the property to collect rents. Don't make that mistake. Doing so not only takes time, but if a tenant is not there (or does not answer the door) and pays late, the tenant could argue that the reason rent was late was because you goofed up by not collecting the rent on time. Make it the tenant's responsibility to get the rent to you—either by delivering it or by mailing it on time. If you have an on-site manager at the property, you can ask tenants to give the rent to the on-site manager, and you could then collect the rent from the on-site manager.

Many landlords do not allow tenants to pay rent in cash, except at the lease signing. They do this because they don't want to have a tenant argue that they paid their rent in cash and either someone stole the money or the landlord forgot he received it. Also, regularly accepting rent in cash can make landlords a target for robbery. Tenants without a checking account can pay with a cashier's check or money order. If you do allow payments in cash, your lease should instruct tenants to never leave cash *without getting a receipt* for the money; you should keep a copy of all receipts.

If you accept a partial payment, make sure the tenant realizes that late fees will accrue until the total rent, together with late fees, is paid.

If a tenant pays rent with a personal check that is dishonored, have the tenant immediately reimburse you—along with the bad-check fee—with a money order or cashier's check. Make sure you have a provision in your lease that requires tenants who have given you a bad check to pay future rent with money order or cashier's check.

Security Deposits

Almost all landlords collect a security deposit from tenants when tenants move in. The security deposit provides protection to the landlord in case the tenant fails to pay rent or damages the property.

Some local laws limit the amount of security (or cleaning) deposits, require that interest be paid on the deposits, and require that the deposits be held in a separate trust bank account.

In deciding how much to charge for a security deposit, consider what other landlords charge. And consider the age and condition of the unit being rented; charge a larger deposit for a newly renovated unit. In many areas, security deposits range from half a month's rent to one and one-half months' rent. Here's a suggestion: Don't have the security deposit be the same as the monthly rent, because tenants may incorrectly assume that the security deposit can be used as the last month's rent. And don't allow tenants to pay the security deposit in installments. Doing so gets you started off on the wrong foot with tenants and doesn't provide the *security* a security deposit is intended to provide. If you know a prospective tenant intends to borrow money for the first month's rent or security deposit, you should probably avoid renting to that person; chances are, the person will quickly get into financial trouble.

Even if state laws don't require you to pay interest on security deposits, consider paying a nominal rate. Tenants appreciate it and feel that they are lucky to have such a nice landlord. Suppose your lease stipulates that you pay interest on security deposits—assuming tenants are current with their rent and other obligations—at 2% simple interest (not compound interest). Say your tenant stays for a total of 452 days with a deposit of $850. Interest = $850 × 2% × 452 ÷ 365 = $21.05.

One of the main landlord/tenant disputes involves the return of the security deposit. Many potential problems can be eliminated by completing an inspection sheet with the tenant when they move in and again when they move out. You can also take photos or videos of the unit before they move in, to accompany the inspection sheet. Make sure the tenant understands that professional carpet cleaning, done between every vacancy, will be deducted from the security deposit.

As tenants are preparing to move, give them a list of things to clean; some tenants have a hard time figuring out what needs cleaning. The list should include: tub, shower, toilet, sinks, countertops, appliances (inside, outside, behind, and under), light fixtures, windows (inside and out), doors, moldings, closets, floors, blinds, cabinets (inside and out), etc. In most cases, tenants don't do a perfect cleaning job, so most landlords hire a professional cleaning person to go in after the tenant is finished, if for no other reason that to "spot" clean. Having the unit cleaned the same way, and by the same cleaner, between each vacancy can alleviate disagreements with tenants; that way, tenants understand you aren't using their security deposit to pay for an *extra good* cleaning job when they move out. Some landlords have a policy of paying the first portion of the cleaning bill (perhaps the first $50); if you use a policy like this, be consistent to avoid complaints that you treat some tenants better than others.

When returning security deposits, let tenants know what amount you need to withhold from the deposit, if any, and why. Consider asking tenants if what you have in mind sounds fair; if you are fair, most tenants will likely agree. Tenants who come away feeling that you have been a fair landlord will be more likely to refer family and friends. In cases where the tenant objects to what you propose (and there are some people who are hard to satisfy), you will have to decide what to do; in many cases you can compromise and both feel good about the compromise.

Periods of Vacancy

Some landlords lose more rent than needed during periods of vacancy. One common mistake is to set the rent too low or too high. If you set the rent too low for the upcoming vacancy, you will not collect as much rent as you could. If you set the rent too high, you will have trouble finding a tenant. To determine what rent should be, find out what similar properties in your area are renting for; do this by investigating properties for rent or by calling landlords and property managers. When you set the rent, consider any fix-up you plan on doing; for example, if you will be painting and installing new carpet, you will likely be able to increase rent.

Your lease should require tenants to give you reasonable notice when they move (such as 30 days). When a tenant lets you know he or she will be moving, ask why. In some cases, it may be related to disturbance from another tenant, something about the property, or the way you run things. Perhaps you can correct the problem and convince the tenant to stay. Even if you can't talk the tenant into staying, you might be able to correct something so it won't happen again.

When you determine that a tenant will be moving, visit the property to determine if any major fix-up is required. If so, make arrangements in advance to have the work done; that way, contractors can start immediately when the tenant moves. If the unit does not require major fix-up and is showable, start advertising immediately. Your lease hopefully gives you the right, with adequate notice, to show the unit to prospective tenants.

One way to advertise is to place a nice sign on the property. The sign can be an effective means of advertising because neighbors, and even your tenants, tell friends or family about your vacancy. You can also advertise in local newspapers and on the Internet. Place notices on bulletin boards of colleges, local stores, and businesses with lots of employees. If your area has rental agencies that assist tenants in finding a place to live, try listing your property with them. When you get a phone call from a prospective tenant, ask how they heard about the property; this will help you evaluate which advertising methods work.

Showing vacant units can be time-consuming. Don't show a unit until it is clean and ready to show. To eliminate unnecessary showings, do a *pre-interview* when prospects call. If you are getting lots of calls, schedule several appointments during the same time frame. Having more than one prospect there at the same time may work to your advantage; prospective tenants will know others are interested in renting from you. If you are showing an occupied unit and your tenant gets annoyed because of frequent showings, you can ask prospects to drive by the outside before arranging an appointment to show the inside.

Take applications promptly and process applications quickly. Remember, each day of vacancy costs you money. Once you have approved an application, get the lease signed as soon as possible (collecting all of the required money at the lease signing). You can then stop showing the unit.

Some prospects will ask you to delay starting rent for awhile. Have a policy to delay rent only a certain number of days past the lease signing. For units that are ready to move into, that might be 5 to 10 days past the lease signing.

To reduce upcoming vacancy periods, consider having leases expire at peak rental periods. For example, if you have a college or university in your area, with a large influx of tenants at the end of August of each year, have your leases expire at the end of August.

Rent Adjustment for Existing Tenants

The rental market changes over time. When rents change in your area, make sure you react. For example, if rents are decreasing (like following a period of overbuilding rental units or during a period when lots of tenants are buying homes), make sure you decrease your rents. If you don't, you will have a hard time renting vacant units, and your existing tenants will move somewhere else where the rent is more reasonable.

If rents are increasing, make sure you increase your rents. You cannot, of course, increase the rent on an existing tenant until his or her lease has expired. For month-to-month tenancies, the lease will state how much notice you must give when you increase the rent.

Don't make the mistake of increasing rents at the wrong time of the year, when vacancies are high; if your tenants do move, it will take you more time than usual to get the units re-rented, and you will probably have to reduce the rent. Most landlords evaluate rents and make rent adjustments on a regular basis (like each 6 months or each year). Do rent increases at a time of year when demand for rental units is the greatest.

When increasing rent for an existing tenant, consider the tenant's past history: paying rent on time, getting along with other tenants, taking care of the property, etc. For tenants you would hate to lose, increase the rent to an amount that is *below* market rent; let them know you are making an allowance because you appreciate having them as a tenant.

Controlling Expenses

Another way of maximizing profits is to control expenses. That does not mean you should avoid repairing things that need to be fixed or avoid upgrading the property. But there are some things you can do to control expenses. For problems reported by a tenant, you may be able to figure out a solution over the phone. For example, if an appliance is not working, you can have the tenant check the circuit breaker. Some problems can be fixed without hiring a repairperson; for example, if a drain is plugged, you or one of your tenants can try using a plunger to remedy the problem.

If you need to hire someone, select people who do quality work, are dependable, and do not overcharge. Occasionally get more than one bid, especially on large jobs. Find a good handyman who knows how to do a variety of repairs. Often, a handyman will charge considerably less than a specialist (like a plumber or electrician). And the handyman can do several things at once with one visit, instead of separate visits by specialists. If you need a good handyman, check with your real estate agent or inquire at a home-improvement center (some of their regular customers are handymen). Chances are, other landlords and property management companies will *not* share names of their handymen because they want to keep them for themselves.

Don't let repairpeople do repairs unattended in occupied units. You don't want to be accused by a tenant that something is damaged or missing. Instead, arrange a time when the tenant will be there. Never give a repairperson a key to an occupied unit.

If you have the time and talent to do some of the upkeep yourself (such as cleaning, yard care, painting, and minor repairs), do it! But consider how long it will take you to do the things during periods of vacancy. For example, it might take you 15 days of spare time to paint a unit, whereas a professional painter can do it 3 days. You might save $300 by doing it yourself, but you could lose more than that in rent by doing the painting yourself.

Controlling Utilities

Water Bill. We can't control the price of water, but we can control how much water is used. Leaky toilets waste a lot of water; worn-out flapper valves stop providing a good seal and allow water to leak 24 hours a day. Worn washers on faucets are another culprit; as the washers age, they become brittle, allowing small leaks. Most tenants do not report leaky toilets or dripping faucets, so check toilets and faucets whenever you or a repairperson are there (including, of course, when the unit is vacant). Consider low-flow showerheads that use less water. If you have an automatic sprinkling system for your landscaping, set it to water during early morning hours, when evaporation is less; and, change the frequency of watering, depending on the season.

Electricity. Most medium and large rental complexes have outside lights and common area lights for which the landlord pays the electricity. Landlords can reduce electricity expense by installing low-voltage flourescent light bulbs, by using timers or electric eyes (so lights come on only when it is dark), and by using motion-detection lights (that come on for a set period of time when someone is detected in the vicinity).

Gas. Some buildings have a hot water boiler (that provides heat to the units) or a hot water tank (that provides hot water to the units). If you are paying to heat the water, installing an energy-saving blanket will reduce heat loss, and save money on the gas bill. If you are paying for the gas on a large hot water tank, consider using a recirculating pump, which circulates hot water through the pipes. Without a recirculating pump, tenants far away from the water heater waste a lot of water—and your money—waiting for the hot water to reach them.

> *Special note:* In some cases, landlords have a clause in their lease requiring tenants to reimburse them for certain expenses. For commercial complexes with more than one tenant, tenants are often required to pay their share of common area expenses, such as yard care, snow removal, outside utilities, and property taxes; the fee is referred to as a CAM (Common Area Maintenance) fee. For residential properties, especially those with master-metered buildings (for example, one gas meter for the entire building), tenants may be required to reimburse the landlord for their share of certain expenses; landlords often hire a company (like Ista or Relms) to assist in billing the tenants for their share (often determined with sub-meters). Having tenants reimburse the landlord can significantly reduce the landlord's expenses.

Controlling Repairs and Upkeep

Painting. One way to save money is to use one brand and color of paint. Not only does it allow you to use leftover paint for the next paint job, but it allows you to easily touch up scratches, rather than having to repaint an entire wall or room. Some tenants may offer to paint if you supply the paint. *Suggestion*: Don't go for the idea unless the tenant is a professional painter. You may end up having to replace door knobs, carpet, light fixtures, switches, etc. because the tenant gets paint on things.

Carpet. Use one style and color of carpeting. Pick one that will likely be available for a few years. If a small section of carpet is damaged, rather than having to replace all of the carpet, you can use a remnant or the carpet from a closet (or other inconspicuous area) to replace the damaged area.

Water damage. Water damage can be very expensive to repair. Make sure land slopes away from buildings. Otherwise, surface water (from rain and sprinkling systems) will run into your buildings. Have the roof inspected regularly to prevent roof leaks. In climates with freezing temperatures, keep units heated when vacant. Otherwise, water inside the pipes and fixtures can freeze, breaking pipes and fixtures; when the ice thaws, water spews everywhere. Not a pretty sight! If attics and crawl spaces have water pipes, make sure they are insulated and adequately heated. Check toilets to make sure wax seals are not leaking. Check caulking around tubs and showers. And check for leaks under sinks; leaks, even slow ones, can cause considerable damage to floors, walls, and units below the leak. Make sure laundry areas and hot water heaters have adequate drainage, so if there is a leak the water has somewhere to safely drain.

Clogged toilets and drains. In rare cases, water does not drain properly because tree roots grow into sewage lines. In most cases, clogs are caused by something tenants do. In many cases, clogs can be solved with a plunger. If you have an on-site manager, the on-site manager should have a plunger and use it to correct the problem. If that doesn't work, and you have to call a drain-cleaning specialist, have the company indicate the cause of the problem on the invoice. If the problem was caused by your tenant, have the tenant reimburse you.

Management Options

The profitability of a rental property is affected by the quality of the management. The question is, Who will handle the management responsibilities? One option is to do the management yourself.

Do the Management Yourself

If you elect to do the management yourself, keep in mind it will likely take more time and energy than you anticipate. That doesn't mean it will be a horrible experience. In fact, you may enjoy it. Here are a few keys to being a good property manager:

Develop a good system.
Make sound decisions, using expert advice.
Be easy to get in touch with and return calls promptly.
Don't let things slide.
Care about your tenants and others you deal with.
Be firm, when called for, in a respectful way.

Hire an On-Site Manager

Often, for rental properties with three or more units, owners hire an on-site manager to assist with certain duties. In fact, in certain areas, an on-site manager is required by law for certain-sized complexes. To avoid a misunderstanding, put the on-site management agreement in writing, spelling out the on-site manager's duties and the fee.

Most on-site managers show vacant units, replace burned-out exterior light bulbs, and keep walkways and common areas free of debris. In addition, on-site managers are the eyes and ears of the owner, reporting any problems with parking, sprinkling system, noise, arguments between tenants, etc.

Some owners have the on-site manager do the landscaping; others hire a professional landscape company. For areas that have snow, the on-site manager may be asked to shovel snow from walkways; a snow removal company is generally hired to remove snow from larger areas, like the parking lot and driveways.

Some owners have the on-site manager process applications from prospective tenants and select tenants. Don't make this mistake! Very few on-site managers have the skill and judgment to decide who will make a good tenant; chances are, after a while, you will have a property full of unsavory tenants.

For smaller properties, on-site managers are usually compensated with an adjustment in rent. For larger properties, on-site managers may be compensated with free rent plus a fee. Regardless of the amount of the fee, having an on-site manager might require paying withholding taxes (FICA and income tax) and paying worker's compensation. Check with your accountant about the requirements.

If an on-site manager is not performing his or her duties (and some do start to slack off after awhile), talk to him or her about it and, if necessary, find another tenant to act as the on-site manager. You can't afford to have things run into the ground by a bad on-site manager.

Tip: Don't leave keys to all of the units with an on-site manager. Someone could break in and steal the keys, giving the thief access to the other apartments. Instead, keep the keys at your home or office. Use a system of identifying the keys that does not reveal the property address or unit number; that way, if the keys do get stolen, the thief won't know what the keys are for.

Get Assistance for Some of the Management Duties

If you don't have enough time to do everything, you can hire someone to help. For example, you could hire someone to do the bookkeeping (prepare deposits, post rental payments to payment charts, pay bills, and prepare reports and income tax summaries).

You could also hire someone to handle the vacancies. A great deal of time is required when there is a vacancy; hiring someone to help with that can free up a LOT of time. This person, referred to as a leasing agent, can oversee getting vacant units fixed up, place ads, show units to prospective tenants, take and process applications, and sign leases. The leasing agent generally does not do any of the actual fix-up or cleaning; he or she only arranges to get it done. Because selecting tenants is such a critical aspects of owning rental property; you don't want to turn this responsibility over to someone you can't trust to select good tenants. If you don't feel comfortable allowing someone else to select your tenants, keep that part of the job for yourself; have the leasing agent do everything else.

You can, of course, hire more than one person to help out. For example, you could hire one person to do the bookkeeping and another person as a leasing agent. Or, if you have lots of properties, you can have more than one leasing agent—each responsible for certain properties. If you do hire someone to assist you in the management, make sure the person's duties are well-defined and separate from those of other people.

Hire a Professional Property Management Company

If you discover you don't like property management, don't have enough time, or aren't good at it, you can hire a professional property management company.

When selecting a property management company, get referrals from your real estate agent and other property owners. After narrowing the choices down, visit with each company to determine what kind of job they might do. Here are some questions to ask:

- What is the management fee? Most property management companies base their fee as a percent of *rents deposited*, often about 6% to 15% of rents. The percent varies from property to property, depending on what the units rent for, the age of the building, quality of construction, turnover rate, and the type of tenants the property attracts. For example, the management fee for a brand new duplex in a nice area of town that rents for $1,500 a unit might be 6% of rents, whereas the fee for an older, worn-out building in a bad neighborhood might be 15% of rents. Some management agreements include an incentive fee, based on occupancy rates.

- How are vacancies advertised (newspapers, Internet sites, signs, etc.)? What will your cost be?

- How long does it take to clean an apartment, and what does it generally cost?

- How many handymen do they use, and what do they charge?

- Will they use some of your repair people, if you ask them to?

- Will they charge a fee to oversee repairs? Some management companies charge a 10% or 20% override fee, based on the actual repair cost. If they do charge a fee and it doesn't seem fair to you, look elsewhere.

- How do they determine how much rent to charge?

- What is their policy on security deposits?

- What type of lease form do they use? Review their lease provisions and any accompanying rules and regulations to see if you approve of what they use. Would they use your lease form if you wanted them to?

- What are their office hours? Who accepts phone calls during evening hours and on weekends?

- Who specifically processes tenant applications and selects tenants?

- Do they order credit reports on prospective tenants? Background checks? What will it cost you?

- What type of summary reports will they provide to you, and how often?

- If the account generates surplus cash, how often will that cash be sent to you?

- How do they handle tenants who are late with rent?

- Will they call you for approval on large-expense items? If so, what's the threshold?

- Will they mind if you visit the property and talk to tenants to evaluate their performance?

- Will they give you names and phone numbers for owners they currently do management for? If so, call the owners to see what they have to say.

Hiring a property management company does *not* mean you should no longer be involved. Keep in mind that a property management company oversees lots of properties; they can't focus exclusively on yours. And because they do not own the property like you do, they will likely not be as *personally* involved as you are. So stay involved as much as possible; consider yourself a part of their team. Let the management team know that you want to be involved. Ask them to contact you when there is a vacancy so you can discuss what to charge for rent, and what fix-up items to do before re-renting (you may want to meet them in the vacant unit to hear their recommendations on what fix-up items to do). Have them call you if they are unsure whether to rent to a particular tenant. Schedule personal visits with the management team to review what's happening with the rental market. Remember, their time is valuable, so keep visits brief.

Drive by the property three or four times a year to see how it looks. If it needs attention, tell the property manager. At least once a year, visit the property with the manager to evaluate the condition of the property. Discuss what you can do to improve the appearance.

You may want to consider visiting with your tenants periodically to see how they like living there. When doing so, don't give tenants your contact info (you don't want them calling you instead of the manager). And while hoping to get some feedback on how the property is being managed, and the type of tenants being selected, don't infer to the tenants that you are *worried* about the property manager's performance. If you are happy with what the property management team is doing, let them know. If there is something they are doing that you are unhappy with, let them know that too; your feedback can be valuable to their future performance.

Of all the steps, Step 9 may cause the most headaches. But having a well-managed property can make a huge difference in the amount of money you will make on a property.

A Final Word

So, here we are, owners of the imaginary Park Place property. Talk about a really slow way to get rich! Now it's time to get serious by finding a *real* property to invest in.

The fact that you finished reading the book means you are ready to consider becoming a landlord. Take your time assembling the right team. Develop a system to find available properties. Quickly eliminate the duds. Carefully evaluate the properties you're interested in by meticulously projecting after-tax cash flows and the resulting IRRs; evaluate enough properties to discover the difference between a good deal and a bad deal. Once you find a property that fits the bill, carefully prepare an offer, with contingencies. If, after doing your due diligence, the numbers don't make sense, ask the seller to modify the terms; if the seller doesn't agree, don't be afraid to walk away from the deal.

Once you become an owner of a rental property, keep the property occupied by good tenants. Care about your tenants, keep the property in good condition, control expenses, and pay attention to details. Finally, be careful to avoid mistakes that trip up most new investors. I mentioned them throughout the book but list some of the very costly mistakes in the next few pages.

Best wishes for success in all of your investment and personal ventures.

25 Costly Mistakes
Novice Investors Make

Mistake #1. Failing to set aside money each month.

Lots of people live paycheck to paycheck, never saving enough for something unexpected (like a car problem or medical bill), let alone for investing. Set some money aside each month, perhaps $200 to $500. Use the money to pay off credit cards, starting with the one charging the highest APR. Next, establish an emergency fund, up to 6 or 9 months of living expenses. Then, continue building the nest egg. Before long, you could have enough to get into a nice investment.

Mistake #2. Not paying attention to rental market cycles.

Rental real estate goes through cycles. Rents increase and decrease as supply and demand change. Vacancy rates change. And values change. Try to identify the cycle in your area by getting input from landlords, property management companies, apartment house associations, and real estate agents who specialize in rental property. Use that knowledge so you can determine when to adjust rents, as well as when to buy and sell rental property.

Mistake #3. Failing to get help from experts.

Some real estate investors think they can do everything alone, without any help. These investors are doomed for failure. Instead of trying to be a one-person football team, build a team of experts. First, find key members of your team: an attorney, income tax advisor, real estate agent, and property management company. Make sure they have lots of experience with rental real estate. Then, assemble other team members, such as a property inspector, contractor/remodeling specialists, repair specialists, handyman, suppliers, insurance agent, appraiser, architect, and a structural engineer. The advice you get from team members will be invaluable.

Mistake #4. Wasting time evaluating duds.

Evaluating a property correctly takes a lot of time. Spending that time on over-priced properties is a waste. To eliminate the duds, determine what buyers of rental property are paying per unit, per square foot, or per dollar of gross rent (gross rent multiplier, or GRM). Use that as a basis to decide which properties are, and are not, worth pursuing. Do full-blown evaluations only on those that pass the test.

Mistake #5. Being too anxious.

Some investors are so anxious to become an investor, they fail to consider if a particular investment meets their basic investment criteria. Always take the time to decide if a particular investment is the best *type of investment* to make, compared to other types of investments. If it is, make sure it is the best available *of that investment type*.

Mistake #6. Investing in an area that is dependent on a major employer.

In some areas, employment is heavily dependent on a major employer or industry. When employment is high, the rental market is strong. Some people invest in an area during a boom period, when rents and prices are high. Then, if employment is cut, the area has a major downturn, with workers relocating to other areas. If you invest in an area that is heavily dependent on a major employer or industry, be cautious; allow for a downturn in the economy.

Mistake #7. Investing in a property that attracts bad tenants.

Not all properties attract the same quality of tenants. For example, a property in a bad area of town doesn't attract the same quality of tenants as a property in a nice area of town. The price may be considerably lower for a property in a bad area. Some investors jump at the lower price, only to be surprised by the type of tenants the property attracts; they are not prepared for the management headaches, the number of tenants who skip out, and the damage caused by tenants. If you decide to invest in a property that targets mediocre or unsavory tenants, be prepared for the extra headaches.

Mistake #8. Overbuilding or buying a property that is overbuilt.

Some investors make the mistake of spending lots of money to fix up an apartment complex in a distressed area of town, only to discover that the area itself will not justify rent over a certain amount, even if the property is in tip-top condition. They have "overbuilt," and may not be able to recoup their fix-up costs. And some investors make the mistake of buying a property that is over-built for the area.

Mistake #9. Biting off more than you can chew.

Don't make the mistake of investing in a property that is larger than your finances justify. When rents are high and vacancy rates low, things are great. But, when rents drop or vacancy rates increase, things turn ugly; the more units you own, the more the problem is magnified.

Mistake #10. Putting all your eggs in one basket.

Diversification reduces risk. Don't get too heavily invested in any one segment of the rental market. When investing in residential rentals, consider owning some two-bedroom units and some one-bedroom units. Perhaps invest some money in commercial rentals too. When one segment of the market gets soft, the other segment(s) of the market may be okay. Some people invest only in commercial rentals, because they don't want the day-to-day headaches that come from residential rentals. But when the commercial market goes soft, it can be very difficult to find tenants and sell properties. And a vacancy period can last forever! Commercial investors, too, should consider diversifying their portfolio, including some residential rentals.

Mistake #11. Leveraging to the hilt.

Some investors buy property by getting huge mortgage loans, with high LTV ratios. You have probably heard late-night infomercials about buying real estate with nothing down. The problem is, you have to pay whatever is owed on the mortgage, with higher-than-usual monthly payments! If the rental market takes a downturn, or if you underestimated expenses, you can have severe cash flow problems. If you don't have additional resources to make it through the rough spots, you will end up in financial ruin.

Mistake #12. Neglecting to project NOI, cash flow, and IRR.

Some investors consider working with numbers a waste of time—they figure they can tell a good investment from a bad investment without spending countless hours running numbers. In some cases, the investment works out. In other cases, it leads to disaster. Generally, numbers do not lie. A carefully projected NOI and cash flow worksheet are valuable in deciding whether to buy a property. If the numbers don't work out on paper, chances are the investment will be a flop. Don't turn your back on this valuable tool.

Mistake #13. Failing to walk away from a deal in which the numbers don't work.

Some investors, when evaluating a property, get emotionally attached to the property and overlook what the numbers say. Remember, investing is a *business*, so don't buy a property just because the property would be one you would be proud to own. If the property doesn't meet your investment criteria, walk away.

Mistake #14. Overanalyzing a property.

Some investors don't spend enough time evaluating a property before buying it. But some investors spend too much time analyzing properties, looking for reasons *not to buy*. They may never buy anything, or miss out on good investment opportunities.

Mistake #15. Failing to get the best financing.

Some investors are so anxious to get a deal closed, they don't take the time to explore financing options. Ask for a *good faith estimate* on several possible loans; the different possible loans don't necessarily have to be from different lenders. Compare loan costs and calculate APRs. Prepare a cash flow worksheet for each possible loan to see which scenario results in the best IRR. You may be pleasantly surprised to find that one particular financing scenario produces a much better rate of return than other options.

Mistake #16. Overemphasizing IRR.

Some investors, when comparing possible investments, make a decision based solely on IRR. While an IRR is a valuable tool in deciding which properties to buy, don't overlook the other investment criteria. If you cannot handle the risk from a certain property or if the cash flows are not adequate, walk away— even if the projected IRR looks fabulous.

Mistake #17. Failing to include contingencies in an offer.

Don't make an offer on a rental property without including certain contingencies. Doing so can be a disaster. Make your offer subject to obtaining financing that is satisfactory to you, subject to a satisfactory review of leases and other documents, subject to satisfactory results from a physical inspection of the property, and subject to satisfactory review of any other issues affecting the property. Make sure the contingencies are carefully worded.

Mistake #18. Rushing through the due diligence period.

The due diligence period is an extremely valuable part of the investment process. Use the due diligence period to learn everything you can about the property, and determine whether what you find is acceptable. Make sure the financing commitment is what you were expecting. Review leases, income and expense records, and other documents provided by the seller. Select a well-qualified property inspector and accompany the inspector inside of every unit. If you discover something bad or that adversely affects the cash flow, redo your operating statement and cash flow worksheet. Don't be afraid to renegotiate with the seller, if needed. If the seller will not budge and the revised cash flow projections don't make sense, walk away!

Mistake #19. Having a bad tenant-selection process.

This may be the most common major goof landlords make. Having good tenants is THE major factor in having a smooth operation. If you have bad tenants, you will need lots of aspirin, and will likely question your decision to invest in rental property. When selecting tenants, use a written application. Ask questions as you review the application. After the applicant leaves, make calls to verify what's on the application. Be sure to get credit reports and background checks. If, after the process is complete, you don't feel confident the applicant will make a good tenant, error on the side of caution by saying no.

Mistake #20. Cutting costs by neglecting repairs.

Some investors figure the best way to help the bottom line (NOI) is to avoid spending money on repairs. Big mistake! The saying "A stitch in time saves nine" definitely applies to owning rental property. Small problems often become big problems if not fixed.

Mistake #21. Cutting costs by personally doing everything.

Some investors, in an effort to reduce expenses, try to do everything themselves: management, yard care, snow removal, cleaning, repairs, painting, and improvements. Doing so can be counterproductive. Only do tasks for which you are qualified; if you are not qualified, hiring yourself can result in a lousy job! Second, vacancy periods may be prolonged while doing the work, so you lose out on rental income. Third, the time spent doing the tasks could possibly be spent more productively; if you can earn $50 an hour at another task and could pay someone $30 an hour to clean your apartments, you would be losing $20 an hour to clean the apartments yourself.

Mistake #22. Forgetting that owning rental property is a people business.

Some landlords focus so much on the bottom line, they forget that the bottom line depends on keeping tenants happy. Owning rental property is a people business. Genuinely care about your tenants and others you deal with. Listen to what they say. Be respectful. Promptly take care of requests for repairs. Happy tenants result in happy landlords. Your tenants will stay longer, and will tell friends and relatives to rent from you.

Mistake #23. Failing to keep the property modern.

Most landlords, after buying a rental property, merely keep things status quo. They don't take the time, or don't have the imagination, to make dramatic changes. By failing to keep the property in tip-top condition and modern, they are losing out on top-quality tenants and top-quality rents. Enlist a creative set of eyes every now and then to give suggestions on what you can do to give the property a contemporary edge. And hire someone two or three times a year to thoroughly clean the exterior of your property to make it sparkle.

Mistake #24. Failing to keep rents current.

Some landlords rarely raise rents, losing out on rental income they could collect. Some landlords make the mistake of raising rents too high; current tenants move elsewhere where rents are more reasonable, and vacancies are hard to fill. Monitor what's happening with rents and vacancy rates in your area. Then, adjust rents to market levels (or slightly below market levels for your good tenants); make the adjustments at times of the year when demand for rental units is the highest.

Mistake #25. Being a big spender.

Some investors, once their investments start producing extra cash, start living a life of luxury—spending extravagantly on homes, cars, and vacations. By doing so, their investments become more risky because the owner has less cash available to cover the investments if things turn sour. Or they lose everything because their investments cannot support their extravagant lifestyle. This is not to say we shouldn't enjoy nice things, but don't *waste* money on unnecessary things. Instead, use some of that extra money for additional investments, to pay off a mortgage loan, or as a cushion in case things take a downturn; there's nothing like having money for a rainy day.

Quick Start with Calculators

Keystrokes for the HP 10BII+ and TI BAII PLUS appear throughout the book. Selected keystrokes for other popular calculators can be requested at *info@getrichslowwebber.com*.

The calculator information shown here and elsewhere in the book is *not* to show you every function of your calculator. For additional explanations, refer to the manual that came with your calculator. The main registers we will use in the next few pages are circled:

Calculator registers. Most keys have more than one function. The first appears on the face of the key.

HP 10BII+. A second function appears in gold on the bottom half of the key. To access the second function, press the gold shift key ⬛🔽 first. The third function appears in blue above the key. To access the third function, press the blue shift key ⬛🔼 first.

TI BAII PLUS. A second function appears in color above the key. To access the second function, press ⎡2ND⎤ first.

Turning on and off. To turn the HP 10BII+ on, press ⎡ON⎤; to turn off, press ⬛🔽 ⎡OFF⎤. To turn the TI BAII PLUS on, press ⎡ON/OFF⎤; to turn off, press ⎡ON/OFF⎤. To save batteries, the calculators turn off if not used for a certain amount of time.

Arithmetic. For the HP 10BII+ and TI BAII PLUS, we do arithmetic as we say it.

Example. Multiply 1,222 by 32.8.

HP 10BII+	TI BAII PLUS
1,222 ⎡×⎤ 32.8 ⎡=⎤ **40,081.60**	1,222 ⎡×⎤ 32.8 ⎡=⎤ **40,081.60**

Notice, when keying in 1,222 we did not key in a comma (there is no *comma* key). The comma is shown in keystrokes for clarity and will show up in the calculator display.

Correcting entries. If we enter a number incorrectly, we can correct our mistake without having to start the problem over again. Pressing the backspace key (← on the HP 10BII+ and → on the TI BAII PLUS) gobbles up the last digit. Pressing ⎡C⎤ on the HP 10BII+ clears the entire displayed number. Pressing ⎡CE/C⎤ on the TI BAII PLUS clears the entire displayed number.

Worksheets. The TI BAII PLUS has two modes of operation: the *standard-calculator mode* and the *worksheet mode* (to guide us through special applications). There are 12 worksheets. To access a worksheet, press the key(s) to select the worksheet. For example, to access the amortization worksheet, press ⎡2ND⎤ ⎡AMORT⎤; to return to the *standard-calculator mode*, press ⎡2ND⎤ ⎡QUIT⎤. The HP 10BII+ does not use worksheets.

Changing sign. We can change the sign of a displayed number by pressing ⎡+/−⎤.

Setting the decimal. We can change the decimal setting as shown below. Both the HP 10BII+ and TI BAII PLUS use the internal, more accurate number, for chain calculations. If we want to use the displayed value in chain calculations we can "round" the internal number to match the displayed number. With the TI BAII PLUS, to see more digits on a displayed number, we must store the number before changing the decimal setting or we will lose the number.

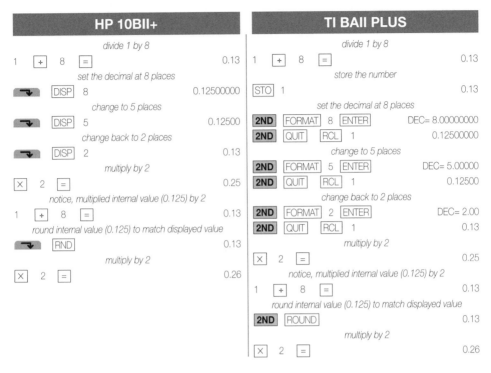

The "round" function is a one-time deal, for that calculation only; for future calculations, the internal, unrounded number will be used unless we use the round function.

Percent problems. Let's do a few examples.

> **Example.** You buy a duplex for $350,000. What is the building value, assuming that the building value is 75% of the total price?

HP 10BII+		TI BAII PLUS	
350,000 [×] 75 [%] [=]	**262,500.00**	350,000 [×] 75 [%] [=]	**262,500.00**

Example. You are thinking of buying an office building. You project the first year's annual rent (called *scheduled rent*) to be $124,000. You project rents will increase 3% each year. Calculate the projected scheduled rents for Years 2 through 5. Round amounts to the nearest dollar.

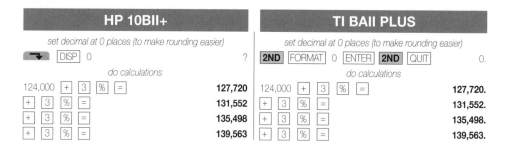

Example. You are thinking of buying an office building. You project the first year's scheduled rent to be $124,000. If you anticipate a vacancy rate of 7%, what is the dollar amount of vacancy, and what amount should you be able to deposit, after vacancy? Round amounts to the nearest dollar.

HP 10BII+		TI BAII PLUS	
set decimal at 0 places (to make rounding easier)		*set decimal at 0 places (to make rounding easier)*	
⬇ DISP 0	?	2ND FORMAT 0 ENTER 2ND QUIT	0.
do calculations		*do calculations*	
124,000	124,000_	124,000	124,000
− 7 %	8,680	− 7 %	8,680.
=	115,320	=	115,320.
set decimal back to 2 places		*set decimal back to 2 places*	
⬇ DISP 2	115,320.00	2ND FORMAT 2 ENTER 2ND QUIT	0.00

Time-saving registers. Let's calculate the total monthly rent on a 72-unit apartment building in which 36 units rent for $850 each, 24 rent for $900 each, and 12 rent for $925 each. One approach would be to write down subtotals and then to add the subtotals:

$$
\begin{array}{rl}
36 \times \$850 = & \$\ 30{,}600 \\
24 \times \$900 = & \ \ 21{,}600 \\
\underline{12} \times \$925 = & \ \ \underline{11{,}100} \\
72 & \mathbf{\$\ 63{,}300}
\end{array}
$$

Here are a few approaches we can use to save time:

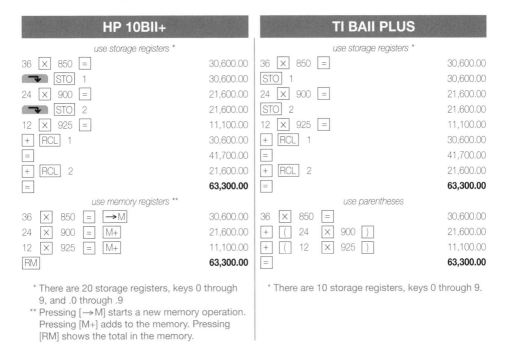

HP 10BII+		TI BAII PLUS	
use storage registers *		*use storage registers* *	
36 ☒ 850 ☐	30,600.00	36 ☒ 850 ☐	30,600.00
⬛ STO 1	30,600.00	STO 1	30,600.00
24 ☒ 900 ☐	21,600.00	24 ☒ 900 ☐	21,600.00
⬛ STO 2	21,600.00	STO 2	21,600.00
12 ☒ 925 ☐	11,100.00	12 ☒ 925 ☐	11,100.00
+ RCL 1	30,600.00	+ RCL 1	30,600.00
=	41,700.00	=	41,700.00
+ RCL 2	21,600.00	+ RCL 2	21,600.00
=	**63,300.00**	=	**63,300.00**
use memory registers **		*use parentheses*	
36 ☒ 850 ☐ →M	30,600.00	36 ☒ 850 ☐	30,600.00
24 ☒ 900 ☐ M+	21,600.00	+ ⦅ 24 ☒ 900 ⦆	21,600.00
12 ☒ 925 ☐ M+	11,100.00	+ ⦅ 12 ☒ 925 ⦆	11,100.00
RM	**63,300.00**	=	**63,300.00**

* There are 20 storage registers, keys 0 through 9, and .0 through .9

** Pressing [→M] starts a new memory operation. Pressing [M+] adds to the memory. Pressing [RM] shows the total in the memory.

* There are 10 storage registers, keys 0 through 9.

We have created videos for the HP 10BII, HP 10BII+, and TI BAII PLUS:

Video #1. Getting Started
(you may want to watch this video now)

Video #2. Solving TVM Problems
(watch this video in conjunction with pages 171–78)

Video #3. Amortization and Cash Flow Problems
(watch this video in conjunction with pages 179–83)

To access the videos, go to *getrichslowwebber.com* (click Calculator Videos).

Additional Practice Using a Financial Calculator

In the next few pages, we will solve a variety of problems with a financial calculator. Keystrokes for the HP 10BII+ and TI BAII Plus are shown. Selected keystrokes for other popular calculators can be requested at *info@getrichslowwebber.com*.

Time-Value-of-Money (TVM) Problems

TVM problems involve five variables:

N   **Total number of periods.** Stated another way, N is the total number of times interest is calculated. If you leave $100 deposited for 10 years and earn interest of 5% compounded quarterly, the *n-value* is 40 (10 years × 4 periods per year = 40 periods).

i   **Interest rate per period.** The annual interest rate divided by the number of periods per year. If you earn 5% compounded quarterly, the *i-value* is 1.25% (5 ÷ 4 = 1.25).

PV   **Present value.** A one-time amount that happens at the beginning of the first period.

PMT   **Periodic payment.** An amount that happens once every period.

FV   **Future value.** A one-time amount that happens at the end of the last period.

Financial calculators have a register for each of the five TVM variables. For the HP 10BII+, the TVM registers are on the top row; the *i-register* is labeled "I/YR." For the TI BAII PLUS, the TVM registers are on the third row down; the *i-register* is labeled "I/Y." We can solve TVM problems using this three-step approach:

1. Clear the TVM registers.

- For the HP 10BII+, press ⟶ [C ALL].
- For the TI BAII PLUS, press [2ND] [CLR TVM].

2. Enter the given data.

- Enter dollar amounts *received* as positive numbers, and dollar amounts *paid* as negative numbers (example: 300 [+/−] [PMT]).
- Enter the periodic rate in the *i-register*; don't use the [%] key.

3. Solve for the unknown.

- For the HP 10BII+, press the register representing the unknown.
- For the TI BAII PLUS, press [CPT] and then the register representing the unknown.

Find What a Single Deposit Will Grow to (Solve for FV)

If we make a deposit into a savings plan, we can calculate the sum to which the money will grow (FV) if we know the dollar amount of the deposit (PV), how long the money is left on deposit (N), and the interest rate earned (*i*).

Example 1. What will $500 grow to if left on deposit for 8 years earning 6% compounded quarterly?

HP 10BII+		TI BAII PLUS	
(1) clear TVM registers		*(1) clear TVM registers*	
⟶ [C ALL] *	0.00	[2ND] [CLR TVM]	?.??
(2) enter given data		*(2) enter given data*	
500 [+/−] [PV]	− 500.00	500 [+/−] [PV]	PV= − 500.00
8 [×] 4 [=] [N]	32.00	8 [×] 4 [=] [N]	N= 32.00
6 [÷] 4 [=] [I/YR]	1.50	6 [÷] 4 [=] [I/Y]	I/Y= 1.50
(3) solve for FV		*(3) solve for FV*	
[FV]	805.16	[CPT] [FV]	FV= 805.16

* *Tip*: For the HP 10BII+, if you press ⟶ and release, then hold down [C ALL], the display will show the P/YR setting (it should always be "1").

If you get a wrong answer, it may be because you don't have your "periods per year" register set at 1 period per year. To set the register correctly on the HP 10BII+, press: 1 ⟶ [P/YR]. For the TI BAII PLUS, press: [2ND] [P/Y] 1 [ENTER], then [2ND] [QUIT].

In Example 1, we entered the $500 as a *negative* amount because we *paid* it into the savings plan. The ending balance ($805.16) is a positive amount because we can take that amount out of the plan if we want to. The savings plan earns interest of $305.16 (the $805.16 we end up with minus the $500 we deposited).

Find What a Series of Deposits Will Grow to (Solve for FV)

In Example 1, we found what a *single* deposit would grow to. In the next example, we will determine what a *series* of deposits will grow to if the deposits are made at the *beginning* of each month and at the *end* of each month. The balance is greater if deposits are made at the beginning of each month because the money starts earning interest sooner. The example shows how we let the calculator know whether the deposits are made at the "beginning" or "end" of each period.

> **Example 2.** Antonio decides to stop drinking soda pop and deposits the $100 he spends on the stuff into a savings plan. If Antonio just turned 20 and can earn 6% compounded monthly, how much will he have in the savings plan when he retires at age 65, assuming deposits are made (1) at the beginning of each month, and (2) at the end of each month?

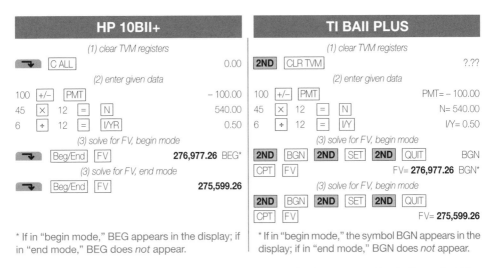

You may wonder when we should have our calculators in "Begin" mode. The payment date (like the first day of each month) does *not* matter. What matters is when payments start. If payments start immediately (at the beginning of the first period) we should be in "Begin" mode. If payments start after one period has lapsed, we should be in "End" mode.

Find the Amount That Must Be Deposited Into a Sinking Fund (Solve for PMT)

Money set aside for a specific purpose is referred to as a sinking fund. For example, you might want to establish a college fund for a child, needing $30,000 in 18 years. Or you might need $25,000 in 5 years to replace an apartment building roof. A *sinking fund* is not a fund that is slowly sinking; it is a fund in which we *sink* money.

Example 3. You want to accumulate $25,000 to replace an apartment building roof in 5 years. You can deposit $1,500 today. If you can earn 7% compounded monthly, what additional amount must you deposit, at the end of each month, to have the $25,000 in 5 years?

HP 10BII+		TI BAII PLUS	
(1) clear TVM registers		*(1) clear TVM registers*	
⬇ C ALL	0.00	2ND CLR TVM	?.??
(2) enter given data		*(2) enter given data*	
25,000 FV	25,000.00	25,000 FV	FV= 25,000.00
1,500 +/– PV	– 1,500.00	1,500 +/– PV	PV= – 1,500.00
5 × 12 = N	60.00	5 × 12 = N	N= 60.00
7 ÷ 12 = I/YR	0.58*	7 ÷ 12 = I/Y	I/Y= 0.58*
(3) solve for unknown		*(3) solve for unknown*	
PMT	**–319.49**	CPT PMT	PMT= **–319.49**

* By dividing 7 by 12, and transferring the result directly into the interest rate register, we enter the *internal, more accurate value* (0.583333333..), regardless of where we have the decimal set. Don't make the mistake of entering a *rounded* rate (0.58); you will get a wrong answer.

Calculate the Yield on an Investment (Solve for i)

Many investments, such as stocks and bonds, produce income *during* the investment. For investments in stocks, stockholders often receive dividends. For investments in bonds, bondholders often receive annual or semiannual interest checks. We can calculate the yield as shown in the next example.

Example 4. You are thinking about buying a 7% $1,000 corporate bond at a price of $1,050. If you do, you will receive $1,000 in 18 years (the $1,000 is referred to as the maturity value). You will also receive interest checks of $35 each 6 months ($1,000 maturity value × 3.5% semiannual rate = $35). Calculate your yield on the bond.

HP 10BII+		TI BAII PLUS	
(1) clear TVM registers		(1) clear TVM registers	
⟶ C ALL	0.00	2ND CLR TVM	?.??
(2) enter given data		(2) enter given data	
1,050 +/− PV	− 1,050.00	1,050 +/− PV	PV= − 1,050.00
1,000 FV	1,000.00	1,000 FV	FV= 1,000.00
35 PMT	35.00	35 PMT	PMT= 35.00
18 × 2 = N	36.00	18 × 2 = N	N= 36.00
(3) solve for unknown		(3) solve for unknown	
I/YR	3.26	CPT I/Y	I/Y= 3.26
× 2 =	**6.52**	× 2 =	**6.52**

If you buy the bond, you will earn 6.52% compounded semiannually. Notice, when you solve for "*i*" you get 3.26. But, remember, the *i*-register represents the interest rate *per period*, in this case the interest rate for each 6 months. To calculate the yield, we must multiply the periodic rate (3.26) by the periods per year (2), getting 6.52%.

You may wonder why your yield is less than the 7% interest the bond pays. Here's why. You are paying a premium for the bond: $1,050 for the $1,000 bond. So why in the world would you be willing to pay a premium for the bond? Here's the reason. The 7% rate the bond pays is apparently better than what new bonds are paying, so you are willing to pay a premium for this bond.

Calculate an APR for an Installment Plan (Solve for i)

We are sometimes allowed to pay a bill over time. In most cases, we are required to pay a bit extra for not paying the bill in full. The extra money is interest, even though the company extending the credit may call it a service fee, administrative fee, or something else. The interest rate we pay on borrowed money is known as the annual percentage rate (APR).

Example 5. You receive your insurance premium notice for a triplex. Instead of paying the $1,200 six-month premium now, the company gives you the option of making 6 monthly installments of $230, starting today. If you elect to pay on the installment plan, what APR will you be paying?

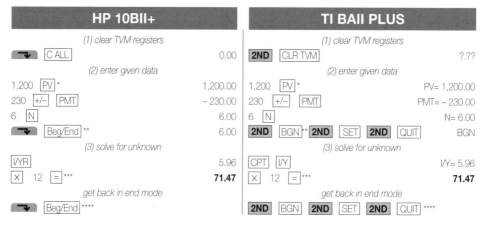

HP 10BII+		TI BAII PLUS	
(1) clear TVM registers		*(1) clear TVM registers*	
⬛ C ALL	0.00	2ND CLR TVM	?.??
(2) enter given data		*(2) enter given data*	
1,200 PV *	1,200.00	1,200 PV *	PV= 1,200.00
230 +/− PMT	− 230.00	230 +/− PMT	PMT= − 230.00
6 N	6.00	6 N	N= 6.00
⬛ Beg/End **	6.00	2ND BGN ** 2ND SET 2ND QUIT	BGN
(3) solve for unknown		*(3) solve for unknown*	
I/YR	5.96	CPT I/Y	I/Y= 5.96
× 12 = ***	**71.47**	× 12 = ***	**71.47**
get back in end mode		*get back in end mode*	
⬛ Beg/End ****		2ND BGN 2ND SET 2ND QUIT ****	

* You are, in effect, borrowing the $1,200, so treat it as a *positive* PV.

** Because the first payment of $230 is due today, put in *begin* mode.

*** When we solve for the interest rate (5.96), we have solved for the interest rate per period (per month); to get the *annual* rate, we must multiply by 12. You may think we should multiply by 6 since you make payments for 6 months, but to get the annual rate we multiply by 12 (not 6), because there are 12 months in a year.

**** The majority of TVM problems are in *end-mode*, so it is recommended that you put your calculator back in end-mode *immediately* after finishing a *begin-mode* problem.

In this example, if you elect to pay on the installment plan you will be paying a whopping 71.47% interest (your APR is 71.47%). You would be much better to get a cash advance on a credit card that charges 18% interest.

Find the Amount to Pay for a Promissory Note (Solve for PV)

Someone who borrows money is generally required to sign a promissory note, which spells out terms of repayment. An owner of a note (a lender) who needs cash may sell the note to a third party. The price is based on the yield the investor demands.

> **Example 6.** You have the chance to buy a promissory note. Five years ago, Maria bought a home from Ted for $195,000 and paid $30,000 down. Maria agreed to pay Ted the remaining $165,000 by making 180 monthly payments of $1,400. She just made the 60th payment. Ted needs some money to start a business and asks you to buy the note from him, in which case you will collect the remaining 120 payments from Maria. If you want to earn 8.5% compounded monthly, how much can you pay for the note?

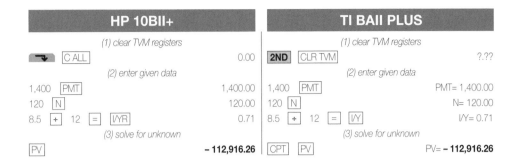

HP 10BII+		TI BAII PLUS	
(1) clear TVM registers		*(1) clear TVM registers*	
〔C ALL〕	0.00	〔2ND〕 〔CLR TVM〕	?.??
(2) enter given data		*(2) enter given data*	
1,400 〔PMT〕	1,400.00	1,400 〔PMT〕	PMT= 1,400.00
120 〔N〕	120.00	120 〔N〕	N= 120.00
8.5 〔÷〕 12 〔=〕 〔I/YR〕	0.71	8.5 〔÷〕 12 〔=〕 〔I/Y〕	I/Y= 0.71
(3) solve for unknown		*(3) solve for unknown*	
〔PV〕	**– 112,916.26**	〔CPT〕 〔PV〕	PV= **– 112,916.26**

Find the Remaining Term on a Loan (Solve for N)

Example 7. Several years ago you got a mortgage loan on a duplex at 6.25% interest. You currently owe $222,094.44 and pay $1,849.29 a month, of which $310 is for taxes and insurance (TI). How many months until the loan will be paid off?

HP 10BII+		TI BAII PLUS	
(1) clear TVM registers		*(1) clear TVM registers*	
〔C ALL〕	0.00	〔2ND〕 〔CLR TVM〕	?.??
(2) enter given data		*(2) enter given data*	
222,094.44 〔PV〕	222,094.44	222,094.44 〔PV〕	PV= 222,094.44
6.25 〔÷〕 12 〔=〕 〔I/YR〕	0.52	6.25 〔÷〕 12 〔=〕 〔I/Y〕	I/Y= 0.52
1,539.29 〔+/–〕 〔PMT〕	– 1,539.29	1,539.29 〔+/–〕 〔PMT〕	PMT= – 1,539.29
(3) solve for unknown		*(3) solve for unknown*	
〔N〕	**268.00**	〔CPT〕 〔N〕	N= **268.00**

You have another 268 months (22 years and 4 months) until the loan will be paid off. The PI portion of the payment is $1,539.29; the TI portion ($310) does not apply to the debt. We entered the $1,539.29 payment as a *negative* because you will be *paying* it. We entered the $222,094.44 as a positive number.

Special note. We have created videos for the HP 10BII, HP 10BII+, and TI BAII PLUS:

Video #1. Getting Started
   (watch this video in conjunction with pages 165–69)

Video #2. Solving TVM Problems
   (watch this video in conjunction with pages 171–78)

Video #3. Amortization and Cash Flow Problems
   (watch this video in conjunction with pages 179–83)

To access the videos, go to *getrichslowwebber.com* (click Calculator Videos).

Here are a few helpful suggestions when solving TVM problems with a financial calculator.

Tip 1 To review values in the TVM registers, press $\boxed{\text{RCL}}$ $\boxed{\text{N}}$, $\boxed{\text{RCL}}$ $\boxed{\text{PV}}$, etc.

Tip 2 It doesn't matter what order the given values are entered in the registers.

Tip 3 Remember to enter the *i-value* as a periodic rate. And don't use the % sign; for 4% compounded semiannually, enter the 2% periodic rate as "2," *not* "2%" or ".02."

Tip 4 When entering the *i-value*, don't round the periodic rate. For example, for a rate of 7% compounded monthly, the periodic rate (7 ÷ 12) is not exactly 0.58 (it is 0.583333333 . . .). By dividing 7 by 12 and *transferring* the result directly into the interest rate register, we enter the *internal, more accurate value* (0.583333333 . . .), regardless of where we have the decimal set. Don't make the mistake of entering a *rounded* rate (0.58); you will get a wrong answer.

Tip 5 Remember to enter dollar amounts *received* as positive numbers and dollar amounts *paid* as negative numbers. When entering a negative number, don't use the minus (–) key; instead use the +/– key: 300 $\boxed{+/-}$ $\boxed{\text{PMT}}$.

Tip 6 Of the three *dollar* variables (PV, PMT, and FV), there must be at least one *negative* amount and at least one *positive* amount.

Tip 7 We must know at least three of the five variables. For some problems, we will know four of the five variables. For problems in which we know only three variables, we solve for a 4th variable, meaning there is an unused register. If we forget to clear the TVM registers, a previous value will remain in the unused register, and we will get a wrong answer!

Tip 8 If an upcoming problem is merely a *variation* of the preceding problem, there is no need to clear the TVM registers; instead just enter the values that are different.

Tip 9 In deciding whether the calculator should be in *begin* or *end mode*, it doesn't matter what day of the month the payment is due. What matters is whether the first payment is made immediately at the beginning of the first period or is due after one period has lapsed. For mortgage loans and car loans, for instance, the first monthly payment is due after 1 month has lapsed (interest is paid in arrears), so we should be in *end mode*.

Tip 10 Most TVM problems are *end mode* problems, so put your calculator back in "end" mode immediately after getting an answer to a *begin mode* problem. If you forget, your answers to *end-mode* problems will be wrong, and you won't know it; that's what we call going through life as a "beginner." Keep in mind that clearing the TVM registers does *not* default to "end" mode.

Amortization

In the next three problems, we will use our amortization registers. (Remember, when amortizing we must have our decimal set at 2 places.)

Calculate Payments for an Adjustable Rate Mortgage (ARM)

With an adjustable rate mortgage (ARM), the interest rate changes at set intervals (like each year). The interest rate is tied to an index (such as the 1-year T-bill rate). Most ARMs provide for a maximum interest rate change each year (annual cap) and during the life of the loan (lifetime cap). Payments change to reflect the new rate.

> **Example 8.** You get a 30-year $60,000 ARM. The interest rate is 7.5% for the first year, 8.25% for the second year, and 8.125% for the third year. Calculate the monthly payment for each year.

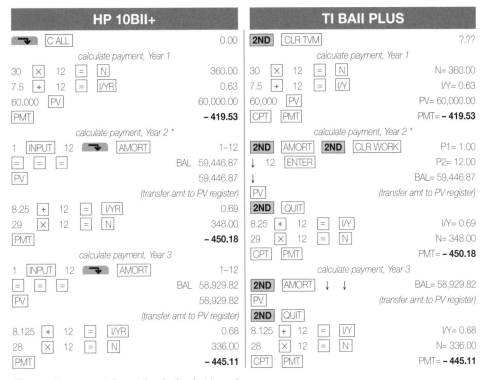

*To amortize accurately, set the decimal at two places.

In this example, we first found a payment for a 30-year 7.5% $60,000 loan; for the second year, we found a payment for a 29-year 8.25% $59,446.87 loan; and for the third year, we found a payment for a 28-year 8.125% $58,929.82 loan.

ARMS often start out with a rate lower than that of fixed-rate loans, but the borrower takes the risk of the rate increasing above that of fixed-rate loans. Many people prefer fixed-rate loans because they dislike the uncertainty of ARMS.

Calculating a Balloon Payment

A balloon payment pays off a loan with one large payment. For example, a payment may be calculated using a 30-year term, but the borrower may be required to pay the lender whatever balance is still unpaid at the end of 10 years; the required final payment is called a balloon payment.

Example 9. You get a 30-year 8.5% $100,000 mortgage loan. You agree to make a balloon payment at the end of 10 years. Calculate the amount of the balloon payment.

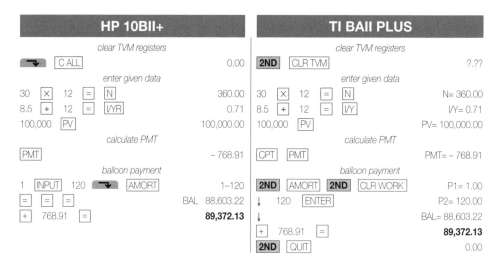

The balloon payment is $89,372.13. Notice, the balloon payment is *not* $88,603.22 (the balance after payment 120 is credited); this is because payment 120 is due at the same time as the balloon payment. So, instead of writing out a check for $768.91 (for payment 120) and another for $88,603.22, you write one check for the total ($89,372.13).

Calculate an APR for a Mortgage Loan

An annual percentage rate (APR) *relates the amount and timing of value received by a borrower to the amount and timing of payments made*. Front-end fees are a form of interest—just paid in advance. So when front-end fees are charged the total interest increases, and the *real* interest rate (APR) will be greater than the stated annual rate.

Mortgage lenders are required to disclose an APR to a borrower. However, the APR they are required to disclose, called a reportable APR, reflects only a few of the borrower's total loan charges: origination fee, points, mortgage insurance, and other fees paid directly to the lender. The reportable APR does *not* reflect loan fees paid to third parties (like for an appraisal, lender's title policy, document preparation, credit report, and recording fees), meaning the borrower's real APR is generally greater than the APR the lender discloses to the borrower.

A reportable APR does not consider that the majority of mortgage loans are paid off early—because borrowers sell the property, refinance their loan, or get extra money to pay off the loan. When a mortgage loan is paid off early, loan costs, for APR purposes, are spread over a shorter period of time, *increasing the real APR* even more. To calculate a *real APR, reflecting an early payoff*:

1. Calculate the monthly payment using the loan amount and note rate.

2. Calculate the remaining balance (using amortization registers) at the designated time.

3. Calculate the APR by putting the remaining balance (the result of the previous step) in the FV register (as a *negative* value, since this amount will be *paid*), changing the N-value, and changing PV to the net proceeds (after loan costs are deducted).

Example 10. You need to borrow $300,000 to buy a rental property. You can get a 30-year loan at 7% interest, with loan fees totaling $7,400. You project you will sell the property or refinance the loan in an estimated 8 years. What is the real APR, reflecting the early payoff?

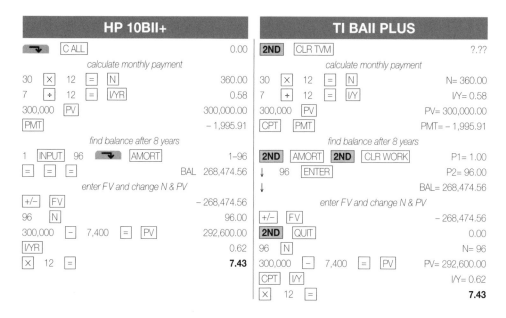

HP 10BII+		TI BAII PLUS	
⬇ C ALL	0.00	2ND CLR TVM	?.??
calculate monthly payment		*calculate monthly payment*	
30 × 12 = N	360.00	30 × 12 = N	N= 360.00
7 ÷ 12 = I/YR	0.58	7 ÷ 12 = I/Y	I/Y= 0.58
300,000 PV	300,000.00	300,000 PV	PV= 300,000.00
PMT	− 1,995.91	CPT PMT	PMT=− 1,995.91
find balance after 8 years		*find balance after 8 years*	
1 INPUT 96 ⬇ AMORT	1–96	2ND AMORT 2ND CLR WORK	P1= 1.00
= = =	BAL 268,474.56	↓ 96 ENTER	P2= 96.00
enter FV and change N & PV		↓	BAL= 268,474.56
+/− FV	− 268,474.56	*enter FV and change N & PV*	
96 N	96.00	+/− FV	− 268,474.56
300,000 − 7,400 = PV	292,600.00	2ND QUIT	0.00
I/YR	0.62	96 N	N= 96
× 12 =	**7.43**	300,000 − 7,400 = PV	PV= 292,600.00
		CPT I/Y	I/Y= 0.62
		× 12 =	**7.43**

In the example, your real APR, reflecting the early payoff, is 7.43%, considerably higher than the 7% stated annual rate.

Calculating APRs is extremely valuable when comparing different loan possibilities. For example, suppose you could get the 7% loan of the above example, or a 7.125% loan with loan costs totaling $3,500. The real APR, reflecting an early payoff, on the 7.125% loan is 7.33% (you can calculate it if you want), which is lower than the 7.43% APR of the first loan. So, you should get the 7.125% loan instead of the 7% loan.

Calculating APRs is also valuable when deciding whether to refinance. To decide whether to refinance, compare the APR on the contemplated loan (the one you are thinking about getting) with the note rate of your current loan. If the APR on the contemplated loan is less, it is probably a good idea to refinance, unless you suspect that interest rates will be lower in the near future.

Solving for Net Present Value (NPV)

When payments change, we cannot use our TVM registers. Instead we use our cash flow registers. When payments change, the interest rate is referred to as internal rate of return (IRR), and present value is referred to as net present value (NPV). We solved for an IRR in Step 6 of the book (see page 88). In the next example, we will calculate NPV.

> **Example 11.** You have the chance to buy a promissory note, in which you will receive 82 monthly payments of $800 (starting in one month), followed by 120 monthly payments of $950. If you want to earn 8.5%, compounded monthly, what amount can you pay for the note?

You will receive a total of $179,600. If you paid $179,600 you would earn no interest. If you want to earn interest you must pay less. *Hint:* Because we don't know the initial cash flow, we enter a zero cash flow at the beginning of the first period.

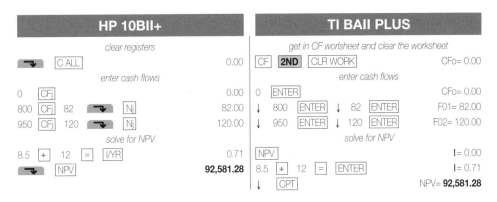

We can review the cash flows we entered as shown below:

> **HP 10BII+.** To review the cash flows, press RCL CFj . The initial cash flow will be shown. Pressing + will show the frequency of that cash flow: it shows that cash flow "0" happened one time. Continuing to press + shows each cash flow, and then the frequency of the cash flow.

> **TI BAII PLUS.** Press CF to get into the cash flow worksheet. Then, press the down-arrow key (↓) to view the cash flows and frequencies.

Additional Practice Using Excel®

In the next few pages, we will solve a variety of problems using Excel. We'll start by solving some time-value-of-money (TVM) problems.

Time-Value-of-Money (TVM) Problems

TVM problems involve five variables:

N   **Total number of periods.** Stated another way, N is the total number of times interest is calculated. If you leave $100 deposited for 10 years and earn interest of 5% compounded quarterly, the *n-value* is 40 (10 years × 4 periods per year = 40 periods).

i   **Interest rate per period**. The annual interest rate divided by the number of periods per year. If you earn 5% compounded quarterly, the *i-value* is 1.25% (5 ÷ 4 = 1.25).

PV   **Present value.** A one-time amount that happens at the beginning of the first period.

PMT **Periodic payment.** An amount that happens once every period.

FV   **Future value.** A one-time amount that happens at the end of the last period.

Excel relies on compound interest formulas to solve TVM problems. We provide the values for the TVM variables and the Excel program does the arithmetic. We solve TVM problems using a three-step approach:

1. **Select the Excel format that represents the unknown value:**

If solving for	Excel format
n	=NPER(i, PMT, PV, FV, Mode)
i	=RATE(n, PMT, PV, FV, Mode, Guess)
PV	=PV(i, n, PMT, FV, Mode)
PMT	=PMT(i, n, PV, FV, Mode)
FV	=FV(i, n, PMT, PV, Mode)

where n = total number of periods (such as 48 or 4*12); i = interest rate per period (such as 9%/12 or .09/12); **PV** = present value; **PMT** = periodic payment; **FV** = future value; **Guess** = estimated periodic rate; **Mode** = 0 if periodic payments start after one period has lapsed (*end* mode); Mode = 1 if periodic payments start immediately (*begin* mode). *Note*: We will use the word "Mode" in place of Excel's word "type."

2. **Enter the given data.** In any cell on an Excel spreadsheet, type the format, substituting known values inside the parentheses. Don't use dollar signs. Use commas only to separate values. Enter dollar amounts as positives if the money is received or negatives if the money is paid.

3. **To solve for the unknown, press ENTER.** The answer appears. A negative value appears in parentheses.

Find what a Single Deposit will Grow To (Solve for FV)

If we make a deposit into a savings plan, we can calculate the sum to which the money will grow (FV) if we know the dollar amount of the deposit (PV), how long the money is left on deposit (N), and the interest rate earned (i).

> **Example 1.** What will $500 grow to if left on deposit for 8 years earning 6% compounded quarterly?

We are solving for FV (the amount at the end of the last period), so:

(1) Select format for FV	=FV(i, n, PMT, PV, Mode)
(2) Enter given data (in any cell)	=FV(6%/4, 8*4, 0, -500, 0)
(3) Press ENTER	**805.16**

Notice, we entered the rate as 6%/4, since interest is compounded quarterly. We entered the initial deposit as a negative because we *deposited* the $500, rather than received it.

Find what a Series of Deposits will Grow To (Solve for FV)

In Example 1, we found what a *single* deposit would grow to. In the next example, we will determine what a *series* of deposits will grow to if the deposits are made at the *beginning* of each month and at the *end* of each month. The balance is greater if deposits are made at the beginning of each month because the money starts earning interest sooner.

> **Example 2.** Antonio decides to stop drinking soda pop and deposits the $100 he spends on the stuff into a savings plan. If Antonio just turned 20 and can earn 6% compounded monthly, how much will he have in the savings plan when he retires at age 65, assuming deposits are made (1) at the beginning of each month, and (2) at the end of each month?

Let's first find the balance assuming deposits are made at the *beginning* of each month (Mode = 1).

(1) Select format for FV	=FV(*i*, *n*, PMT, PV, Mode)
(2) Enter given data	=FV(6%/12, 45*12, -100, 0, 1)
(3) Press ENTER	**276,977.26**

Now, let's find the balance assuming deposits are made at the *end* of each month (Mode = 0).

(1) Select format for FV	=FV(*i*, *n*, PMT, PV, Mode)
(2) Enter given data	=FV(6%/12, 45*12, -100, 0, 0)
(3) Press ENTER	**275,599.26**

You may wonder how to determine the mode (begin or end). The payment date (like the first day of each month) does *not* matter. What matters is when payments start. For problems in which payments start immediately (at the beginning of the first period), the mode = 1; if payments start after one period has lapsed, the mode = 0.

Find the Amount That Must Be Deposited Into a Sinking Fund (Solve for PMT)

Money set aside for a specific purpose is referred to as a sinking fund. For example, you might want to establish a college fund for a child, needing $30,000 in 18 years. Or you might need $25,000 in 5 years to replace an apartment building roof. A *sinking fund* is not a fund that is slowly sinking; it is a fund in which we *sink* money.

Example 3. You want to accumulate $25,000 to replace an apartment building roof in 5 years. You can deposit $1,500 today. If you can earn 7% compounded monthly, what additional amount must you deposit, at the end of each month, to have the $25,000 in 5 years?

(1) Select format for PMT	=PMT(i, n, PV, FV, Mode)
(2) Enter given data	=PMT(7%/12, 5*12, -1500, 25000, 0)
(3) Press ENTER	**(319.49)**

Notice, we entered $1,500 as a negative because it was *deposited*, and we didn't enter the amount with a comma between the "1" and "5." That's because commas are used only to separate values. Likewise, we didn't enter the $25,000 with a comma after the "5."

Calculate the Yield on an Investment (Solve for i)

Many investments, such as stocks and bonds, produce income *during* the investment. For investments in stocks, stockholders often receive dividends. For investments in bonds, bondholders often receive annual or semiannual interest checks. We can calculate the yield, as shown in the next example. Here are a few things to keep in mind when using Excel to solve for a rate:

- A "guess" is required because Excel uses an iterative (guess-and-check) method for calculating the rate. If the program can't find a result within 20 tries, the "#NUM!" error is returned, in which case we must enter a better guess. For consistency, we will base our initial guess on an annual rate of 12%.

- If the answer does not appear as a percent or does not have 2 decimal places in the percent: right-click on the cell, click Format Cells, highlight Percentage, adjust the decimal setting to 2 places, and then click OK.

- If the answer is not an *annual* rate, multiply by the number of periods per year to get the *annual* rate.

Example 4. You are thinking about buying a 7% $1,000 corporate bond at a price of $1,050. If you do, you will receive $1,000 in 18 years (the $1,000 is referred to as the maturity value). You will also receive interest checks of $35 each 6 months ($1,000 maturity value × 3.5% semiannual rate = $35). Calculate your yield on the bond.

(1) Select format for i	=RATE(n, PMT, PV, FV, Mode, Guess)
(2) Enter given data	=RATE(18*2, 35, -1050, 1000, 0, 12%/2)
(3) Press ENTER	3.26%

Note: If the answer does not appear as a percent, or does not have 2 decimal places in the percent: right-click on the cell, click Format Cells, highlight Percentage, adjust the decimal setting to 2 places, and then click OK. The answer of 3.26% is the *periodic rate*, not the annual rate. We must multiply the periodic rate by 2 to get the annual rate. Additional steps are shown, assuming the answer appears in Cell A1:

In any blank cell, type: =A1*2

Press ENTER.   The answer appears: **6.52%**

> If the answer does not appear as a percent or does not have 2 decimal places in the percent: right-click on the cell, click Format Cells, highlight Percentage, adjust the decimal setting to 2 places, and then click OK.

You may wonder why your yield is less than the 7% interest the bond pays. Here's why. You are paying a premium for the bond: $1,050 for the $1,000 bond. So why in the world would you be willing to pay a premium for the bond? Here's the reason. The 7% rate the bond pays is apparently better than what new bonds are paying, so you are willing to pay a premium for this bond.

Calculate an APR for an Installment Plan (Solve for i)

We are sometimes allowed to pay a bill over time. In many cases, we are required to pay a bit extra for not paying the bill in full. The extra money is interest, even though the company extending the credit may call it a service fee, administrative fee, or something else. The interest rate we pay on borrowed money is known as the annual percentage rate (APR).

> **Example 5.** You receive your insurance premium notice for a triplex. Instead of paying the $1,200 six-month premium now, the company gives you the option of making 6 monthly installments of $230, starting today. If you elect to pay on the installment plan, what APR will you be paying?

For this problem, payments start immediately, meaning the Mode is 1, not 0.

(1) Select format for *i*	=RATE(*n*, PMT, PV, FV, Mode, Guess)
(2) Enter given data	=RATE(6, -230, 1200, 0, 1, 12%/12)
(3) Press ENTER	5.96%

The answer of 5.96% is the *periodic rate*, not the annual rate. We must multiply by 12 (since there are 12 months in a year) to get the annual rate. Use the same procedure shown before, getting: **71.47%**. *Note*: You may think we should multiply by 6 since you make payments for 6 months, but to get the annuial rate we multiply 12, because there are 12 months in a year.

In this example, if you elect to pay on the installment plan you will be paying a whopping 71.47% interest (your APR is 71.47%). You would be much better to get a cash advance on a credit card that charges 18% interest.

Find the Amount to Pay for a Promissory Note (Solve for PV)

Someone who borrows money is generally required to sign a promissory note, which spells out terms of repayment. An owner of a note (a lender) who needs cash may sell the note to a third party. The price is based on the yield the investor demands.

> **Example 6.** You have the chance to buy a promissory note. A little over 5 years ago, Maria bought a home from Ted for $195,000 and paid $30,000 down. Maria agreed to pay Ted the remaining $165,000 by making 180 monthly payments of $1,400. She just made the 60th payment. Ted needs some money to start a business and asks you to buy the note from him, in which case you will collect the remaining 120 payments from Maria. If you want to earn 8.5%, compounded monthly, how much can you pay for the note?
>
> | | |
> |---|---|
> | (1) Select format for PV | =PV(*i, n*, PMT, FV, Mode) |
> | (2) Enter given data | =PV(8.5%/12, 120, 1400, 0, 0) |
> | (3) Press ENTER | **(112,916.26)** |

Find the Remaining Term on a Loan (Solve for N)

> **Example 7.** Several years ago you got a mortgage loan on a duplex at 6.25% interest. You currently owe $222,094.44 and pay $1,849.29 a month, of which $310 is for taxes and insurance (TI). How many months until the loan will be paid off?
>
> | | |
> |---|---|
> | (1) Select format for *n* | =NPER(*i*,PMT, PV, FV, Mode) |
> | (2) Enter given data | =NPER(6.25%/12, -1539.29, 222094.44, 0, 0) |
> | (3) Press ENTER | **268.00** |

You have another 268 months (22 years and 4 months) until the loan will be paid off. The PI portion of the payment is $1,539.29; the TI portion ($310) does not apply to the debt. We entered the $1,539.29 payment as a *negative* because you will be *paying* it. We entered the $222,094.44 as a positive number.

Amortization

The next few examples involve amortization for a mortgage loan, in which we calculate interest, principal, and remaining balance. As of the printing of this book, Excel does not have an amortization program that is precise, unless we create an Excel spreadsheet that rounds the interest portion of each payment to the nearest penny. We will use the =FV format to *approximate* an unpaid balance.

> *Note*: For future examples, we will show solutions on one line, instead of using the three-step approach.

Calculate Payments for an Adjustable Rate Mortgage (ARM)

With an adjustable rate mortgage (ARM), the interest rate changes at set intervals (like each year). The interest rate is tied to an index (such as the 1-year T-bill rate). Most ARMs provide for a maximum interest rate change each year (annual cap) and during the life of the loan (lifetime cap). Payments change to reflect the new rate.

> **Example 8.** You get a 30-year $60,000 ARM. The interest rate is 7.5% for the first year, 8.25% for the second year, and 8.125% for the third year. Calculate the monthly payment for each year.

PMT, Yr 1:   =PMT(i, n, PV, FV, Mode) → =PMT(7.5%/12, 30*12, 60000, 0, 0) → **(419.53)**

BAL, End Yr 1:   =FV(i, n, PMT, PV, Mode) → =FV(7.5%/12, 12, -419.53, 60000, 0) → (59,446.88)

PMT, Yr 2:   =PMT(i, n, PV, FV, Mode) → =PMT(8.25%/12, 29*12, 59446.88, 0, 0) → **(450.18)**

BAL, End Yr 2:   =FV(i, n, PMT, PV, Mode) → =FV(8.25%/12, 12, -450.18, 59446.88, 0) → (58,929.83)

PMT, Yr 3:   =PMT(i, n, PV, FV, Mode) → =PMT(8.125%/12, 28*12, 58929.83, 0, 0) → **(445.11)**

In this example, we first found a payment for a 30-year 7.5% $60,000 loan; for the second year, we found a payment for a 29-year 8.25% $59,446.88 loan; and for the third year, we found a payment for a 28-year 8.125% $58,929.83 loan.

ARMS often start out with a rate lower than that of fixed rate loans, but the borrower takes the risk of the rate increasing above that of fixed rate loans. Many people prefer fixed rate loans because they dislike the uncertainty of ARMS.

Calculating a Balloon Payment

A balloon payment pays off a loan with one large payment. For example, a payment may be calculated using a 30-year term, but the borrower may be required to pay the lender whatever balance is still unpaid at the end of 10 years; the required final payment is called a balloon payment.

> **Example 9.** You get a 30-year 8.5% $100,000 mortgage loan. You agree to make a balloon payment at the end of 10 years. Calculate the amount of the balloon payment.

PMT: =PMT(i, n, PV, FV, Mode) → =PMT(8.5%/12, 30*12, 100000, 0, 0)
               → (768.91)

BAL, Yr 10:   =FV(i, n, PMT, PV, Mode) → =FV(8.5%/12, 120, -768.91, 100000, 0) → (88,603.20)

Balloon PMT: The balance after payment 120 is $88,603.20. But, payment 120 is due at the same time as the balloon payment, so the balloon payment is: $88,603.20 + $768.91 = **$89,372.11**

Calculate an APR for a Mortgage Loan

An annual percentage rate (APR) *relates the amount and timing of value received by a borrower to the amount and timing of payments made.* Front-end fees are a form of interest—just paid in advance. So when front-end fees are charged the total interest increases, and the *real* interest rate (APR) will be greater than the stated annual rate.

Mortgage lenders are required to disclose an APR to a borrower. However, the APR they are required to disclose, called a reportable APR, reflects only a few of the borrower's total loan charges: origination fee, points, mortgage insurance, and other fees paid directly to the lender. The reportable APR does *not* reflect loan fees paid to third parties (like for an appraisal, lender's title policy, document preparation, credit report, and recording fees), meaning the borrower's real APR is generally greater than the APR the lender discloses to the borrower.

A reportable APR does not consider that the majority of mortgage loans are paid off early—because borrowers sell the property, refinance their loan, or get extra money to pay off the loan. When a mortgage loan is paid off early, loan costs, for APR purposes, are spread over a shorter period of time, *increasing the real APR even more*. The next example shows how to calculate a *real APR, reflecting an early payoff*. We will use the following process:

1. Calculate the monthly payment using the loan amount and note rate.

2. Calculate the remaining balance (FV) at the designated time.

3. Calculate the APR by letting the remaining balance (the result of the previous step) be the FV value (as a *negative*, since this amount will be *paid*), changing the N-value, and changing PV to the net proceeds (after loan costs are deducted).

Example 10. You need to borrow $300,000 to buy a rental property. You can get a 30-year loan at 7% interest, with loan fees totaling $7,400. You project you will sell the property or refinance the loan in an estimated 8 years. What is the real APR, reflecting the early payoff?

PMT: =PMT(*i, n*, PV, FV, Mode) → =PMT(7%/12, 30*12, 300000, 0, 0) → (1,995.91)

BAL, Yr 8: =FV(*i, n*, PMT, PV, Mode) → =FV(7%/12, 8*12, -1995.91, 300000, 0) → (268,474.63)

APR: =RATE(*n*, PMT, PV, FV, Mode, Guess) → =RATE(8*12, -1995.91, 292600, -268474.63, 0, 12%/12) → 0.62%

> *Note*: If the answer does not appear as a percent, or does not have 2 decimal places in the percent: right-click on the cell, click Format Cells, highlight Percentage, adjust the decimal setting to 2 places, and then click OK. Because the answer (0.62%) is the periodic rate, multiply by 12 using the same procedure we used before, getting **7.43%**.

In the example, your real APR, reflecting the early payoff, is 7.43%, considerably higher than the 7% stated annual rate.

Calculating APRs is extremely valuable when comparing different loan possibilities. For example, suppose you could get the 7% loan of the above example, or a 7.125% loan with loan costs totaling $3,500. The real APR, reflecting an early payoff, on the 7.125% loan is 7.33% (you can calculate it if you want), which is lower than the 7.43% APR of the first loan. So, you should get the 7.125% loan instead of the 7% loan.

Calculating APRs is also valuable when deciding whether to refinance. To decide whether to refinance, compare the APR on the contemplated loan (the one you are thinking about getting) with the note rate of your current loan. If the APR on the contemplated loan is less, it is probably a good idea to refinance, unless you suspect that interest rates will be lower in the near future.

Solving for Net Present Value (NPV)

When payments change, the interest rate is referred to as internal rate of return (IRR), and present value is referred to as net present value (NPV). We solved for an IRR in Step 6 of the book (see page 93). In the next problem, we will calculate NPV.

Example 11. You have the chance to buy a promissory note, in which you will receive 82 monthly payments of $800 (starting in one month), followed by 120 monthly payments of $950. If you want to earn 8.5%, compounded monthly, what amount can you pay for the note?

Enter the cash flows in Column A. Because we don't know the initial cash flow, we enter a zero cash flow at the beginning of the first period (in Cell A1).

Cell A1:   0

Cells A2 through A83:   800

> *Note*: Enter 800 in Cell A2, and then copy and paste to other cells.

Cells A84 through A203:   950

> *Note*: Enter 950 in Cell A84, and then copy and paste to other cells.

In Cell B1, use the NPV format: =NPV(i, A2:A?)+A1

In Cell B1, type: =NPV(8.5%/12, A2:A203)+A1
Press ENTER. *The answer will appear*: **92,581.28**

Forms

The following pages include a few common forms:

Operating Statement
Projected Cash Flow Worksheet (During Ownership)
Projected Sales Proceeds
Residential Rental Application
Inspection Sheet

You can download forms for free from our website: *getrichslowwebber.com*. The forms contain basic information. You may want to tweak the forms to include things you consider important.

We are not including forms for an offer to purchase or a lease agreement because laws and customs vary from state to state. It is essential that the forms you use contain provisions and wording that conform to local laws and customs.

Location _____   **OPERATING STATEMENT**

Type of Property _____

Time Period _____   *Notes & Comments*

1. Scheduled Rental Income   _____   _____

2. – Vacancy & Credit Losses @_____%   _____   _____

3. Effective Rental Income   _____   _____

4. + Other Income   _____   _____

5. Gross Operating Income   _____   _____

    Operating Expenses

6. Property Taxes   _____   _____

7. Property Insurance   _____   _____

8. Off-site Management   _____   _____

9. On-site Management   _____   _____

10. Repairs & Painting   _____   _____

11. Water & Sewer   _____   _____

12. Gas   _____   _____

13. Electricity   _____   _____

14. Advertising   _____   _____

15. Accounting & Legal   _____   _____

16. Licenses & Permits   _____   _____

17. Supplies   _____   _____

18. Yard Care   _____   _____

19. Trash Removal   _____   _____

20. Snow Removal   _____   _____

21. Cleaning, Interior   _____   _____

22. Cleaning, Exterior   _____   _____

23. _____   _____   _____

24. _____   _____   _____

25. Total Operating Expenses   _____   _____% of Line _____

26. Net Operating Income (NOI)   _____

Projected Cash Flow Worksheet (During Ownership)

Purchase Data	
Property	
Purchase Price	
Down Payment	
Amount Borrowed	

Mortgage Data		
	1st Mortgage	2nd Mortgage
Loan Amount		
Interest Rate		
Term (yrs)		
Monthly Pmt		
Loan Costs		

Depreciation Data	
Building %	
Building Value	
MACRS Life	
Full-Yr Depreciation	
Month of Purchase	
Month of Sale	

NET OPERATING INCOME

	Year 1	Year 2	Year 3	Year 4	Year 5	Year 6
1. Scheduled Rent						
2. – Vacancy						
3. = Effective Income						
4. – Operating Expenses						
5. – Other Expenses						
6. = NOI						

CASH FLOW BEFORE TAX

7. – Annual Debt Service						
8. –						
9. = CFBT (Line 6 – 7 – 8)						

TAX LIABILITY OR SAVINGS

10. NOI (Line 6)						
11. – Interest – 1st Mortgage						
12. – Interest - 2nd Mortgage						
13. – Depreciation Bldgs						
14. – Amortized Loan Costs						
15. –						
16. –						
17. = Taxable Inc (or Loss)						
18. If Loss, Amt Allowed						
19. × ___ % Tax Rate =						

CASH FLOW AFTER TAX

20. CFBT (Line 9)						
21. + Tax Saved						
22. – Tax Paid						
23. = CFAT						

Projected Sales Proceeds

ADJUSTED BASIS	
1. Original Basis	
2. + Improvements	
3. – Depreciation	
4. = Adjusted Basis	

GAIN (AND RESULTING TAX)		(B) Recapture	(C) Capital Gain
5. Selling Price Yr _____			
6. – Selling Expenses			
7. – Adjusted Basis (Line 4)			
8. = Gain			
9. – Suspended Losses			xxxxxxxx
10. = Reportable Gain			
11. Tax Rate	xxxxxxxx		
12. Tax	xxxxxxxx		

CFAT FROM SALE	
13. Selling Price (Line 5)	
14. – Selling Expenses (Line 6)	
15. – Mortgage Balance	
16. = Sales Proceeds Before Tax	
17. – Recapture Tax (12B)	
18. – Capital Gain Tax (12C)	
19. = Sales Proceeds After Tax	

Residential Rental Application

<table>
<tr><th rowspan="6">LIST ALL OCCUPANTS</th><th>Name</th><th>Date of Birth</th><th>Social Security #</th><th>Driver's License #</th></tr>
<tr><td></td><td></td><td></td><td></td></tr>
<tr><td></td><td></td><td></td><td></td></tr>
<tr><td></td><td></td><td></td><td></td></tr>
<tr><td></td><td></td><td></td><td></td></tr>
<tr><td></td><td></td><td></td><td></td></tr>
</table>

<table>
<tr><th rowspan="4">EMPLOYMENT</th><th>Your First Name</th><th>Employer</th><th>Supervisor</th><th>Phone #</th><th>Employed Since</th><th>Monthly Salary</th><th>Job Discription</th></tr>
<tr><td></td><td></td><td></td><td></td><td></td><td></td><td></td></tr>
<tr><td></td><td></td><td></td><td></td><td></td><td></td><td></td></tr>
<tr><td></td><td></td><td></td><td></td><td></td><td></td><td></td></tr>
</table>

<table>
<tr><th rowspan="3">PRESENT LOCATION</th><td>Address</td><td>Your Phone #</td><td>How Long</td></tr>
<tr><td>Landlord</td><td>Landlord Phone #</td><td>Rent</td></tr>
<tr><td colspan="3">Why Moving?</td></tr>
</table>

<table>
<tr><th rowspan="3">REFERENCES</th><th>Name</th><th>Relationship</th><th>Phone #</th><th>Address</th></tr>
<tr><td></td><td></td><td></td><td></td></tr>
<tr><td></td><td></td><td></td><td></td></tr>
</table>

<table>
<tr><th rowspan="3">VEHICLES</th><th>Year</th><th>Make & Model</th><th>Color</th><th>License Plate #</th></tr>
<tr><td></td><td></td><td></td><td></td></tr>
<tr><td></td><td></td><td></td><td></td></tr>
</table>

<table>
<tr><th rowspan="5">OTHER</th><th>Your First Name</th><th>E-mail Address</th><th>Cell Phone</th></tr>
<tr><td></td><td></td><td></td></tr>
<tr><td></td><td></td><td></td></tr>
<tr><td></td><td></td><td></td></tr>
<tr><td>Pets, if any</td><td></td><td>Smoking?</td></tr>
</table>

I (we) hereby warrant that the above information is correct and complete. We authorize the landlord to inquire with any of the above sources to verify information. We also authorize the above sources to divulge pertinent information to the landlord or their agents; this includes credit reporting services giving credit reports, background checks, etc.

_____	_____	_____	_____
Applicant's signature	Date	Applicant's signature	Date

Inspection Sheet

Address and Unit # _____

	Item	New	Good	Detailed Description of Any Defects	NR*	L*	T*
GENERAL ITEMS	Items at Entrance						
	Floors						
	Walls & Ceilings						
	Windows, Sills, Screens						
	Drapes, Blinds						
	Doors						
	Lights, Switches, Plates						
	Closets						
BATH	Tub, Shower, Toilet						
	Sink, Vanity, Cabinets						
	Mirrors & Accessories						
KITCHEN	Countertops & Cabinets						
	Range & Refrigerator						
	Sink, Disposal, Taps						
OTHER							

* Indicates who will correct defects, if any: NR = not required; L = Landlord; T = Tenant.

I (we) have personally inspected the unit we will occupy and agree that this represents an accurate account of the condition.

_____ _____   _____ _____
                                                                     Landlord   Date

_____ _____
            Tenant(s)   Date

Glossary

adjustable-rate mortgage (ARM). A mortgage loan in which the interest rate is adjusted at set intervals, based on a specified interest rate index.

adjusted basis. Basis (cost) of an asset minus accumulated depreciation.

alternative minimum tax. An additional federal income tax, levied as a result of having certain tax preference items on a person's income tax return.

amortized loan. A loan repaid with periodic payments of equal amount.

annual percentage rate (APR). The "real" annual rate paid for borrowed money, the disclosure of which is required by the Truth in Lending Act. The APR is designed to help borrowers compare interest rates.

appreciation. In investment terminology, an increase in value.

bad check fee. A fee charged to a person for writing a check that has insufficient funds.

balloon payment. A single, often large, payment on a loan at an agreed-upon time that pays whatever balance is still owed.

bear market. Situation in which investors are pessimistic about the overall economy and stock market. *See also* bull market.

bull market. Situation in which investors are optimistic about the overall economy and stock market. *See also* bear market.

capitalization rate (cap rate). An indicator, expressed as a percent, found by dividing a property's Net Operating Income by its value.

capital gain. Profit from the sale of a qualifying investment as a result of the value increasing.

cash-on-cash return. An indicator of value, expressed as a percent, found by dividing the first year's projected cash flow (before tax) by the amount of money invested.

certificate of deposit. A special savings account in which the depositor agrees to leave money for an agreed-upon period of time.

collateral. An item of value (such as a car or real estate) that is pledged by a borrower. If the borrower defaults on the loan, the lender can sell the collateral and use the proceeds to repay the loan.

common stock. Ordinary stock in a corporation, with no guaranteed dividends but typically with voting rights.

compounding period. The amount of time that occurs between interest calculations. For example, if interest on a savings account is paid quarterly, the compounding period is three months.

contingencies. Conditions, if they occur, that can void an offer to purchase property.

conventional loan. The basic type of mortgage loan.

corporation. A business entity that sells shares of stock to investors who become owners of the corporation.

corporate bond. A written promise of a corporation to repay a specified sum on a certain date, usually with interest during the term.

cost segregation method. A depreciation method that separates building components into different categories, each with a different depreciable life.

counteroffer. A counter proposal to an offer, outlining the acceptable terms or conditions different than those proposed. A counteroffer is not valid unless accepted by both buyer and seller.

credit loss. A loss of income because someone does not pay what he or she owes.

dealer property. Real estate that is purchased with the intent to resell.

depreciation. The amount claimed as an expense because of an asset's loss of usefulness. Depreciation expense is only a "paper" entry, not a cash outlay. *See also* modified accelerated cost recovery system (MACRS).

diversification. Investing in a variety of things rather than putting too much money in a single investment.

dividend. For corporate stock, a distribution of corporate profits to stockholders.

double taxation. A situation in which earnings are taxed twice. For example, corporate profits are taxed; then any remainder that is distributed to stockholders is taxed again.

due on sale clause. For a mortgage loan, a provision that requires the borrower to pay the loan in full if the property (or any part) is sold.

early termination fee. In some lease agreements, the penalty the tenant must pay for terminating the lease (rather than being required to keep paying rent).

earnest money deposit. Money that accompanies an offer to purchase property, designed to show a seller that the buyer is serious (earnest) about buying the property.

equity-type investment. An investment that can increase or decrease in value; the rate of return is uncertain. *See also* fixed-return investment.

escrow account. For mortgage loans, an account maintained with a lender for payment of property taxes and/or insurance.

FHA loan. A mortgage loan in which the lender is insured against loss by the Federal Housing Administration (FHA).

fixed-rate loan. A loan in which the interest rate remains fixed for the entire loan. *See also* adjustable-rate mortgage (ARM).

fixed-return investment. An investment in which the rate of return is fixed. *See also* equity-type investment.

future value. The value of something at a specified time in the future (at the end of the last "period"). For savings plans, future value represents what a deposit or series of deposits will accumulate to over time. For investments, it is the value at the time the investment is liquidated.

general partnership. A partnership in which all partners are liable for the debts of the partnership. *See also* limited partnership.

graduated equity mortgage (GEM). A mortgage loan in which the payments change at set intervals.

gross rent multiplier (GRM). A relationship between price and rents, found by dividing price by gross rent.

income statement. *See* operating statement.

installment sale method. A method of reporting gain, in which the seller reports the gain as the money is received, instead of all at once.

interest-only mortgage. A mortgage loan in which the borrower pays interest only (no principal) for the first few years.

internal rate of return (IRR). An interest rate earned; it considers the dollar amount and timing of each cash flow.

joint tenants. A form of ownership in which two or more people own property together; when one dies, his or her share goes to the surviving joint tenant(s). *See also* tenants in common.

late fee. For tenants, a fee charged for paying rent after a specified date.

lender's policy of title insurance. *See also* policy of title insurance. A lender's policy of title insurance guarantees the lender (rather than the buyer) that title is as stated in the policy.

letter of intent. An informal letter from a buyer to a seller, preceding a formal agreement, that spells out the main points the buyer and seller need to agree upon. A letter of intent is not binding on either party; it is simply a way to start the negotiations.

leverage. Using borrowed money to control more investments than could otherwise be controlled.

limited liability company (LLC). A special type of business ownership that limits the personal liability of its owners.

limited partner. A type of partner in a limited partnership who is not actively involved in the business or personally responsible for the partnership debts.

limited partnership. A type of partnership in which some of the partners (called "limited partners") take no active role in the business and are not personally responsible for the partnership debts. *See also* general partnership.

loan-to-value (LTV) ratio. The loan amount divided by the value of the property, generally expressed as a percent.

MACRS. *See* modified accelerated cost recovery system.

maturity value. For a bond, the principal amount which must be repaid to the investor on the maturity date.

Modified Accelerated Cost Recovery System (MACRS). The method of depreciation required on all federal income tax returns for property placed in service after 1986.

money market account. A savings account similar to a passbook account, except a minimum balance must be maintained and the account generally has check-writing privileges.

mortgage broker. A "middle man" who matches borrowers with lenders.

mortgage insurance. A guarantee by a private company or governmental agency that insures a lender for an agreed-upon sum in the event a loan is not repaid.

mortgage loan. A loan secured by real estate.

municipal bond. A bond issued by a state or local government.

mutual fund. An investment fund in which numerous people contribute; the money in the fund is then invested in specific investments on behalf of the group of investors.

negative amortization loan. A loan in which the payment is not enough to cover interest; as a result, the unpaid balance increases.

net operating income (NOI). Income, less operating expenses, of a business or venture.

net present value (NPV). The present value of future cash flows for a cash flow problem (one in which the cash flows change from period to period).

note rate. The interest rate stated on a promissory note.

operating statement. A financial summary that shows the revenues and expenses of a business or venture. Also referred to as an Income Statement.

origination fee. For mortgage loans, this is a one-time front-end fee charged by the lender (often expressed as a percent of the loan amount).

period. *See* compounding period.

personal property tax. A tax levied on property other than real estate.

points. A one-time front-end loan fee for getting a loan with a rate lower than the prevailing rate. Each point is 1% of the loan amount.

policy of title insurance. A guarantee from a title company that title to a property is as stated in the policy. If title is flawed, the title company is obligated to cure the flaw or pay the owner of the policy a pre-determined amount of money.

preliminary title report. A report from a title company showing how title is vested, mortgage loans against the property, and any other items that affect title to the property. *See also* policy of title insurance.

prepayment penalty. A penalty charged to borrowers of some loans for paying the loan off early.

present value. In a time-value-of-money problem, the value of something at the beginning of the first period. For savings plans, present value is the initial one-time deposit. For investments, it is the initial investment. For loans, it is the loan amount. Present value can also be the discounted value (in today's dollars) of amounts to be received in the future.

profit and loss statement. *See* operating statement.

promissory note. A written promise to repay a loan.

property tax. A tax levied on real and personal property by local governments.

real APR. The APR from the borrower's standpoint. The borrower's real APR is often higher than the reportable APR because certain loan costs are not used in calculating the reportable APR.

real estate. Land, buildings, and other improvements attached to the land.

real estate investment trust (REIT). A corporation that focuses on real estate investments.

real estate professional. A special IRS classification that allows certain individuals to deduct all passive losses (not just $25,000 per year).

recapture portion of gain. The part of gain from the sale of real estate that is a result of taking depreciation.

reconstructed operating statement. An operating statement representing projected realistic income and expenses for the future, rather than historical data provided by the owner.

rent roll. A written summary showing names of all tenants, rents, security deposits, etc.

reportable APR. The APR that a lender must report to a borrower in accordance with the Truth in Lending Act. *See also* annual percentage rate (APR).

secured loan. A loan that is secured by something of value (such as a car or real estate). *See also* collateral.

security deposit. For tenants, a deposit the tenant gives to the landlord for the purpose of providing protection to the landlord in case the tenant fails to pay rent, or damages the property.

seller disclosure statement. A written statement from the seller of a property, disclosing what problems, if any, the seller knows about the property.

---

seller financing. For mortgage loans, a loan in which the seller of the property provides the financing to the buyer.

sinking fund. A fund set up to accumulate a certain sum on a specified future date.

Starker exchange. *See* 1031 tax-deferred exchange.

stock. Ownership in a corporation.

stockholder. An investor who purchases stock in a corporation.

straight-line depreciation. A depreciation method that assumes the asset loses an equal amount of usefulness during each year.

tax bracket. For income taxes, this is the rate that is applied to the highest dollar of taxable income.

tax rate schedules. Schedules used to calculate income tax.

tenants in common. A form of ownership in which two or more people own property together; when one dies, his or her share does not go to the other people—it goes to his or her heirs. *See also* joint tenants.

1031 tax-deferred exchange. A transaction in which the seller, if he or she meets certain qualifications, can defer reporting the gain from the sale of a property.

U.S. securities. Various types of bonds issued by the U.S. government, including T-bills, Treasury notes, Treasury bonds, and savings bonds.

VA loan. A mortgage loan in which the lender is partially insured against loss by the Veterans Administration (VA). The borrower must be a qualified veteran.

yield. An investor's rate of return.

zero-coupon bond. A type of bond that pays no periodic interest; instead the bondholder buys the bond at a discount and receives the face value at maturity.

Index

My Contact Information & Notes

(real estate agents, real estate attorneys, tax advisors, property managers, lenders, property inspectors, general contractors, handymen, electricians, plumbers, painters, roofers, suppliers, insurance agents, appraisers, architects, structural engineers, utility companies, landscapers, trash removal, snow removal, cleaning, tile installers, pest control, advertising, etc.)

My Contact Information & Notes

My Contact Information
& Notes

My Contact Information & Notes